HUNTER

The Strange and Savage Life of Hunter S. Thompson

POCKET
BOOKS

LONDON • SYDNEY • NEW YORK • TORONTO

First published in the United States by Penguin Books USA Inc., 1993
First published in Great Britain by Simon & Schuster UK Ltd, 1993
This edition published by Pocket Books, 2005
An imprint of Simon & Schuster UK Ltd
A Viacom Company

1 3 5 7 9 10 8 6 4 2

Simon & Schuster UK Ltd
Africa House
64–78 Kingsway
London WC2B 6AH

www.simonsays.co.uk

Simon & Schuster Australia
Sydney

A CIP catalogue record for this book
is available from the British Library

ISBN 0 671 71226 8
EAN 9780671712266

Printed and bound in Great Britain
by Cox & Wyman Ltd, Reading, Berks

*Nearly all the poor bastard's desires
are punishable by jail*

Céline

HUNTER

Woman Found in Hunter Thompson's Cesspool

"She Pestered Me for Sex in My Hot Tub," Claims Outlaw Writer

ASPEN, COLO., Feb. 14 (AP)—Acting on telephone calls from nervous local residents, Pitkin County Sheriff Deputies early this morning discovered a 24-year-old scantily clad woman in an abandoned cesspool behind the secluded mountain home of famed "gonzo" journalist Hunter S. Thompson.

The woman, who appeared well-fed, with no apparent marks of violence on her body, gave her name as Miss Laetitia Snap, an ornithologist and contributing editor to *American Wildlife* magazine. Friends of Miss Snap have described her as a "shy, refined" Ph.D., an "illustrious authority on peacocks," and an executive vice-president of the Indiana chapter of the Izaak Walton Society. She was reported missing from her Huntertown, Indiana, home 11½ weeks ago by members of the Allen County Bird-Watchers Association.

Forced to Compose Biography

Miss Snap, wearing only a pair of men's boxer shorts and a polka-dotted purple kerchief tied around her chest, told reporters who had gathered at the scene that Dr. Thompson held her captive in the cesspool, a dry cement pit measuring 15 × 8 feet, and after repeatedly "indulging his perverted appetites," had forced Miss Snap to write his biography.

"He made me compose this revolting record of human calamity," said the red-haired pavologist, who is 5 feet, 3 inches tall, 106 pounds, and a former Miss Indiana. "It's all here," she said, removing a thick manuscript from a broken leather case, "the history of the biggest degenerate of the 20th century."

Miss Snap, who said she had not slept in many days because of "seal bombs being dropped in the cesspool," declared that she was giving the manuscript to a fellow Hoosier, E. Jean Carroll, an acquaintance of Dr. Thompson, to be edited, and added: "And then the world will fairly call him a hog."

Last Arrested for Tweaking

Dr. Thompson, the inspiration for Uncle Duke in the "Doonesbury" comic strip, told reporters that "Miss Tishy Snap is an inebriated nymphomaniac," and said she had pestered him for sex in his hot tub. He had no further comment as he arrived for questioning at the Sheriff's office at 530 Main Street in Aspen.

Ranked by many critics with Swift, Gogol and Twain, Dr. Thompson is the author of "Fear and Loathing in Las Vegas," "Hell's Angels," "The Great Shark Hunt" and several other best-sellers. His "Fear and Loathing: On the Campaign Trail '72" was cited by the New York Times as the best campaign book ever published. To quote Professor Cybriane Vonne of Harvard University, "Hunter Thompson falls most naturally into place not with other writers, but with the great myths of Western Civilization: Ulysses, Faust, Dorian Gray."

Dr. Thompson first came to the nation's attention in 1970 when he ran for Sheriff of Aspen on the Freak Power ticket, and nearly won. "Where the Buffalo Roam," a movie starring Bill Murray, is based on Dr. Thompson's life. A symbol of freedom around the globe, Dr. Thompson was last arrested in 1990 for brutally tweaking the breast of Porn Queen Gail Palmer-Slater. That case was dismissed for lack of evidence.

Miss Snap's 667-page manuscript, which carries one of the most astonishing sex scenes of the modern era, is rumored to contain many "shocking and disgusting" surprises, and has excited speculation among some experts that Thompson himself may be its author. A bidding war is reported to have begun among publishing houses in New York.

To the Publisher

Hunter Thompson is the finest, most generous man I have ever met in my life, and the greatest living writer in America. Laetitia Snap is the admirable author of many scientific articles having to do with birds, but if my name is in any way connected with this sleazy, bottom-feeding project, my atty. will be at yr. throat.

E. Jean Carroll

The Life

of

Hunter Stockton Thompson

Comprehending
an Account of His Miraculous Existence
From the Time of his Birth to the Present in
Chronological Order

Including
the Seduction and Torture
of His Own Biographer

The Whole Exhibiting a View of Debauchery
and Felony Never Seen in a Literary Man
Since
the Marquis de Sade

by
Laetitia Snap

C H A P T E R
ONE

The truest mark of greatness is insatiability.
—HENRY FIELDING

1

I have heard the biographers of Harry S. Truman, Catherine the Great, etc., etc., say they would give anything if their subjects were alive so they could ask them some questions. I, on the other hand, would give anything if my subject were dead.

He should be. Oh, yes. Look at his daily routine:

3:00 p.m. rise
3:05 Chivas Regal with the morning papers, Dunhills
3:45 cocaine
3:50 another glass of Chivas, Dunhill
4:05 first cup of coffee, Dunhill
4:15 cocaine
4:16 orange juice, Dunhill
4:30 cocaine
4:54 cocaine
5:05 cocaine
5:11 coffee, Dunhills
5:30 more ice in the Chivas
5:45 cocaine, etc., etc.
6:00 grass to take the edge off the day
7:05 Woody Creek Tavern for lunch—Heineken, two marga-

ritas, two cheeseburgers, two orders of fries, a plate of tomatoes, coleslaw, a taco salad, a double order of fried onion
rings, carrot cake, ice cream, a bean fritter, Dunhills, another
Heineken, cocaine, and for the ride home, a snow cone (a
glass of shredded ice over which is poured three or four jig-
gers of Chivas)
9:00 starts snorting cocaine seriously
10:00 drops acid
11:00 Chartreuse, cocaine, grass
11:30 cocaine, etc, etc.
12:00 midnight, Hunter S. Thompson is ready to write
12:05–6:00 a.m. Chartreuse, cocaine, grass, Chivas, coffee,
Heineken, clove cigarettes, grapefruit, Dunhills, orange juice,
gin, continuous pornographic movies.
6:00 the hot tub—champagne, Dove Bars, fettuccine Alfredo
8:00 Halcyon
8:20 sleep

O! It just *hails* cocaine in the Doctor's house. I once saw him
put cocaine on his virile member and ask a Republican speechwriter to snort it off. She did. An ugly little skinny thing. Fortu-
nately she had sense enough not to chop it into piles first with a
razor. But I'll treat of his virile member later, when I get to that
part.

He is almost completely bald.

Once I found a picture of him with hair. For crying out loud!
I said. I lost it all at once, he said. At what age? I said. The year
I was supposed to die, he said. You were supposed to die? I said,
my ears pricking up. When I turned twenty-seven, he said. Why?
I said. Well, he said, that's how I had worked it. You knew you
were going to die? I said. Well, I *planned* on it, he said. Oh, really!
I said. He shook his head; had he *had* any hair he would have torn
it out. It's been confusion ever since, he said.

We were watching *Caligula* during this conversation. The Doctor held a big white Hitachi Magic Wand Vibrator in his hand.
About the size of a tire jack. I have it all on tape. I have everything
on tape, I have the Doctor on tape begging me to put everything
on tape if any *lawyers* happen to be interested.

Anyway, I was talking about biographers. Some biographers
harbor secret prejudices in their hearts for the individuals they are
writing about. I do not. I unrestrainedly hate Hunter Thompson.

I flatter myself, perhaps, but I am convinced that no biographer in the world ever loathed his subject as I loathe Hunter Thompson. Of course, I am in an unusual position here, in the cesspool. And naturally, to be perfectly frank, I did not always shudder at the detestable character whose crimes I am about to record. No, in the beginning I was rather——well, come now! I liked him better than his peacocks; if that doesn't give you some idea nothing will! Having said this much by way of introduction, I commit the following pages to the candor of the public.

2

It all began the evening I received the fax. It was Tuesday, July 16. I was sitting in my kitchen eating a hard-boiled-egg-and-mayonnaise sandwich. My picture had just appeared in a *New York Times* article about the Giant Cassowary. It was on the front page of the science section. I was wearing a Speedo bathing suit. I give you my word, Reader, if it hadn't been for that Speedo, there would have been no fax signed, "Love Doc."

To be perfectly frank, I might as well have been stark naked.

He asked me to call him. I did. He kept up a line of chatter and screams on the phone of which I did not understand a twentieth. I remember he frequently yelled: **GET OFF THE JEEP, YOU FUCK!** This would be followed by a blast of something called the pig-squealer. **TAKE THAT! GODDAMN IT!** he would cry. A second phone rang continually during our conversation. **FUCK YOU!** he would shout, **I TOLD YOU I WASN'T HOME!**

One time it rang and it was Ed Bradley, the *60 Minutes* correspondent. The two of them made plans to go to the hardware store and buy bug lights. The next day the Doctor sent a chartered plane to Indiana with an invitation to visit his 7,000-acre estate in Woody Creek, Colorado, the better to observe his birds, which he said were "trained to clear out schools for the blind and rooms full of small children."

As if I, Laetitia Snap, did not know the Thompson Peafowls! Had he not bred the only flock in the world above 8,000 feet, forty degrees north of the equator, obliterating the 7,806 record noted by Colonel W. W. Tott (1823–1897) in the temperate Palni Hills of India? Was Hunter Thompson not rumored to possess the most dazzling cock outside Punjab? But as for knowing *what* Dr. Thompson was, aside from the fact that he was some sort of writer, perforce, perforce, I was like a rack of lamb thrown to a Turkey Vulture.

One look was apparently enough for him.

I was hastened into his big red car with the white top *down* and transported at terrifying speed from the Aspen Airport to Owl Farm (huh!), his log domicile deep in the mountains outside rugged Woody Creek.

There he plied me with Chartreuse (I who never tasted liquor in my life!). Indeed the plying started in the car at ninety-one miles an hour when he handed me a margarita in a paper cup he had bought at the airport bar.

When I refused to let go of the dashboard, he turned on his blinking signal, stomped on the brakes, swerved into the weeds at no less than sixty miles an hour, and after coming to a standstill in a cloud of dust, with the huge engine rumbling, in the hot glare of the sunset, he subjected me to such large amounts of that Mexican intoxicant, that even now I am wondering in the dampness and silence of the cesspool if it did not contain Spanish Fly. I found Dr. Thompson so —————— attractive! Hairless and sweaty like something in the jungle.

"Should I have lipstick on?" he asked, turning off the car, which he called "the Shark."

His voice was deep and velvety. It rolled and vibrated like a cello. Not that he ever vocalized a complete word, no, sometimes it was just the vowels, other times the consonants, sometimes it was some other system, and in the intervals of articulation he produced various sounds as if he were locked in an iron lung face down in a drawer of nylons.

"You don't know what it's like having *hundreds* of ideas coming into your mind at once, Miss Tishy," said the Doctor, as I rummaged in my purse. I handed him a tube of Tempting Red. He applied it with the dexterity of a Revlon counter girl, turning from side to side, looking at himself in the rear-view mirror, sucking in his cheeks and pushing out his lips, saying, "Poooch! Poooch!"

"I can't imagine!" I said.

"Trying to control them," he said, smiling coquettishly. Then, dropping one shoulder and reaching under the seat, he took out a small round flat black steel container. He removed the lid, looked

inside, sighing and raising his eyebrows a little, licked the thing all over with zest, and put the lid back on.

"Is that cold-sore medicine?" I asked.

"Yes," he said, softening his voice. "The mountain air. Everything affects me."

"Oh!"

"Everything," he said, even softer and more passionate.

"You're a highly sensitive human being, Doctor!"

"Everything, yes."

He dropped his head to one side, his yellow plastic cigarette holder between his teeth catching the last gleams of the sun.

"It must drive you mad being that sensitive," I said.

"It does!" he said, giving a thump to the steering wheel. "It does," he said more gently. "That's true." He glanced at me hesitantly out of the corner of one eye. "It's nice that we can talk this way."

He was wearing aviators. Such a shy fellow!

His face kept changing color. He was unable to move a single muscle in his body naturally. Big-nosed, big-boned, six-five at least, with an unbecoming khaki bush hat on his head snapped up on *both* sides, a knit bike glove on his right hand, a red plaid short-sleeved shirt, khaki pants with pleats, low-cut Chuck Taylor All Stars, white socks, a black silk pilot's jacket with "Messaluna—Beirut" embroidered on the back, a United States Secret Service patch sewn on the left front and a Pitkin County Sheriff's Deputy badge pinned on the right, he was without exaggeration the worst-dressed chap I ever beheld in my life.

"Did you bring the cocaine?" he asked.

"Cocaine!" I cried.

He handed back my lipstick.

"Well. My niece is waiting," he said.

"Your niece!"

"I have to take you to the Jerome [hotel] now."

"But the *peacocks!*"

"I have so many things to do," he said, flexing his big knees.

"What do you have to do?"

"Get drugs."

"Drugs!" I eyed him. The aviators flickered with two green streaks of light. Had I thought he was serious I would have lost consciousness and fallen on the Shark's floor. "And then what?" I said.

"Do the drugs," he said.

"Get the drugs, do the drugs, and then what?"

"Pass out."

"And then?"

"Get more drugs."

"Ah."

"Do more drugs."

"Ah."

"And pass out."

"Ah!"

"You're a very opinionated broad," he said, smiling and giving my thigh a whack.

It was a test.

But no matter. He kept a survival kit in the Shark. It contained matches that lit in the wind. And he squandered the whole box for me in the breeze on the way to Owl Farm.

3

Don't torment yourself, Tishy, what does it matter, drunk or not. I confess I was out of my mind. I liked him, in short. He showed me the house. It was hard to believe how woody it was! In the living room he had a big fireplace and hundreds of speakers connected to a tape player. He put on Los Lobos, his favorite, and flopped down on the couch.

"This is *our* song, Miss Tishy," he said.

It was so loud I couldn't hear it.

Next stop, the bedroom. There were guns in the corner, guns on the floor in boxes, guns in cases——the room was chock-full of guns, guns thronged all about the bed. There were also a number of big electric fans with whirring blades like airplane propellers. When much, much later I used to awake, I would see him holding up the skirts of his bathrobe, trembling all over and sweating, staggering as close as he could to the walls so as to not take himself off at the knees.

THE CLOSET:

14 madras shirts
8 pair of khaki trousers

10 Hawaiian shirts
2 plaid sports jackets
1 blue seersucker sports jacket
1 green silk suit
19 pair of white low-cut Chuck Taylor All Stars

This list does not include his homely shorts wardrobe or the stacks of "Hunter S. Thompson" T-shirts he kept on his bookshelves. I clapped both hands to my forehead in amazement. "People give them to me," he said, rocking back and forth on the balls of his feet——anything to maximize his pleasures. "What for?" I said, "do you wear them?" "I give them to other people," he said, rocking happily. "The T-shirts are revolving."

One leg was longer than the other.

He set off for the study, what a walk! Neck stretched out like a Thai court dancer, extraordinary pitch to the pelvis, one elbow raised behind him, spine curved in an S, legs darting and lunging like an Indiana University Pom-Pom girl.

"Don't turn around, Miss Tishy!" he cried when we reached the office. Then he disappeared through a door. I heard crashing and straining in the next room. At some point he fell, I believe, or flung himself to the ground; that's how it sounded. His screams drew me to the door. Then there was silence, then more crashing and cursing. At last he called hoarsely, COME IN!

I opened the door halfway and put my head in. It was dark. After a moment, I could see the gonadal glow of a bubbling hot tub, and behind it, what we Hoosiers call a make-out couch, with leather cushions.

"I built the whole thing myself," said the Doctor proudly.

So much for the house. We returned to the kitchen for a blast of the pig-squealer. "This sound was obtained by tying a boar in the middle of a field and twisting his nuts with a pair of Harley-Davidson pliers!" he yelled cheerfully.

I never saw anybody so happy to be entertaining in my life.

The walls, the cabinets, the refrigerator, the top of the stove, and the lampshades were covered with newspaper clippings, faxes, poems, photos, reminders, letters, Polaroids, peacock feathers, lists, posters, leaflets, telegrams, memos, transcripts, tickets, statements, summonses, bulletins, cards, addresses, phone numbers, drawings, almost every square inch, like a cocoon, and he had a big IBM typewriter set up on the kitchen counter. He said this was where he wrote. The novel he was writing was called *Polo Is My Life*. Random House had given him a million dollars for it. "A million dollars!" I snorted. He said he had been working two months and had three pages completed.

"But I'm getting an editorial assistant," he said, and showed me his pictures of Filipino mail-order brides. His favorite was Anna Maria, 5'3", swimming, dancing, and postcard collecting. We ate chocolate cake. "Don't you want a glass of milk with that?" I asked. This stunned the Doctor. "Milk curdles the underside of my brain tissue," he said, "in the cortex."

His fork was in his hand. His eyes were fastened on my bust.

"Dr. Thompson!" I cried.

"Oh! Sorry!" he said.

He could discern it, I suppose, distended from my tiny shoulders, in my tight, dove-gray maillot, under my Calvin Klein suit jacket, jutting from my slender torso.

"I can see it trembling, Miss Tishy," he said.

"Dr. Thompson!" I cried again. "I'm here to see the peafowls!"

I tried to stand. My legs felt like they had taken a side blast from a tranquilizer gun.

"I can't help it, my dear," he said, pouring me another Chartreuse, "it puts me in the mood to write."

I'VE JUST HAD A NASTY INTERRUPTION ...

Well, I'm not stopping. The beast stands up there holding the lid of the cesspool and shouts down at me. Well, I'm *not* answering him.

4

Good. Fine. Now I've lost my concentration. This whole chapter, which I have been manipulating so delicately despite lacerating emotional and physical pain, calling up my first tender impressions of the dumb bastard, is ruined. Well, it can't be helped. What I write now will not be equal to what I had in mind when I was in a relatively good humor and merely besotted with misery, but the reader will have to put up with it.

The Doctor, finishing his cake, stood up and said he could not write a word until he freed my nipple and if he freed my nipple he could write at least two pages this very night, indeed probably more, so why didn't I read these three pages he had written already while he positioned me on a stool beside the couch in front of the TV in the kitchen and videotaped the whole operation?

"In what posture do you want me to be reading this?" I asked, smiling and nodding toward the camera. I might as well have been picking cherries, I was so shnockered.

"Well," said the Doctor, ruminating. "I want to free the nipple from this side. So then I should put the camera over ahhhhh here, right? [scratching his bald head] So ahhhhhh you should be turned in this direction." He hurled some newspapers and flashlights off the coffee table.

"You're the cinematographer!" I cried. Indeed, he had cameras set up on tripods all over the house.

I shook down the pages in my hands and began reading.

"What's a 'hooter'?" I said.

"Why don't you keep going?" said the Doctor, plunging his fingers into his glass of Chivas Regal and shoving them up his nostrils.

"Because I can't think what a hooter is."

"Nobody cares what you think," said the Doctor, stepping out from behind the camera.

"Well!" I cried, smacking him with the papers.

"Read! Read!" he said, taking my lapels between his fingers and thrusting them apart, "or I'll beat you!"

"You *bent* the pages."

"They're in *your* hands."

" 'The woman is a hooter.' "

"Read that again," said the Doctor, endeavoring to remove my suit jacket and fling it. "I like the way your voice jumps. I find it exciting."

"I'm fatigued with saying, 'The woman is a hooter.' "

"How would you like a taste of the long knuckle?" said the Doctor.

I continued reading.

"OK, now sit *very* still, Miss Tishy!" said the Doctor, assuming his position and bending towards my bust. I smelt a lovely smell. It must have come from the Chanel face cream he slathered himself with. The smell alone would have softened a hedgehog.

"Do you have the scissors?" I said.

"Read! Read!"

"EEEEEEEEEEEEK!"

"Sorry," said the Doctor.

"Well, you're too high. Pray, let me assist. [guiding his fat fingers] The tip's right there."

"Read! You're almost at the end!"

"OUCHHHHHHHH!"

"Oh! God!" cried the Doctor, the top of his bald head glowing like a Rome apple. "Hold still! Hold still!"

[Snip.]

And my nipple burst through like an exploding tooth paste cap. I can't tell you how pleased and happy Dr. Thompson was. He even darkened the aurae with blood red lipstick. "Almost looks like an ad for CBS," he said, tickled.

5

And then something odd happened. Odd things always happened around the Doctor because he himself was so odd it was like dealing with an extraterrestrial, but after he actually *did* compose two new pages on his special paper with the picture of the naked brunette with the ring through her labia while taking many a respite to admire, and even endeavor to suck and chew, the nipple, he handed me the pages.

"They're lost," he said sadly. "They'll all be lost. Lost forever."

"What do you mean?" I said.

"No one will ever see them except you," he said. Dawn was breaking. He was standing, but his knees seemed sapped.

"Why?" I asked.

He looked at me sadly and said nothing.

"But they're giving you a million dollars!"

He whispered very faintly, "Lost."

"You ordered me to put everything on my tape recorder. It's all here!" I said.

Utter Silence.

"All right!" he said suddenly. "Lighten up!"

A horn went off.

"What's that?" I said, jumping.

"Those fucking birds get in front of the motion sensor," he said.

"The peacocks!" I cried.

"Those stupid little bastards!" he said. "Come and see." And we went outside and when I beheld the Doctor lope out on the lawn between the sprinklers and heave a bucket of honeydew rinds at his cocks, and heard them shrieking **"PEHAUN PEHAN,"** and saw them shaking the crests on the crowns of their metallic blue heads, erecting their ocellated trains and strutting toward the Doctor rattling and shivering their feathers, it seemed to me, Reader, I had never seen a bird till that moment.

"You'll stay with me, Miss Tishy, won't you?" the Doctor whispered.

And everywhere, as the sun came up, there was the look of something extraordinary about to happen. What answer did I give the Doctor? Did we return to the house to free another nipple? Did Anna Maria, the Filipino mail-order bride, arrive? These are questions which will be answered after the first biographical section. But now we are going to turn back the clock. Yes, good-looking Reader, we are going to observe Hunter S. Thompson year by year, beginning at the beginning so as to produce in the end a picture of the man whose vices are enough to fill every bagnio between here and Terre Haute.

And in fact, if the Reader does not like my comments alternating with the biographical sections, I suggest he buy two copies of the book and read them simultaneously.

C H A P T E R
TWO

The word "Hunter" sounded strange in Mama's ears;
she imagined that a hunter must be some sort of
ferocious beast.

—LEO TOLSTOY

1

COMMONWEALTH OF KENTUCKY
BUREAU OF VITAL STATISTICS
CERTIFICATE OF BIRTH

Full Name of Child: Hunter Stockton Thompson
Place of Birth: Norton Infirmary, Louisville, Kentucky
Sex: Male *Legitimate?* Yes *Full Term?* Yes
Date of Birth: July 18, 1937 *Weight* (N.O.R.): 11 pounds
Father: Jack Robert Thompson, White, 42, Horse Cave, Ky
Mother: Virginia Davidson Ray, White, 29, Louisville, Ky
Father's Trade: Insurance engineering, First Kentucky Fire ·
  Insurance Co. 10 years
Mother's Trade: Housewife, 1½ years

Are you a Negro? No? Well, the thing I remember about going
over to Walter Kaegi's when we were about ten or eleven is
that Hunter used to say, "Let's go over to Kaegi's and fight the
niggers."
Because Kaegi's house backed up to Beargrass Creek, which

runs through a culvert at that point. And for some reason there were black guys on the other side of the culvert. I don't know if they lived there or what. But there would be taunts and bricks and stuff thrown. And then somebody would charge.

—NEVILLE BLAKEMORE, childhood friend of HST; Louisville lawyer

Beargrass Creek was a concrete culvert going through Louisville. And black dudes would be walking down there and we would ambush them. We'd have BB guns with us. When they'd come down the creek, we'd shoot at them. And well, of course, the result was absolutely predictable. They'd come boiling up out of the creek, and they're much bigger than us. They're black guys, and, of course, we'd run like mad, screaming and hollering, into Walter Kaegi's house and lock the door. And we'd hide in there.

And that became part of the Hunter mythology. "Let's go shoot 'em in the creek!"

—GERALD TYRRELL, known as "Ching," childhood friend of HST; retired executive vice-president of a bank; partner of The Dickens Group, a Louisville literary agency

He was like Charles Manson. He had his followers. Hunter was a force to be reckoned with, I'm telling you! He had a little reign of terror. We would quake at the sight of him. We would always travel in little groups of twos and threes and you would always try to catch a little shot to see if Hunter would be around.

He would swagger. He was in perpetual motion. Today they would use a term like "hyperactive." Everybody thought Hunter would end up in prison or dead or something. He was fearless. He knew structure and power. He was manipulative. If he wasn't the top banana the game plan changed.

—CHILDHOOD NEIGHBOR, four years younger than HST; name withheld by request

Hunter was the pole around which trouble would occur. He was a good-looking boy who could out-think you and out-perform you. But I believe he had great sadness. He was a serious, important child. Chairman of the Board of the gang. He knew how to bestow attention. His approval was extremely important because he had so many skills. And so you spent your whole time bouncing up and down waiting for Hunter to approve.

I remember there was a lot of stress involved in being around Hunter. You didn't want to cross him. He would become physically aggressive and physically violent. With his fists. And kicking. He was well coordinated and also effective. He would win. He would rile somebody up and then he would go at them like a windmill. He had a bad temper as a child. Also he had this way of standing *outside* any problem, so he never got caught.

Lying was the thing he did best. He did it with total cool and total confidence.

> —JOHN BRUTON, childhood friend of HST; South American businessman

I was afraid of the guy. And I still am. Always unnerved by his presence. Always minding my p's and q's and watching my step. Why? To my knowledge all he ever did was twitch my ears at the dining room table. He did it until I was ready to kill him. I pleaded with everyone at the table. "Can anyone do anything about this guy?" And it used to take until I was actually ready to burst into tears. And my mother would say, "Hunter, for God's sake!" or "Damn it!" When she was really mad she'd say, "Damn it." And everybody would freeze. But that's the only physical contact we ever had.

[We had dinner] every night at a large dining room table. Set with mats and with fine china. We always ate at the dining room table. Never ate in the kitchen.

> —JIM THOMPSON, HST's youngest brother; former disc-jockey; man of letters; currently working on his memoirs.

Hunter was difficult from the moment of his birth.

> —VIRGINIA RAY THOMPSON, HST's mother

He was always a pain in the ass. When World War Two was going on, oh, hell, we had to have been about five or six, maybe, and I went over to visit Hunter one time, and I had a stupid doll that was something made out of a piece of thin plywood, just this cut-out doll that you painted clothes on. And it was the days when you just didn't get toys so easy. And so that day I go over to see Hunter and he grabs my doll and smashes it over a tree.

—JUDY WELLONS WHITEHEAD, childhood friend of HST; businesswoman in Mexico

I remember the Thompson family was looked down on because they weren't nice people in the sense that when the parents were concerned, no one ever thought of calling Mrs. Thompson or Mr. Thompson. All I remember is there was this despair of Hunter because Hunter was incorrigible and you couldn't do anything about it because you couldn't talk to his mother. It was the kind of thing where there would never be anything like calling on them or dealing with them because they were *part* of it. Mrs. Thompson couldn't control her boy.

She could never cope with Hunter. She was sort of weak and dithery. A desperate, ineffective woman. I remember her as just covered with woe. The house itself was just messy. But she had a droll sense of humor. My own mother did not like Hunter, which added, of course, to the appeal.

—JOHN BRUTON

2

Let's say Hunter was not born into enormous affluence. And the Louisville we both grew up in was so free-form—the forties and fifties. The fabric of society was tearing. The whole business of integration, the influx of industry started corrupting this very sleepy, stable world of Southern society that lasted through the Second World War. And then all of a sudden, all bets were off! Everything was exploding! The city was growing at a phenomenal rate. All the old institutions were being fragmented and de-

centralized and there was absolutely nothing you could hang
your hat on.

> —PORTER BIBB, childhood friend of HST; former
> publisher of *Rolling Stone;* currently Director of
> Corporate Finance for a major investment firm.

Louisville? Louisville is a tight-assed town. Hunter, Walter Kaegi,
Ching Tyrrell, Neville Blakemore, Duke Rice, Judy Wellons—she
lived in a very large house on Willow; John Bruton's house was
enormous, his parents had a chauffeur, we all lived in what is now
called the Cherokee Triangle. It has eleven or twelve streets. Old
frame houses, big trees, big yards; like yuppies and preppies live in
the Triangle now and there are a lot of the old guard still there,
and they've just kept it up. Hunter lived on Ransdell in a stucco
house with a big front porch.

> —"GINNY DANIALS," childhood friend of HST;
> entrepreneur; does not wish her true name
> revealed

3

When his father was alive he used to sit on the front porch with
his little radio and watch us play in the front yard. His dad was
a lot older. He was a retired, white-haired, stone-faced guy who
didn't say much. He was a big sports fan. He would listen to the
Louisville Colonels baseball team sitting on the porch. I think
Hunter respected him. His mother had no power over him, but
had great influence. His father could discipline him, up until the
end.

> —GERALD TYRRELL

I remember that his father may have occasionally whipped Hunter.
I mean in those days. And I think he used a razor strap. I recall
Hunter using the term "whipped in the snoshole."

> —WALTER KAEGI, childhood friend of HST;
> professor of history at the University of Chicago

——Tell me about your father.

—— (Silence)

—— You never talk about him.

—— Well, read what I've written!

—— I've read everything you've written. You *never* mention him.

—— (Silence)

—— Tell me about him.

—— He had a great outlook on life.

—HUNTER THOMPSON interview*

4

We played war over at Walter Kaegi's house. We had helmet liners and we would put them on like we were little soldiers. And we'd go over to Walter's and he'd make us java. You know, we'd drink some java. Actually it was tea and he made it very sweet and full of milk, you know, just like soldiers, see?

We all had armies. Lead soldiers. Second World War guys. At one point we made tanks in Hunter's basement out of wooden blocks with great spikes for cannons and we also had places where we could hide our soldiers inside. Then we went over to Neville Blakemore's house and played war with him and stole all his good soldiers. We put them in the bodies of our tanks. There was one machine gunner that was just an absolute beauty, you know, a World War One-type machine-gun guy, and we all coveted it. Hunter stole it. He got it. And when we returned to his basement afterwards we opened up our tanks and found that we had half of Neville's soldiers. And Neville kept saying, "I seem to have lost my soldiers. What happened?" We all said, "We don't know. We haven't seen them." Of course they were in the bellies of our tanks.

—GERALD TYRRELL

---

*All interviews with all individuals were conducted by the author unless otherwise noted.

The forties, after all, were *very* different from the fifties or the sixties. Remember that. Hunter went through World War Two. There were scrap-metal drives, we collected grease, there were air-raid drills, and blackouts. And looking at the culture of boys in that period—there was a radio culture. A comic book culture. We used to listen to *Sergeant Preston*. There was a cowboy thing. *The Lone Ranger*. Television didn't exist. We went to the movies on Saturdays, the matinee.

And we boys had a code of honor among ourselves. We had rules. They were not imposed by need, and were very strong.

In fights Hunter's technique was always to provoke action and then do something startling. To throw the other person off balance, physically as well as psychologically. He created situations of confusion and perhaps even fright or disorientation.

In the wars there would usually be five or six boys to a side. We were usually bare-chested and wore helmet liners, army surplus from World War Two, and carried Daisy air rifles, BB guns and, of course, rocks. A lot of Louisville had vegetation. Lots of squirrels, rabbits, minks. So there were places for ambushes. There was a woods near us. There were plenty of rocks. Our mothers were terrified. Because of course we could have been blinded by the BB guns and the rocks. But this was Kentucky. And Hunter is very Kentucky. Kentucky is a very violent place.

—WALTER KAEGI

Then we all got bullwhips. Hunter sold his army to buy his bullwhip. And we'd go to Lash LaRue movies. Lash could take somebody's cigarette right out of their mouth. So we practiced on tree branches. We put poppers on the ends so we could crack them even better. And then we'd go strolling through the neighborhood with our bullwhips and there's somebody's mailbox, hey, we'd go pop that mailbox. Make a big dent in that mailbox. We'd pop tree branches as we'd go along. Now there was a rumor that Hunter popped a cat, but I was not with him. I never saw Hunter hurt an animal. But there was a rumor that Hunter took the bullwhip to the cat and made the fur fly.

—GERALD TYRRELL

That hat he often wears in pictures is the same style as a Confederate cavalry hat and that goes back to elementary school. He was a tall boy with high cheekbones and certainly by the fifth grade he was wearing a Confederate hat. Flapped. In the autumn months I remember he wore a zipped brown leather jacket. Also I remember him wearing an Army jacket with insignia on it. And the boys would wear the Cub Scout shirt without the pants. Which also tended to look like a cavalry uniform.

We did a lot of reading at the Highland Branch Library. This was after World War Two and before the Korean War. And we boys just *constantly* read about war. Mainly the Civil War. We knew quite a bit about the Southern generals and read in detail about the battles. Next to us on Bates Court there was a woods, and that's where we played North-South. That's the critical thing, North-South. We passed letters back and forth over enemy lines. Hunter was General Thompson of the Virginia Second Cavalry. His base was Fort Lee. Mine was the Army of Central Georgia. We made special control stamps and special cancellations.

—WALTER KAEGI

I've always felt like a Southerner. And I always felt like I was born in defeat. And I may have written everything I've written just to win back a victory. My life may be pure revenge.

—HUNTER THOMPSON interview

Hunter was a Southerner, but Rhett Butler and Hunter had *nothing* in common.

—JUDY WELLONS WHITEHEAD

5

I remember that we played doctor with the girls. One of the girls was M———. She is now a very proper lady. She married a guy named ———. We had a room off our garage and we played doctor there. Hunter and a bunch of us took her into the back room and we had her pull her pants down and we looked and I remember somebody drew what it looked like on the wall. It was marvelous. Dear M————. Her father was one of the most respected doctors in Louisville!

—JOHN BRUTON

You know I gave Hunter his first writing job when he was ten. I started and edited *The Southern Star*. It was printed on my father's office mimeograph machine. Later I hand-set with rubber type. It was four cents a copy. I published and edited it for three years.

—WALTER KAEGI

HAWKS A.C. TURN PRO

FORM ALL-STARS

The Hawks A.C. have changed the name of their club to the Highland All-Stars. . . .
Coach Brecky Speed is a great help to the team. Players get paid about 20–25¢ a month.

—HUNTER THOMPSON, *The Southern Star* (written when he was twelve years old)*

Hunter organized a baseball team one year. It was called the Cherokee Colonels. Hunter, of course, was the shortstop. And everybody in those days did a bit of stamp collecting. Hunter and Duke Rice formed a stamp company and sold to the little guys. To earn more money we'd go to Walgreen's and buy those cheesy folding stools for a buck apiece and then we'd take them to the infield at the Kentucky Derby and sell them for five dollars each. Then we'd bet the money. There was virtually *nowhere* we couldn't go as

---

*See Bibliography for a complete list of HST's works.

youngsters. We had the run of the city. Downtown was ours! Bikes gave us an awful lot of mobility. We were really very fearless little boys. On Saturdays we went to the movies with bean-shooters. The trick was to get a whole mouthful of beans and blow them out like a machine gun. This is what we did in the movies in those days. And then Hunter discovered girls.

The girl that he discovered was Judy Wellons. Hunter walked down the street with his saunter and kind of hit her on the arm, and I thought this was awful. What's he messin' around with girls about?

—GERALD TYRRELL

We got off the bus and my dog always used to come and meet me. My little dog named Dubby. She was just this little black dog. Whenever my sisters and I would fight, the dog would get all excited and bite my sister. And so I was telling Hunter this story, and, "So," I said, "you better never hurt me while my dog is around because she'll bite you," and Hunter said, "Oh, yeah?" And I said, "Yeah." So he hauls off and kicks my dog across the street.

—JUDY WELLONS WHITEHEAD

6

Mother's about five eight or nine. Pretty substantial. But not fat, either. Robust, I guess. She's never worn slacks or pants one day in her life.

Mother had to leave the University of Michigan because the family ran out of money. She was a swimmer and she played tennis. She rode horses. This is back in the 1920s. At one point in her life she owned a horse.

. . . My mother would give us a long leash. Let us go as long as we wanted on our own until we messed up and then—there *might* be discipline. Maybe. She was not a nagger at all. But she had three boys. There was Hunter, then my brother Davison, who was three years younger. And then me. She had an awful leather strap that she kept in the drawer with the cloth napkins. And she would bring out that strap. It was horrible-looking. It had a buckle on it. And that was all she would do. She'd say, "Well, let's see here. We've got this strap. What are we going to do with this strap?" And that would quiet us down. I cannot remember ever being hit by my mother.

She would probably admit today that she spoiled us rotten. If she had to do it over again, she probably would have clamped down a little harder. We all made C's in school.

—JIM THOMPSON

I think there is something of the Southern belle about Virginia Thompson, though Southern belle is not a fair description because it implies a shrinking violet or an empty, mannered type of youthful femininity which is very old-school. This is not Virginia Thompson. She is a brilliantly insightful realist. She hates decorum for the phony sake of appearing proper.

—JEFF PORTER, close friend of the Thompson family

My mother is sharp. She's intelligent, but not in a bookish, schoolish kind of way. She has a very dry humor, pretty cynical, but she would probably stake a claim to being an optimist. She's kind of a stiff-upper-lip optimist. Even in the face of absolute tragedy. I rarely see her cry. I've never seen her raging mad. She's solid. Even-keeled. A Roosevelt Democrat, good strong liberal, a strong libertarian. She doesn't know it, but she's almost radical in that regard.

. . . But my mother was not at all physical. She never hugged and kissed us. Never. I don't remember ever being touched by my mother in an affectionate way. Hell no. There wasn't any of that in my family.

—JIM THOMPSON

—— How's your mother?

—— She's at home sharpening her teeth.

—HUNTER THOMPSON interview

My mother was not particularly feminine. She carried her suffering, I would say, respectfully, as a woman. But I don't think she was out there to win anybody's heart. I never saw her flirt or romance or carry on.

. . . Sex was not a big issue around our house. It wasn't discussed. When it came time to, uh, talk about sex, my mother gave me a book. Probably the same with Hunter and Davison, called *Being Born*. I remember we were fascinated by it because it showed a woman's breasts. She was getting ready to breast-feed her baby. And we would all turn to that page and gather round and look at this picture. And it showed cows and baby cows and baby sheep. Sex was really downplayed. *Really* downplayed.

—JIM THOMPSON

The girls just loved Hunter. And gosh, I remember going down at the Highland Presbyterian Church to a youth group called The League. It was every Sunday afternoon at five o'clock. That's where we did our first close dancing. We'd turn the lights out, and we had the jukebox, and do that close dancing. And the girls, they always wanted to dance with Hunter.

Susan Barnes was there, known as Susan Peabody. When Hunter came back here for the Castlewood Reunion in 1990, she's the one he wanted to see. He asked me to give her a call.

—GERALD TYRRELL

Have you heard about the bracelet Hunter gave me? This ID bracelet, an engraved, silver ID bracelet with my name on the front and his on the back? Just the names. Just first names. Susan and Hunter. I don't remember ever kissing Hunter. He was not forward excepting his wildness. Hunter, sexually, was shy. And so was I.

—SUSAN PEABODY BARNES, childhood sweetheart

We all joined the Sunday school class because we could ahhhh, we had special activities. At night we had all taken up smoking pipes. We would go to the Walgreen's drugstore across from the library.

And we got pipes of tobacco. And sneaked out of the Sunday school and smoked our pipes on the stairs of the church.

—HUNTER THOMPSON interview

—— Did the Presbyterian teaching about free will affect you?

—— It didn't matter to me what the fuck they were doing.

—— Did it influence your life?

—— I paid *no* attention.

—— But you live so existentially.

—— Sunday school was a fun gang.

—— Did you ever pray?

—— (Rolls his eyes)

—— When you were young? Did you go through a holy period?

—— No.

—HUNTER THOMPSON interview

Probably it's not important, but I realized I told a tale wrong and want to correct it. The story about my dog who would always protect me. I think I said that Hunter kicked the dog—WRONG! He slapped the hell out of *me*. He wanted to see if my dog would attack anyone who hurt me as I claimed. Of course the dog did nothing while I reeled in whirling stars. I don't know how I got that so wrong. As I remember, Hunter always liked dogs.

—JUDY WELLONS WHITEHEAD, in a midnight fax

Oh, he was a fox! I mean, well, you daydreamed about Hunter. At twelve I'd go home to my bedroom and think, "God I'd like to kiss Hunter, I'd like to pull his pants down and see what his penis looks like."

He was just sexy. Sexy, but beyond that. There was a quality in Hunter that I think has always stayed with me, that I always look for in a man. This arrogance. He had a walk that was cool. I wonder if he still walks that way.

And he was a leader. Hunter was the leader of the gang which
we had—I still have this fantasy! I daydream of being in bed with
Hunter. If Hunter and I ever got together, good God!

I met him at twelve. I had just moved to the neighborhood.
And I went out to play. And I was introduced to the kids on the
block. And there was this big buildup and then they said, Here's
Hunter. And his first question to me was, "Are you a Yankee or
a Southerner?"

And I said, "I don't know, I think I'm a Yankee or something."
So he said, "That's the *wrong* choice." And I had this little hat on.
And he took my hat and he threw it down in the mud. And I
fought, and I mean we actually fought. And he said, "From now
on you're going to be a Southerner. This is it."

A lot of girls felt like I did. But a lot of girls were afraid of
Hunter. Because he was dangerous. They said that he was wild.
But he *thrilled* me. When we had slumber parties, it was like,
"OOOOOoooooo, Hunter!"

Hunter would be the one that we would try to call and ask,
"What do you look like naked?" But some girls said, Oh, my
mother thinks he's just too wild. But I never said that, because I
secretly always wanted to be—Hunter's girl.

—GINNY DANIALS

I was down from Shelbyville seeing Hunter. We were either walking or riding our bikes. But anyway we were over on Lexington
Road where there was this little grocery store. And Hunter walked
in that grocery store and just picked up what he wanted, candy
bars, potato chips, and I think he even took a soft drink, and put
it in his pocket, and just walked out! Scared me to death! I said,
"My Lord, I'd be in jail for that!" Walked right on out. I never
have forgotten it! It scared the hell out of me, to tell you the
truth.

—LEWIS MATHIS, childhood friend; lawyer in
Shelbyville, Kentucky

Hunter and I met these guys from Shelbyville at Presbyterian
camp. And we started visiting back and forth. We loved going up
to the Shelby County Fair. That's where we saw our first stripper.

She was in a tent and not particularly attractive. She was old, or she seemed old to us little boys at the time. And not very glamorous. This was sort of the end of the stripping circuit out there in rural Kentucky. But there was a sort of anatomical interest in little boys, especially Hunter.

They weren't really wonderfully smooth strippers like you would get in a burlesque house, with the long gloves. They had music. They'd be on the stage, lit up so we could see them. And they took off their outfits, and they did remarkable things with Ping-Pong balls and with cigarettes.

I remember the stripper popping a Ping-Pong ball out of her vagina, which we all thought was pretty amazing! And she smoked a cigarette with her vagina. She just stuck it in there and Hunter, Lewis and I clapped.

—GERALD TYRRELL

The strippers were just in an old tent. And they got up on the stage. And people would start throwing money at them. We didn't have any money. So Hunter tried to steal some from the girls off the stage.

—LEWIS MATHIS

7

COMMONWEALTH OF KENTUCKY
BUREAU OF VITAL STATISTICS
CERTIFICATE OF DEATH

Name of Deceased: Jack R. Thompson*
Date of Death: July 3, 1952
Autopsy? Yes
Condition Directly Leading to Death: Cerebral Embolus
Interval Between Onset and Death: Minutes
Other Significant Conditions: Virus Bronchopneumonia, Chronic
     Recurrent Thrombophlebitis, right leg

---

*HST's father

C H A P T E R
THREE

Meanwhile, I am undressed and subjected to the
most impudicious fondlings. . . .
—THE MARQUIS DE SADE

1

Did he actually free my nipple? Incredible! *On film?* Astonishing!
Who did he think I was? A runway model for mammography candidates? These memories sent a thrill of panic through me. I fell to
shivering and gnashing my teeth in agony. What's more, it felt as
if an iron band had been clamped around my head and I began to
think the top of my tongue had been dragged on a hook up and
down the stairs.

O! Why had I come? Why had I drunk that Chartreuse? *Who*
was this man? What tormented me beyond endurance as I opened
my eyes at 2:55 p.m.——2:55, Reader!——was my imbecilic sub-
missiveness to Dr. Thompson. Had he asked me to pierce myself
from knees to eyebrows with labia rings I would have!

To exasperate myself as much as possible against the dirty cad,
instead of getting out of bed (I was in "Juan's room," whoever
that was, in the basement) I propped myself up in the pillows, and
though half distracted, began examining the Polaroid pictures the
Doctor had insisted we take of one another the previous night.

They contained no actual outrages, thank God! the shame
would have killed me (I remember he kept asking questions about
the Miss Indiana contest and inquiring whether there was a "burly
lesbian matron who ran her fingers under the plump breasts of the

young contestants," and many times as he aimed the camera at me, he hollered, "Now that's a fashion shot for sure!"); but in every picture of *him*, in the lines of his long flat cheeks and fat tree-shrew nose, in the space——a veritable veld!——between his nostrils and upper lip, in each and every one of his features, in fact, he appeared a different man. "You don't look like you look," I had said. *"I'm not who I am,"* he had answered.

While puzzling over this chameleon and deciding to pack my bags at once, I unfortunately heard the Doctor upstairs in the kitchen yanking back and forth on a venetian blind, shouting **GODDAMN IT, YOU BASTARD!** and perhaps ripping it entirely from the window and stamping on it; I couldn't tell, the noise was so violent——and, Reader, I am ashamed to say, before I knew what was happening, my heart . . .

. . . It leapt, Reader, L-E-A-P-T, Smirking Reader. That flesh marked for sacrifice leapt like a fat frog on a lily pond. Never in my life was I so flabbergasted. The idea that I actually *liked* Dr. Thompson!——this was too much, too much for poor Tishy!·

Trembling with fear and emotion, I put on my best outfit and went upstairs to the kitchen.

The Doctor was sitting at his typewriter rocking back and forth, smoking a Dunhill, drinking a glass of Chivas, reading the *USA Today* sports section, and watching a golf tournament.

The venetian blind was in the sink.

The top of his bald pate glowed with health in a rich rhubarb shade. He smacked me on the neck with a rolled-up *Denver Post* and I fancied he glanced for a moment at my bust, with a smile, which caused the blood to rush to my cheeks. He said he had just awakened. He was attired in a handsome blue bathrobe with the word "SkullBoy" written across the back. I almost admired him. He handed me a Bloody Mary, I handed it back, he handed me the Bloody Mary again, I handed it back, and so on, to and fro, till, excited by the struggle, I had drunk the whole thing. He increased the volume on the TV and eyed it distrustfully.

A minute passed.

"There're no goddamned trees on that golf course!" he cried suddenly, and thumped the kitchen counter with his fist so hard his Dunhill butts jumped in the air.

I turned my eyes to the screen.

"Look!" he cried, pointing with one hand and opening the drawer beside him with the other. "Not a fucking tree!"

The TV screen was the size of a card table.

"Do you see any trees?" he cried, riffling about in the drawer and pulling out a big Ziploc freezer bag.

"I don't see any trees," I said.

"I've been watching, goddamn it!" he said, taking down a knife that was hanging above him and cutting the bag along two seams, opening it and spreading it out flat. "And I haven't seen a god-damned tree!"

There was a fine white powdery residue of what I guessed must have been confectioners' sugar all over the inside of the bag. This he scraped off neatly with the knife and ate. A starving child from the Guadalajaran slums could not have been more thorough.

"What kind of fucking golf course *is* that!" he cried, and then he held up the bag and examined it for missed spots. A whole line of snowy, powdery confectioners' sugar had gathered in the seam. He probably kept Mexican wedding-ring cookies in the bag, I conjectured, because he bent over and licked it. I must say, I would have done the same myself. I adore Mexican wedding rings!

"It's supposed to be the *Championship!*" he cried, licking up and down the bag. He had a tongue like a Great Pyrenees. "And the bastards have chopped down every goddamned tree!"

"Where's it being played?" I asked. "Do you have any more cookies?"

"Scotland!" he cried, taking another empty dusty powdery bag out of the drawer and beginning to cut it open. "Not a god-damned tree in the whole fucking country!"

Before they pulled back with an aerial shot revealing literally acres and acres of trees, poor Dr. Thompson had cut, scraped and licked five bags. And I must say he seemed very relieved.

2

After a chap named Martin paid a short visit and left four new big Ziploc bags filled with confectioners' sugar for the Doctor——really now! I began to smell a rat. Was the Doctor keeping a Mexican baker as a lover?——it was decided we would go to lunch at the Frying Pan.

The Frying Pan was about eight or nine miles away in a little town called Basalt. This necessitated an emotional upheaval about which car the Doctor would drive, the Shark or the Jeep, a discussion which Dr. Thompson conducted with hysterical zest unusual even in a male, and which he did not quit till he had run down all the minutest particulars like Little Al before the Indianapolis 500 (of which I was Princess, by the by). This was followed by a long search for the keys with the Doctor loping back and forth through the house repeating in a low mournful voice, "Those cocksuckers! Those cocksuckers!" and then coming to a complete standstill with his arms dropped to his sides and his mouth hanging open in utter bewilderment as he spied them on the key rack.

Next he had to fill two short-stemmed, wooden-bowled pipes with a substance I strongly, *strongly,* suspected was in violation of every law of nature and decency——Reader, I believed the Doctor possessed marijuana!

Have ruth upon me!

Then, handing the loathsome pipes to me, he said, "Here, Miss Tishy, put these in your pocket," and while I, benumbed with fright, sank down in a chair——had I not had three Bloody Marys I would have run out on the road and flung myself in the ditch——he prepared his snow cone (Chivas with ice) "for the drive";——driving and drinking, yet!——then he couldn't find the bomb he said he wanted to throw into the Woody Creek Tavern on the way to Basalt, then he found it but said it was coming apart and would have killed him and this gave him a good laugh while he was looking for the other bomb which he couldn't find either, well, yes, he did find the other bomb but he mislaid it again; then he couldn't find the keys he just had, then the alarms had to be set, then he sent me to look for the automatic garage door riser, then he was undecided as to what he should wear, and at last, garbed in white boating pants, a white "INTERNATIONAL POLO—100TH ANNIVERSARY" polo shirt, a white "INTERNATIONAL POLO—100TH ANNIVERSARY" baseball cap, white socks, and white Chuck Taylor All Stars, he was ready; and this, mark you, Reader, was the shortest time the Doctor ever took leaving his house.

It started to pour.

We entered the garage.

"Don't worry, Miss Tishy. If we drive fast enough we won't get wet," said the Doctor, heaving himself like a big squid into the spanking red convertible.

He settled his drink in the caddy, lit a cigarette, spread out his arms and legs as if he was sitting in a deck chair at the Indianapolis Marriott, and then, glancing in the rear-view mirror and mashing on the gas, pulled out of the garage at thirty-five miles an hour in reverse.

The peacocks, excited by the rain, their heavy trains erected and quivering, were dancing in the driveway. We shrieked past them with the noise of a jet exhaust, spun 180 degrees, and then hurtled through the gates accelerating to 112 (0 to 110 in 13.4 seconds), and by God, as I clutched those grass pipes and prayed to Jesus for a state trooper to stop us, it was true, we had not felt a drop!

Suddenly the Doctor braked.

"Goddamned slow-moving fucks!" he cried, pulling up behind a ranchero and pounding the steering wheel. "Ye Gods!" Rain was drenching his new Polo hat. "Goddamn bastards!" His cigarette was wet clear through. "Get up off the floor, Miss Tishy!"

3

After his steak ("charred *very quickly* to cinders just on the outside"), potatoes, taco, beans, rice, two margaritas from the Frying Pan, a margarita and three dozen oysters from Chefy's across the street, and the glass of Chivas he brought with him, the Doctor, his long face reminiscent of a Royal Tern, sat under the dripping eaves of the Frying Pan smoking one of his marijuana pipes.

Oh! It wafted up and down Basalt with the odor of a burning tire dump. Four screwdrivers were barely enough to give me courage to sit through it.

4

Hunter S. Thompson!

He ate like a wild dog.

Had he injected the rust off the table leg into his bloodstream, I would not have been surprised.

Now here, the Beast's just dropped something into the cesspool. One moment. Ah! Two frozen bean and cheese burritos and a carton of sanitary napkins. I can tell you right now, I have enough sanitary napkins to swaddle myself up to the waist until menopause. And if I ever get out of here I'm going to kill him.

5

Now where was I? I've just spent an hour defrosting those hideous burritos over the space heater. So what was I talking about? Well, Egads! I can't remember what I was——ah, he made me suck four or five times on the marijuana pipe after he veered off the road and drove up a culvert, the Shark bucking and zigzagging like a big flapping goose.

Red monkey flowers came up to the windows.

He rolled the top down. Then he put his arm around me, and in addition, he had the most beautiful bloodshot brown eyes you ever saw. Oh, those eyes were perfect mud pools! And thick, hairy black eyebrows like a hawk owl. I only noticed them after the four or five sucks on the marijuana pipe. I thought he was going to kiss me. I struggled and trembled, and waited for him to unleash his instincts. And then he spoke: "I have a present here from Alexander Haig."

I opened my eyes.

He was reaching into his jacket, the black Messaluna-Beirut jacket with the Pitkin County Sheriff's badge and Secret Service patch. He pulled out a Kodak snapshot envelope.

"Alexander Haig wanted you to have this, Miss Tishy," he said, opening it.

He removed a white piece of thickish, blottery paper with perforations.

"What's that?" I said.

"I don't know," said the Doctor.

"I've never seen anything like it," I said, frowning.

"Neither have I," said the Doctor, whispering.

He tore off two small squares. He put one in his mouth and handed me the other.

"Take yours," he said.

"What is it?" I said.

"Just put it in your mouth and chew it," he said. "Like this."

He drew back his lips and showed me how to make the tiny mastications.

"What is it?" I said.

"Trust me," said the Doctor.

"What is it?"

"I'm not telling you. Just *do* it."

I looked into his eyes. Living velvet.

"I want to see if you trust me," he said, chewing.

"Then tell me what it is," I said.

"Acid," he said, smiling.

"Acid!" I screamed.

"You've got to do it with me. We have to do this *together*, Miss Tishy."

Then he pried open my lips and penetrated my mouth with the murderous chemical.

Oh! Why hadn't he just thrown me on the seat and ravished me instead! O dreadful! Now what would become of me? How much time did I have before I jumped out the Big Window like Art Linkletter's daughter? How long, O Lord, before my head blew up like a rancid peach?

I sighed and howled.

"Now, don't swallow it," said Dr. Thompson, smiling. "Just chew it."

6

DR. HUNTER S. THOMPSON'S HOT TUB LIST:

Bowl of cherries
Bowl of strawberries
Plate of Dove Bars
Bottle of Chartreuse
Bottle of champagne
Glasses
Bottle of Chivas
Marijuana pipe
Little black flour grinder
Bean-shooter
Confectioners' sugar

[I had seen the Doctor poking the bean-shooter up his nostrils and snorting——well now, it couldn't be confectioners' sugar, could it now, Reader? What on earth could it be? I saw him with the bean-shooter up his nose twenty times before it hit me. Then I sat rooted to the spot. I nearly went out of my mind. It was ...... COCAINE! There could be no doubt about it, ... COCAINE! Reader! I was stupid with shock. The blackguard! The villain! But then a thick fog descended; all the lights went dim as the first wave of acid came over me.]

Dunhills
TarGards
Lighter
Selection of fine terry-cloth robes
Towels
Appropriate movie
[*Unthinkable,* starring the renowned slut Tamara. Oh what a picture, Great God! A dog in heat behaves with more decorum. In the opening scene the nasty jade makes love to herself, then the sister, then the brother, then the sister *and* the brother, then another sister arrives and makes love to the younger sister, then the Doctor got bored and put on *Caligula.*]
Pink feather boa

Over the tub the Doctor hung the pink feather boa. He petulantly flicked at it from time to time before he turned off the lights and replayed the *Caligula* Beheading Scene.

"Oh! Almost forgot ha ha!" he cried, and left the Hot Tub Room.

A minute later he returned with one of the video cameras and for the next thirty or forty minutes he scuttled up and down the steps between the office and Hot Tub Room with the tripod.

Then he readjusted the dangle of the feather boa, opened and closed the sliding doors to the back yard, flustered the curtains, brought in a vase of peacock feathers to decorate the make-out couch, I can't go on, and when all was ready, with the camera aimed at the center of the water, he shifted his eyes in my direction——No. I'm going to quit. Go on! Go on, Tishy!

I was perched fully clothed in my Donna Karan black turtleneck sweater and tight black leggings on the side of the tub waiting for the next wave of the acid to hit. The Doctor was stark naked beneath a royal-red robe. And then the appalling moment the Reader has been fearing. The Doctor reversed *Caligula* to the Beheading Scene again, shucked his wrapper and, howling like a sea lion, plunged into the thrashing water.

What with the magnification of the bubbles, the underwater lights, the Jacuzzi vibrations, the heat, the steam, the marijuana, the Chartreuse and the acid, the Doctor's doodle looked to be a half a yard long and as big around as the calf of my leg. With four or five cullions, besides. "Miss Tishy," said the Doctor. "Take off that sweater!"

And to my utter astonishment, without so much as a protest, I pulled it off over my own head and threw it out the door onto the deck! I, myself, sat on the edge of the tub for a moment and stared, pop-eyed, at the woolly thing. I must have looked quite a sight in my black lacy bra, because the Doctor had suddenly stopped watching *Caligula* and had turned about in the water and was gazing up at me.

Perhaps I was even a delicious sight, for I have very finely developed plump round bubbies, very firm, very smooth, very white, indeed one of the male judges of the Miss Indiana Pageant suffered a stroke during the swimsuit competition, I had caused such tumultuous excitement——and I am not saying this to brag; my abdomen is like marble, and it must have offered quite a contrast, the sight of my tightly swathed buttocks so beautifully relieved by the white intake of my young back and abdomen, and above, the lacy, feathery bra and the bursting bubbies.

"Hand me a strawberry, Tishy, dear," said the Doctor in a husky voice.

And as I turned to reach behind me, the Doctor pulled me into the agitated swirl. Lord! I felt his huge rough hands gliding all over my bubbies! and in the most private parts of my person, as I struggled to come up for air. "Doctor!" I shrieked, breaking the surface. "Take these *off*!" he said, pulling at my leggings.

"Never!"

"Off!"

"No! No! No!" I cried, and heaved my haunch up on the side of the tub, my tresses streaming, and demurely sipped my Chartreuse.

"OFF, Miss Tishy!" said the Doctor, suddenly pulling a knife from the wall. We both stared at it in surprise; he even paused a moment and tested the sharpness with the tip of his thumb. Indeed, he kept knives of all descriptions in every room. This particular knife had a nine-inch blade and was lashed to a three-foot-long bamboo handle and looked to be modeled on the short fighting spears used by Telefomin warriors in New Guinea.

"Off with your pants!" he cried.

"Put that away!" I shrieked, laughing, whereupon he seized my right ankle, lifted my leg out of the water, pulled the material up and slashed off the bottom of my leggings.

I smacked him on the head with the nearest object, a towel! "Oh, Stop! Stop!" I screamed, and oddly enough even though I was terrified out of my wits and was screaming at the top of my lungs, I could still hear myself laughing hysterically. He took a second swipe and hacked my leggings off at the knee——I was certain that after he slashed off all the material, he would start on my epidermis, cut through to the dermis, the connective tissue, and so on till he chopped down to the marrow of my bones.

At some point, I don't know which, my bra was snapped off my body and thrown into the bowl of cherries.

"WHERE ARE YOU WHEN I NEED YOU, MIKE TODD!" I cried.

"Mike will be of no help to you now," said the Doctor, grasping my other leg and cutting a gigantic slit in the thigh.

He was making great sweeping slashes now, holding the stretchy material out and then streaking the knife through the air and slicing, the pieces of material flying and floating about us. Once he passed within half an inch of my stomach, and on another whack he actually took some fine hairs off the front of my knee. And I was still laughing. On the last pass, he slashed the material straight up to my waist, tore the shreds from my body and threw them out the door, over the deck, into the leopard lilies.

My black lace silk panties he popped at the hip with one manly pull.

"Now, Miss Tishy," he said, rolling over to the opposite side of the tub and propping one arm on the side, "isn't that better?" And thus my second day at Owl Farm drew to a close.

Did the Doctor offer any further freedoms? And what about the peacocks? Would I ever remember the reason for my visit? And when would the acid kick in? These are questions which will be answered after the next biographical section. Because now, well-built Reader, we are going to return to the salad days of

Hunter S. Thompson. If you will recall, when we last saw our young hero, and here I advise you to turn to the first photo section and look at his hideous high school photo, and if you find it unhandy to keep turning back and forth between the photos and biographical notes, I advise you to buy a third copy of the book; as you will recall, when we last met our young rapscallion he was shooting at Negroes and stealing money from strippers.

C H A P T E R
FOUR

His unparalleled vices saved him from oblivion.
—EDWARD GIBBON

1

A story in the Louisville *Courier Journal*, June 16, 1955:

Tearful Youth Is Jailed
Amid Barrage Of Pleas

Should I Give Him Medal? Judge Asks Mother; Even Victims of Park Theft Try to Intercede

Juvenile Court Judge Louis H. Jull yesterday ordered
a tearful high school senior to County Jail for 60 days.
When the 60 days are up, Jull said he will make a

final disposition of the case of Hunter S. Thompson, 17, of 2437 Ransdell.

Thompson was one of three youths involved in a scrape in Cherokee Park early in the morning of May 11.

They were accused by police of robbing Joseph E. Monin, 20, of 1824 Bonnycastle . . . At the time Monin and another youth were parked near Hogan's Fountain with two girls.

NO TESTIMONY HEARD

There was no testimony at yesterday's hearing. In a pre-hearing conference, Jull was told by probation officers and attorneys that there were important conflicts in the testimony of the two couples in the parked car, and the three accused of parking alongside them and robbing them.

These discrepancies, he was told, concerned chiefly whether there was any mention of a gun during the scrape. Jull said he had studied the statements given by all seven and was aware of the conflicts.

Jull disposed of the case of one of Thompson's companions first. He placed Ralston W. Steenrod, 17, of 4328 Rudy Lane, on probation to the court. Unlike Thompson, Steenrod had no previous record.

THIRD YOUTH FINED

Sam J. Stallings, 18, of 1822 Fleming Road was just over juvenile age and was tried Saturday in Domestic Relations Court. He was fined $50 for disorderly conduct amended from armed robbery.

Jull continued Thompson's case only after long and emotional pleading by Thompson's mother, Mrs. Virginia R. Thompson, young Stallings' father, S. J. Stallings, and Thompson's attorney, Frank Haddad.

At first, Jull said that "as a last resort," he was going to turn Thompson over to the Youth Authority. Those appearing in Thompson's behalf concluded that the Youth Authority would then commit him to Kentucky Village at Greendale [a sentence that would run for three years—Ed.] and "That would ruin him for life."

HAD APPEARED MANY TIMES

Jull explained that Thompson had been before the court many times as a result of three previous arrests and had always promised to mend his ways, but never had.

Thompson's previous offenses, Chief Probation Officer Charles Dibowski said, involved drinking and destruction of property.

... Both Stallings and Attorney Haddad begged that Thompson be given a little extra time "so we can work something out." They said Thompson wanted to get in the Air Force "which would make a man of him."

... The two young couples who were in the car the night of the offense were spectators at the hearing. When Jull said Thompson would have to go to jail, one of the girls blurted out, "But he tried to help us!"

... The girls told a reporter that they had not known Thompson at the time of the offense but were now on first name terms with him ...

Hunter had an exotic appeal for the very richest girls in Louisville. I mean Arabella Berry [name changed], her father was one of the two or three richest people in five states. He shot at Hunter one night when he brought Arabella home late.

Arabella was the youngest of—there were several sisters. They were all famous. They were just the greatest party girls imaginable. And hospitable to a fault. You'd come in and there's—if you're thirsty, sweep the liquor cabinet and pull out a case of bourbon or whatever you need.

We all felt that this was *owed* to us, especially because we were male, and especially because we were accepted males. We were in such demand! The mothers of the debutantes would put up with the most tremendous amounts of outrage on the part of the males just to keep enough people there to have partners for their daughters to dance with and sit at dinner parties with.

When Arabella Berry's father shot at Hunter, that was not a singular event. That happened all the time. I mean, other fathers shot at people. It was a hokey chivalrous society where people would say, "How dare you lay a hand on my daughter!" On the other side, the daughter was the most experienced fourteen-, fifteen-, sixteen-, seventeen-year-old imaginable. Everybody was playing this charade. The father was acting like a good Southern father was supposed to act. And the daughters were just trying to get along.

> —PORTER BIBB, childhood friend of HST; former publisher of *Rolling Stone;* currently Director of Corporate Finance for a major investment firm.

I was expelled from school once—for rape, I think. I wasn't guilty, but what the hell. We were in the habit of stealing five or six cases of beer on weekends to drink. That night was the Friday night after my expulsion. We did our normal run and stole about five or six cases. We took one of them and put it on the superintendent of schools' lawn at one o'clock in the morning and very carefully put twenty whole bottles right through every pane in the front of his house. . . . We deliberately took about ten minutes to put them through there because we knew they'd never get the cops there in ten minutes.

> —HUNTER THOMPSON, in an interview with Ron Rosenbaum in *High Times,* September 1977

It was the end of a social era. When you got to be sixteen in Louisville and you were in this certain echelon of male acceptability, every single night in the summer, from the day that school ended until the day that school started, every day of the Christmas vacation, there was a major, major party. Sometimes two, and sometimes three, given by the debutantes.

That was the system.

And what this meant was extravagant, free alcohol, for underage drinkers. I mean total free bars. Not bottles, cases. Anything you wanted. And it all had the blessing of the establishment of Louisville. The mayor, the mayor's daughter, or the banker's daughter or Sallie Bingham, whose father owned the newspaper, or whatever. You were untouchable. Hunter was in Athenaeum, the most prestigious literary association in Louisville, and so he was untouchable. We all started drinking at about fourteen.

I'm talking about bashes. In homes, clubs. They'd have a ball, then they'd have a breakfast starting at four and ending at dawn.

Then there'd be a luncheon. Then there'd be a tea. And you got to the point where you were totally cavalier. You'd steal six bottles of gin, get totally drunk, wake up twenty-four hours later and know that there were three more parties. And it just went on and on and on.

—PORTER BIBB

I had been out baby-sitting and was walking home and all of a sudden—well, this was the guy that Hunter got in all that trouble with, Sam Stallings, who was just this horrible asshole. Hunter and Sam pulled up and they were obviously drinking, and Sam was driving. Sam was such a horrible person. Just horrible! Evil. And he was evil from the time he was a child. I mean, I knew him in school. He didn't think anything of breaking somebody's arm, or hurting somebody real bad. He was kind of real soft and fat. He was one of those kind of kids.

And they pulled up, and they said, "Get in the car, Judy." Well, you know, with Hunter, I'd do anything for Hunter. I always just loved him. So I got in the car.

And they got really violent with me. I mean Hunter too. And I ended up jumping out of the moving car to get away from them. I hurt myself real bad.

I had to tell my parents I fell up the steps coming into my house because I was so banged up. I jumped out of a moving car!

I jumped out and ran as fast as I could, home. Bleeding and all.

—JUDY WELLONS WHITEHEAD, childhood friend of HST; businesswoman in Mexico

I come from one of Louisville's first families. My mother was a Clark. George Rogers Clark of the Lewis and Clark expedition settled in Louisville. One of my grandmothers lived on an estate outside of the city, which became part of the University of Louisville. My other grandmother lived in the neighborhood that Hunter lived in. It was a very nice, upscale, upper-middle-class neighborhood. Hunter and I came to know each other through the semi-social, semi-serious Athenaeum Literary Association, which included twelve or fourteen people each year from all over the city—there were probably eight or ten schools represented—

sophomores, juniors and seniors. It was a very big deal. And if you got in, and if you stuck around Louisville, you were *made* for life.

It was a hundred-year-old organization. Very, very seriously taken. It published every year a literary magazine. The ostensible purpose was we met every Saturday night, and after a little proto-col of business, each week somebody had to render something, had to give a reading of a poem or short story or some nonfiction piece of writing that he had created. And we would comment on it.

Ching [Tyrrell] and Neville were members. Hunter was the Censor. The Censor was meant to cease and desist any activity—starting with writing—that was not up to standard. It was an hon-orary position. I don't think *anyone* at that time *ever* thought Hunter was going to have a career as a writer.

The best of these things ended up in the Athenaeum Literary Magazine. Robert Penn Warren was a member. The ostensible rea-son was literary. The real purpose was the members presented the debutantes each year when they came out in Louisville. It was a glorified, upscale stud farm.

—PORTER BIBB

Hunter went to jail several times. Never for any lengthy period of time. After he and several others trashed the filling station on Bardstown Road, I know he ended up in jail. They caused some serious damage. And I think that might have been the time the po-lice came and got him from Male High. They came and they took Hunter away in handcuffs. I was at Male then. I did not see him being taken away, but others did.

—GERALD TYRRELL, known as "Ching," childhood friend of HST; retired executive vice president of a bank; partner of The Dickens Group, a Louisville literary agency.

We moved into a place across the street from a gas station which we broke into and robbed on three consecutive nights. They were raving mad. Big hounds tied up. It was a family of goddamn hill-billies. The idea that anyone would hit them three nights in a row. The second night was bad, but the third night they had a goddamn army out there! They brought in all kinds of cousins and everything. Three nights in a row, Christ.

> —HUNTER THOMPSON as quoted by John Faxton,
> *Aspen Aces & Eights*, Spring, 1992

White bucks, khakis, white button-down Brooks Brothers shirt, leather belt, and a Shetland sweater. That was the uniform. Crew cut. We all wore crew cuts.

Castlewood Athletic Club was a feeder to Athenaeum. It was like a farm system. And Hunter was a big star of Castlewood. But only a very small proportion of Castlewood guys got into Athenaeum. Very small proportion. And that gave Hunter a lot of currency. So he was kind of multilevel.

He hobnobbed with several cliques. The very top athletes who were untouchable in high school, they all knew Hunter. He was a gentleman athlete. He was not a competitive athlete. He never went out for anything. I don't know why. I always wondered. I thought he could have played football. He was probably not quick enough for basketball. And Hunter was also friends with the real shady element. The greaser element.

> —PORTER BIBB

There was somebody who broke into churches, broke into schools, petty vandalism. Notes were left: "The Wreckers." A lieutenant on the police force shadowed Hunter for a year. But he couldn't pin it on him. To this day nobody knows if Hunter was the Wrecker.

> —GERALD TYRRELL

—— Are you the Wrecker?

—— Call the AAA or ask Robin Leach.

> —HUNTER THOMPSON interview

2

Hunter had all the freedom he needed. My mother gave him carte blanche. Take the car, take the keys, come back any time you want ... He often stayed out all night long. And my mother would sit up. She would sit there at the window. I hated to see Mummy sitting up smoking down by the window. She'd get very worried ... And Hunter just abused his freedom and eventually ended up with a little jail time. He was just up to mischief. He wasn't a bad rotten kid.

My mother always hammers the point that Hunter was innocent. The other two were guilty because they had pull.

—JIM THOMPSON, HST's youngest brother

When Hunter started getting into trouble, part of our minds said, "Wow! This guy has balls!" and the other part was just shocked. ... I have a feeling it had to do with his father's death. And his mother was a pretty good alcoholic. That was probably the big key. Hunter was very private about it.

About his whole family. He was full—he was just filled, filled, filled with anger.

—SUSAN PEABODY BARNES, childhood sweetheart

Hunter has an older half-brother, Jack Jr., the son of Hunter's father by a previous marriage. Jack was raised in another town by his mother's relatives and the three Thompson brothers rarely saw him. He was much older, fifteen years or so. At one time he was quite handsome. Jack's a reactionary Republican and a raging alcoholic. The doctor told him if he doesn't stop drinking he'll die, but Jack doesn't pay any attention.

—LOUISVILLE FRIEND, name withheld by request

My mother's father had a drinking problem. He had a terrible time with alcohol. And then she did. My own mother. Several major bouts after she lost her husband in 1952. I've been around so many hideous circumstances involving alcohol, that I cannot even picture getting drunk once. I've seen the ugliest possible side to that whole story.

My grandmother moved in with us after my father died. Lucille Hunter Ray. The infamous Memo. Hunter holds her up on a pedestal. She was a great woman, a strong solid person, definitely an equal ... Very old, beautiful flowing white hair. She had it all hairpinned up. She wore those funny old-lady shoes with the big toe sticking out at the end. And she'd always wear these ancient dresses. Brooches. And she had a girdle. One day she showed me how it worked. She wore it, I think probably every day. She was quiet. She was stately. She was sensitive, but she wasn't a fluttery type at all. She never lost her temper.

... She saw us through all those drunken episodes when we were young. She'd pull us aside and say, "Your mother is sick. She's not feeling well." And, of course, the sickness would be preceded by all sorts of hell-raising, screaming and struggling and crying and slamming of doors. And my mother's "sick."

Hunter had a real short fuse with all this stuff. I don't think he has ever gotten over it. I remember once seeing him. He had a little fit. The phone was on the landing on the steps. There were two stairs down to the first floor. I saw him, probably once or twice, three times, when my mother was racing to the phone to call for help, ripping the wire out of the wall and knocking her back. Terrible, terrible image.

So it wasn't like she was tumbling down fifty stairs and being severely injured. Brutal, brutal scene. Horrible, horrible scene. Screaming. And Hunter did not handle it very well at all. He was intolerant and mean.

—Jim Thompson

Virginia was a serious alcoholic. Hunter pushed her down the stairs one time. Or maybe a couple of times. He couldn't put up with it at all as a kid. He didn't know how to deal with it any other way. It was the only way he had to try and stop her from drinking. I don't think he had a great childhood, myself.

And so when Virginia was down and out, like when she was on one of her binges, then I would go over and, you know, kind of clean up the house. Hunter *never* talked about his mother's drinking.

He beat her once. Pretty bad. I came over and tried to help her and bring her soup and stuff like that. He was in his room. But he wouldn't acknowledge that I was there. My mother would say, "Oh, Virginia's drinking again." Mother would go over and see her. My mother couldn't deal with her at all. Then I'd go over and get some food into her. That was really what I'd try and do. She was always in her bed. But she'd be incoherent. Slovenly, you know, just slovenly.

All the responsibility of the family fell on her shoulders and she couldn't handle it. On the other side, you have to know that Virginia was a very smart, funny, creative person. If Hunter were your son, wouldn't *you* drink?

—CHILDHOOD FRIEND, name withheld by request

Hunter drinking during school was really a myth. He wouldn't drink and come to school, he'd leave school and drink.

—GERALD TYRRELL

Louisville is a big alcoholic place. The two biggest industries are liquor and tobacco. There are about twenty distilleries in and around Louisville. Plus the tobacco plants. And then there's the gambling—well, no, there's no gambling. You don't gamble on horses. Horses are a sure thing.

—PORTER BIBB

Hunter didn't have any respect for his mother at all. None. He said terrible things about her back in those days like she wasn't fit to live. He was really angry.

He was angry all the time, because his family life was such shit. You know. Well, it was. And they had this little boy, Jim, that was a little shining golden boy. And everybody made over Jim, and Hunter was just going through all these terrible things.

He lost his father, those were unhappy years for him. But Athenaeum saved him. Ching saved him. That's the only thing, that was his anchor.

—JUDY WELLONS WHITEHEAD

3

There was certainly more than an implied code with the institutions Hunter grew up with. I'm talking about Castlewood Athletic Club and the Athenaeum. With Castlewood it was a self-governing group where there was serious hazing to get in. And very much a sense of elitism. He was also oriented towards a Southern chivalry, a twisted chivalry.

Have you heard of Athenaeum Hill? That was where we had our parties. This was an important deal to Hunter. We'd go up to the top after Athenaeum meetings or whenever and have bonfires. Basically we'd go up there with girls and we'd drink a lot of beer and make out. We'd sing and tell stories, all the things you do around a bonfire while you're drinking as much beer as you possibly can.

You know in *Fear and Loathing in Las Vegas,* early in that book, he wrote about the glee of gathering his supplies—forty-two tabs of this, two bags of grass, and so on. That's exactly the way he was in high school. He loved gathering up for the big party. He thought that was grand! "We have seventy-one beers!" The important thing wasn't that we had beer, but that we had *seventy-one* beers, and we had two and a half quarts of bourbon and we had a pint and a half of gin, and we were going to have a big party. He had a unique glee in planning. And when I read that part in the book, I said, "Same old guy."

—GERALD TYRRELL

He had a lot of confidence. It came from an intuitive understanding that he was smarter, stronger and quicker than the kids we were running with in society. You could pick up a lot of confidence knowing that the people who were the establishment, the power structure, were not that impressive.

—PORTER BIBB

Hunter drove an unusual vehicle between his sophomore and junior year. It was homemade. It had an old gasoline washing machine motor in it. You sat on top of this seat and held on. And Hunter went everywhere on that thing. It had four wheels. It had two wheels in front and two bigger wheels in back, with an open top, a windshield and a steering wheel. We *all* wanted to ride and go places in it.

—GERALD TYRRELL

The only man in my life until the time I was fourteen years old to tell me that he loved me was Hunter. . . . He was dashing. I remember when he literally carried my books, and rode the bus home with me. And I remember his arm touching mine and I remember the hairs on my arm stood up straight.

We went to Atherton together. And then he switched to Male. Within six weeks. I don't know what happened. I know that he got into some kind of trouble and I think they asked him to leave.

—LOU ANN MURPHY ILER, childhood sweetheart;
artist. HST still has her picture up in his kitchen.

Lou Ann was everybody's dream girl. She was lovely. I remember her in long, very long dresses and floppy socks.

Hunter either left or got kicked out of Atherton. Or had trouble with the football team. The football team reportedly beat him up. Roughed him up. Because he had already started to talk about Male High and they sort of helped him make up his mind, let's say, to leave.

—WALTER KAEGI, childhood friend of HST;
professor of history at the University of Chicago

Louisville Male High School was one of the most prestigious public schools in the country. They sent people to Yale, Harvard, Princeton. They had teachers who turned down professorships at Ivy League colleges. The year that I graduated from Male, they brought girls in. That was almost as cataclysmic as introducing blacks. And it became Louisville Male and Girls. And the next year, after we left, they introduced blacks. All of this was in a tremendous state of turmoil.

—PORTER BIBB

4

Some people say Hunter changed when his father died. But I say
it was *more* than that. Hunter was really keen on sports. The big
organizer. He was shortstopping the baseball team. He wanted to
be the quarterback of the football team. But at Castlewood, he
was just an end. He was on the Highland Junior High basketball
team. He wasn't a starter, but he was on there. And then the tenth
grade happened, and he hadn't grown—everybody else grew. He
didn't get his growth for another year. Then, of course, he shot up
four or five inches. But when he didn't get his growth, and when
it became very apparent that he was not a gifted athlete, and he
was not *going* to be a gifted athlete, and his fantasies were about
being an athlete, and with the death of his father, all this caused
him to look for another outlet for his energy. And he started getting into trouble.

—GERALD TYRRELL

I went on to Princeton. Ching [Tyrrell] and [Porter] Bibb went to
Yale. My theory of Hunter's "dissaffection" from society is based
on family circumstances and economics.

If you go look at the houses where Hunter lived and the houses
where many of his contemporaries lived, you'll see that there's a
difference in circumstances that's still apparent today.

And I think when it became the spring, somebody asked
Hunter, "Where are you going to college?" And he said, "I don't
know. I don't know, but somewhere." I overheard that, and I
imagined at the time there was almost desperation or frustration
in his voice.

I thought that Hunter's circumstances were such that the family
simply couldn't afford to send him away to college anywhere. And
that by this point he had compromised—had gotten a bad record
at Male, and probably couldn't have earned one bit of a scholar-
ship.

So I think that he saw his contemporaries carrying on, and he
was unable to do so himself. And this turned from hurt and disappointment to anger and rage and frustration. I think that ac-
counts for some of the violence and vandalism, too.

Ching really disagrees with me. He says that it started in

Castlewood. And that Hunter couldn't compete athletically with a lot of those people and then came the death of his father. Whatever it was, Hunter was definitely frustrated.

I don't think it was a single event or a single episode. No. I think it was a cumulative effect—of losing out. You're running and you can't catch up and all of a sudden you're still running and everybody else is pulling ahead, through no fault of your own particularly.

But I should say that the latter years in high school, he was becoming, to a degree, sinister.

—NEVILLE BLAKEMORE, childhood friend of HST;
Louisville lawyer

When we were all growing up in Louisville, I would hear these stories about this absolute terrorist, Hunter Thompson. He was the local madman. I briefly went out with his brother Davison, and then married one of Hunter's best friends, Billy Noonan.

Now, I know Neville Blakemore pretty well. He comes from a very fancy family. He married a fancy person. But Neville's got it *wrong*. I think Hunter always *hated* what Louisville stood for. What it stood for then and what it will always stand for. It's a boring, provincial, middle-class, family-oriented town that has nothing going for it except the Derby two minutes a year.

The bottom line is Hunter would not have wanted to fit in. Believe me. Both Ching Tyrrell and Neville came from families whose Louisville roots go way back and they met this wonderful iconoclastic kid. And Hunter couldn't *wait* to get out of there!

—ANNE WILLIS NOONAN, friend of HST; artist

Did you know Owl Creek is the name of a country club here in town? In fact it's real near where Louise Reynolds used to live. Reynolds of Reynolds Aluminum. Hunter used to date her. Maybe she's the one who got away.

—NEVILLE BLAKEMORE

I don't know how we parted. I don't know when we broke up. Yes. I remember. My mother laid down the law. She said if I ever saw Hunter again, I would *never* see him again. I would be sent away.

I don't think Hunter ever knew how much I loved him. I want to tell him now. I want him to know it. Every time I was getting ready to tell him a long time ago, he would do something destructive and I couldn't tell him.

—Lou Ann Murphy Iler

I used to go visit him in jail. That's where Hunter started writing. That's where he took a correspondence course and started writing. Before he left for the Air Force. He was about to graduate from high school. But he couldn't graduate because he was in jail. He was seventeen years old! Terrible. But Sam Stallings didn't go to jail. And Ralston Steenrod, he didn't go either.

Everybody else had money. And got out and went to college. Steenrod went on to Princeton. And Hunter was the only one, cause he couldn't afford, nobody could afford to pay his way. So he went to jail.

The jail was horrible. It was just dirty, the Jefferson County Jail. Oh, it was just nasty. When I went to visit him it was through one of those glass [partitions] with smudged-up lip prints. I mean, he was such a child to be going through this, and those horrible people that were in there with him.

He didn't cry. But he was sad. He wasn't Hunter at all. He looked terrible, you know, like everybody looks in jail, he wasn't eating anything. And he was so ashamed. He was just really embarrassed. I mean, his life had just been taken away from him! And Hunter was not a person you would ever confine, I'm sure you can see that now, so you couldn't picture him confined. And it was just—he was *seething*.

But that's really where he started writing. It was the beginning of his life all over again.

—Judy Wellons Whitehead

5

HEADQUARTERS
Eglin Air Force Base, Florida

23 AUG 57

ATTN: BASE STAFF PERSONNEL OFFICER
PERSONNEL REPORT: A/2C HUNTER S. THOMPSON

A/2C Hunter S. Thompson, AF 15546879, has done some out-
standing sports writing, but ... this Airman, although talented,
will not be guided by policy ... He has little consideration for
military bearing or dress and seems to dislike the service and
want out as soon as possible. ...

W. S. Evans, Colonel USAF
Chief, Office of Information Services

(Printed as a Foreword in *The Great Shark Hunt*)

Visiting dignitaries from all over the world would come to Eglin
Air Force Base and we'd fly by and drop bombs. ... The only
thing an enlisted man like Mr. Thompson had to entertain himself
was the beach, or he could hunt or fish. The girls were in Pensa-
cola, at least fifty miles away. So for a guy who—how can I say
this? For a guy who wants to go to town and do a little dancing
and drinking and go home, there weren't many places.

They had the airmen's club. They could get a drink there. But
I tell you what. Eglin Air Force Base was not the choice base that
GI's wanted to go to. It was desolate and not much going on. I'll
tell you another thing we used to have. We had a lot of drownings.
There was a terrible, terrible undertow there. And guys would go
out swimming and of course, they're gone. I'd tell them every
week. We had all kinds of pamphlets. I had every Monday or Sunday night a death on my hands that I had to process.

The barracks were real nice. Concrete type barracks. Two guys
per room. And our dining halls were pretty popular. There weren't
many guys missing the evening meals at the base. They had
chicken, seafood, shrimp, a lot of oysters, deep-fried oysters, veg-

etables, anything that was in season, they'd whip up some pies, sometimes on a leaner day, Jell-O.

We had a good football team. Bart Starr was on it. Good basketball team. Nice golf course. Good baseball team. No, I can't recall any sportswriting by Mr. Thompson.

—JAMES JARDON, squadron commander, Eglin Air Force Base, during HST's hitch

I played basketball at Eglin when Hunter was the sportswriter for the base paper. And he made up the craziest stories! A little something would happen in the gym and he'd make a great big story! When I left Eglin he wrote that I was going up to the Boston Celtics! He had one story where I hit nine forty-foot jumpers, and then he took a picture of me reenacting a ninety-foot jumper that I threw the length of the floor.

The last trip I made with him, we went to New Orleans. I had a new car. A brand-new Chevy Bel Aire. I won the money for it at the blackjack table in Thule, Greenland. I don't remember much about the trip to New Orleans. Hunter burnt a hole in the seat. We had a lot of beers. Hunter had a great sense of humor. We spent an awful lot of time together. The only time he got strange was when he started writing.

We never talked literature. I'm from Montana. He probably thought I wasn't intelligent enough. Now tell me. What's Hunter famous for? Oh! Is he? I didn't know that. I'll be durned! I'll be durned! Uncle Duke? I'll be durned!

—GENE ESPELAND, Air Force buddy of HST; famous Montana basketball coach

At one point, in Florida, I was writing variations on the same demented themes for three competing papers at the same time, under three different names. I was a sports columnist for one paper in the morning, sports editor for another in the afternoon, and at night I worked for a pro wrestling promoter writing incredibly twisted "press releases" that I would plant, the next day, in both papers.

—HUNTER THOMPSON, *Fear and Loathing: on the Campaign Trail '72,* Straight Arrow Books, 1973

I was at Stevens College. I hadn't spoken to Hunter in about a year and a half. I don't know how he knew where I was. He had been flooding the U.S. Government with as much correspondence as he could trying to get out of the Air Force.

Anyway, it was late at night. The middle of the night. I don't know where he got the number. My room was right across the hall from the pay phone on our floor. And it was ringing and ringing and no one answered it. So I got up and answered it. And it was Hunter.

He was at Eglin and he said all hell was breaking loose. He told me, and I remember his exact words. He said, "I may not surface for a while. If you read about anything in the paper and you don't hear from me, get me a lawyer."

He was hell-bent on getting out of the service. And he was going to get out anyway he could.

—Lou Ann Murphy Iler

NEWS RELEASE

Eglin AFB, Florida (Nov. 8) . . . A reportedly "fanatical" airman had received his separation papers and was rumored to have set out in the direction of the gate house at a high speed in a mufflerless car with no brakes. An immediate search was begun for Hunter S. Thompson . . .

—Office of Information Services

(Printed as a Foreword in *The Great Shark Hunt*)

C H A P T E R
FIVE

It is a truth universally acknowledged, that a single
man in possession of a good fortune must be in want
of a wife.

—JANE AUSTEN

1

Good. At last. I was going to the bathroom. Finally! Awfully un-
pleasant, the Doctor's bathroom. His lipsticks everywhere, a human skull on the table, teeth cleaners, shavers, pluckers, foot
powders, packages of Dunhills littering the carpet, *Playboy*
magazines. Disgusting! The beast! Behind the toilet hung a
sign:

BEWARE $100 FINE
NO CIGARETTE BUTTS, TAMPONS,
KOTEX, SCUMBAGS, DILDOS,
CIGARS, ALLIGATORS,
GOLDFISH, DOGS, JEWELRY,
KIDNEY STONES
IN THE TOILET

Well, it was almost too much. Really. My underpants were
down around my ankles, I was clutching my skirts up to my neck
so as to not touch anything, and what am I compelled to look at,
Reader? A cyclops owl, hideously deformed. It said:

FOR SHERIFF—HUNTER THOMPSON

Sheriff! Naturally my bladder constricted to the size of a Brazil nut. And the Doctor probably had a video camera behind the mirror, too. Oh, he was a regular Rob Lowe of the literary world. I wouldn't be surprised if he hasn't shot thirty or forty tapes of his honored guests relieving themselves. Indeed, I was thinking of calling a cab and riding into town so that I could go to the bathroom there, but I said to myself, Laetitia Snap! You've piddled on the mountaintops of New Guinea, you've piddled in the headwaters of the Nile, you can piddle in the Doctor's bathroom. It was just then that I heard a moan.

I snapped my panties up. It was a little after five o'clock p.m. and the Doctor was still in his bedroom. I quickly washed my hands, noticed a message written on Coconut Grove Hotel stationery on the wall above the light switch which said: "hire an assistant," quickly dried my hands on a clean gray towel, and went down the hall to the bedroom. I opened the door, and peeped in.

The windows were covered with thick wool blankets, the guns thronged about, a lady's head with a bird of paradise mask gleamed on the oak bureau, the lamp by the bed gave off a violet glow, and there the Doctor sprawled——in the brutish gale of the fans, drowned in sweat up to the eyelids.

I tiptoed through the blowing plants. The blue-and-orange-quilted, yellow-and-orange-sheeted, maroon-and-saffron-pillowed, king-sized mattress with his body was on the floor. Beside him was a tray of pill bottles——sinus medicine, cold medicine, two bottles of Valium, a bottle of Halcyon; a jug of strawberry lemonade, cigarettes, TarGards, a half-dozen plastic lighters, the big, dimly lit lamp ("I always sleep with the lights on, Miss Tishy"), *The Washington Post,* and a box of pink Kleenex.

"Dr. Thompson," I whispered. "You're all sweaty!"

He looked like he had fermented in his sleep.

"I don't feel well," said the Doctor, opening both eyes halfway.

"What's the matter?" I said.

A pensive expression crossed the upper part of his face. His nostrils were dribbling like a shower nozzle.

"I'm dying," he said.

I felt his head. It was as cool as a marble ball.

"I was thinking I should go to the hospital," he said in a flat voice.

And to think only ten hours before he was slashing at my britches like a matador! Which reminds me, that acid? My night was most fidgety. I woke up at 3:00 p.m. quite exhausted, my pajamas in disarray, the covers on the floor, and a pair of Benwa balls in my vagina. Reader! If only those lips could have spoken! It would have been something worth reading. I myself was unscathed. A lump here and there, perhaps. I remember the Doctor, vaguely, *vaguely*, explaining the Benwa balls were a present from Richard Burton.

I do not recollect anything else except that I did not know they were Benwa balls; in fact I had never seen Benwa balls, to be frank, I had never heard of Benwa balls; no, the only thing I was absolutely certain of was that I was Elizabeth Taylor. Wait. I also recall the Doctor saying: "She's shuddering. I'm watching her as she staggers sideways and falls. I rush to her side! Don't worry, my dear. I don't want to penetrate you. I just want to suck on your back." And I remember I went to bed almost directly after this in "Juan's room."

"The hospital!" I said, suddenly alarmed. The Doctor did look a bit off——the top of his head had shrunk like an old potato and his breath smelled like a henhouse.

I took his pulse, after spending a good amount of time searching for it. It was 120. Then it zoomed up to 280. Then it dropped to 72 and beat like a tom-tom. I felt his head again. It was hot as a radiator.

"I'll call an ambulance," I said.

"Go get Deborah," said the Doctor, referring to his secretary, who lived next door, and, summoning his remaining strength, turned his boiling head toward the wall.

2

The Doctor sick! The Doctor dying! I hastened out of the house, across the driveway past the tractor and his BSA motorcycle, fretting so that I hardly noticed two Thompson cocks, their long trains rhythmically undulating behind them, flying in a circle over the ranch. At any other time I would have dropped in my tracks. To give you some idea of the Thompson fowls' athletic ability and physical endurance, Reader, the longest recorded flight of a peacock is 1,200 meters (the peahen has achieved twice that distance). It is also an historical fact, however, mentioned by Plutarch among others, that a peacock flew over Alexander the Great's palace the day he died, the same occurred on St. Helena with Napoleon, and, indeed, a cock wearing black taffeta bows around his ankles and his entire harem flew over the gazebo on the country estate of Diana Vreeland on the morning of her demise; in fact, flying peafowl are always a sign of impending disaster and death——"Deborah! Deborah!" I flourished my fists on the cabin door.

A beautiful girl appeared in a short circular skirt and cowboy boots.

"The Doctor, for the love of God!" I cried.

She hurried out the door with a frightened look, walked swiftly across the yard to the main house, passed through the kitchen, turned down the hall, and just before she entered the bedroom, she stopped, and, with her hand on the doorknob, said to me, "How many pages did Hunter get last night?"

"Pages?" I cried furiously. And she disappeared into the bedroom, shutting the door in my face.

3

My spirits were so much oppressed, what with the Benwa balls and the Doctor's health, I just roamed the house; don't worry, I'm not going to describe it again. Deborah came out of the bedroom. I rushed to her. She was a Pi Phi from Purdue. "He just needs something to eat," she said. She took a big pitcher of orange juice out of the refrigerator and removed a glass from the cabinet, and then vanished back into the bedroom.

Forsooth!

4

The Doctor appeared fifteen minutes later.

He wore his light blue SkullBoy robe with the darker blue elephant-print lining. He was barefoot. His feet were quite large. The big toe alone was the size of a drumstick. His face, which had been such a steaming caldron, was now completely bleached. A pair of glasses hung on his hairy chest from a black cord around his neck and also his "five-thousand-year-old" emerald on a gold chain.

5

The Doctor had entered the kitchen at 6:30 p.m.

Then and there the Doctor and Deborah executed their *danse du matin*. In other words:

THE DOCTOR	DEBORAH
1. Lights a Dunhill.	1. Hands him a Chivas.
2. Sits down at the counter.	2. Hands him his ashtray.
3. Increases the TV volume.	3. Switches on his little coffee-cup warmer.
4. Snorts up a gob of cocaine.	4. Brings him a mug of coffee.
5. Lights another Dunhill.	5. Hands him another Chivas.
6. Rips down the venetian blind/curtain.	6. Lays out his vitamins.
7. Snorts up a gob of cocaine.	7. Hands him a fruit compote.
8. Looks around, points to his empty Chivas glass, and so on and so forth.	

The whole comedy was accomplished while the Doctor rocked back and forth in front of his *New York Times* and flipped between CNN and an exhibition Canadian Football League game. Needless to say, no one spoke during this little performance or made the slightest allusion to his croaking. No. The first time the Doctor opened his lips was when a fax came in.

"Is that from Rosenthal?"

From his rich Mexican ocher color, I could see he was back to so-called normal.

"No, it's from Bullet," said Deborah. (The Doctor received twenty or thirty faxes a day, a story in itself.) "He wants to know if he should talk to Perry or Whitmer."

"THESE MOTHERFUCKING MAGGOT BIOGRAPHERS!" yelled the Doctor.

"Biographers?" I said. "What biographers?"

"Three different people are writing biographies of Hunter," said Deborah.

"Really!" I said, staring at her, saucer-eyed.

I was astonished. Why would anybody write a biography of the Doctor?

"It's so bad I can't even answer my telephone!" cried the Doctor, getting off his chair. "Degenerate little paparazzi!" He dumped his ice cubes in the sink. "One of them has been sending out quarts of cheap wine to everybody she thinks I ever met. The other two are badgering my mother, who is eighty-five years old! I won't take this sleazy, low-rent harassment!"

"Look!" I said, only half listening. "Rocket's going for a touchdown!"

"Eight-five years old!" exclaimed the Doctor, taking a dishrag off the faucet. "And they crawl on her like a pack of maggots." He started rubbing the scrape marks on the bottom of the sink. "A surly mob with names like Z. G. Carol and P.O.W. Whitmer and PeePee Perry."

"Notre Dame's greatest receiver!" I said.

"Discount gossip-mongers!" said the Doctor, switching to a Brillo pad and starting to clean around the drain. "Dull-edged publicity-seekers!"

"Notre Dame's in Indiana, you know," I said. La! How the Doctor went on!

"The Pimp, the Cunt and the Hack!" cried the Doctor, getting out the Comet.

Gads. Take off the beads and wipe his nostrils and Dr. Thompson was President of the NRA.

"The maggots have stolen my life!" yelled the Doctor. "I don't have the time or the money"——He suddenly stopped cleaning the sink and stared at me.

Then he looked away, frowned, walked over to the counter, quickly scrawled a big wet "X-NAY" across the fax, handed it to Deborah and said, "You know what we should do"——he stopped short again, and suddenly reached out and seized my arm. "I must like you!" he said, and burst into an affectionate smile.

Yes, half the evening long, Reader, you don't think he is going to live till midnight, and then next minute, Surprise! he's Hemingway at the bullring.

"Ahhhhhhh, Miss Tishy," he said, pulling me next to him.

"What?"

"Guess."

"What?"

"Guess."

"*What?*"

"You are going to write a biography."

"Of whom?"

"Me."

"You!" I cried.

He chuckled happily.

I backed away. "I'm working on my Giant Cassowary book,"
I said.

"No, no, my dear." He pulled me closer.

"I have a contract with Indiana University Press," I said, disen-
gaging his hand, which was sliding toward my rump.

"I'll get you a half-million advance from a *real* publisher." He
leaned back against the sink and embraced me around the waist
with both arms. "It'll be the one *true* biography! We'll make up all
my secrets!"

I saw it couldn't go on like this. A book about Dan Rather you
would expect. *He* is a journalist. But the Doctor! Even Geraldo
Rivera, at a pinch, would not have surprised me. But the Doctor!

"Of course," he said, lowering his voice, "I would get eighty-
seven percent of your advance for my troubles. It's only fair. Goddamn it!" he cried joyfully, giving me a hearty embrace.

"Doctor . . ."

"It will have to be a *rush* job, naturally."

"Doctor, listen . . ."

"And we'll publish it in an elegant Gonzo Edition. It will be
printed on blotter paper and bound in elephant hide, tusks and
all."

"Doctor, I'm serious!" I said, struggling in his manly arms.
Have I mentioned how tall the Doctor is? A monster, huge. With
biceps as big as cantaloupes. "Thank you for the compliment," I
said, wiggling and tussling. "I am quite sensible of the honor you
do me. Take your hand out of there, please. But shouldn't your life
be written by someone who admires you? Likes you? Someone
who has never met you, for instance?"

"Now, now, Tishy, let's get started. Run get your tape recorder."

"Really, Doctor! I'm *not* writing it!" I cried peevishly, and broke out of his grasp after whacking him twice with a plastic Venus he kept on the counter.

6

At dinner, the Doctor opened his box of pizza "with everything" and looked inside. His face fell. "There's never *enough* everything," he said sadly.

7

Even after the Benwa balls I felt my hymen was still intact. A piece of gristle of some importance to me, I need not tell *you*, amply endowed Reader! Yes. I preferred death to ignominy. But now I asked myself. It was apparent the Doctor was disposing himself for a criminal attempt. And the Benwa balls were a unique and perfect example of his art, but really now, was it not time to know what *true* love was, at last? For I had a suspicion the Benwa balls did not probe true love to the bottom.

These innocent thoughts were interrupted when the Doctor announced he had selected a New Wave XXX-rated movie. "What's New Wave?" I asked him, all atwitter. "No dialogue," said the Doctor, "and no men."

He then asked me sit on the side of the hot tub in my Norma Kamali swimsuit and watch the girls in the movie sporting and gamahuching one another as he lugged in the Chartreuse, the bowl of cherries, the Chivas, the Dove Bars, the feather boa, a plate of fettuccine Alfredo, the tripod, and the video camera. I was growing quite agitated. Was he planning to call in Deborah and have us romp like she-otters with the Jacuzzi jets? Or was he going to hold me under water and gamahuche my virgin notch? He then stepped through the sliding doors to the yard and——disappeared.

Vanished! You could have bowled me over with a Benwa ball. Five minutes later I heard him yelling at . . . whom? (Deborah? No, it definitely was not Deborah) another female, another female. And then CLANG! the sliding door shot back and the doctor staggered in carrying a short, naked, platinum-blonde woman.

Because of the dim light, to tell the truth, I could not see what she looked like.

"This is Mona," said the Doctor.

Her mouth was wide open in a rigid, startled expression. I am of a nervous, high-strung disposition myself. It was difficult to compose my mind to think, but I could not help noticing she was staring at the TV, where one of the actresses was thrusting her riding crop between the other actress's legs and twiddling her privates.

"None of that!" said the Doctor, grabbing the young lady by the hair and wrenching her head back. Her arms shot up in supplication.

A savage beast would have been less cruel.

"Doctor Thompson!" I screamed, clawing at his robe.

This roused him even more.

He grasped the young woman by the neck and flung her onto the make-out couch.

8

She ricocheted off the cushion and bounced into the tub, and floated there, face down, her hair fanning out. Sweet Mona! How the Doctor loved her! She had a bright red gash between her legs. Her plastic nipples were pointed like oil funnels, and her eyebrows arched like Claudette Colbert.

"Now then, Miss Tishy," said the Doctor, seating himself on one of the underwater ledges in the tub, and resting a glass of Chivas on Mona's coccyx. "Three maggots are cashing in on my life."

"I won't write your dumb biography!" I cried sulkily. Mona had been enough to make me almost lose my senses. Then the riding crop. I was in no mood.

"Now, now, my dear. What would be a solution to this problem?"

He glanced at me and ceased speaking.

I was arching my spine, grasping my ankles and floating on my back.

"MISS TISHY!" he shouted.

"What?"

"Three maggots are cashing in on my life!"

"I heard you. I heard you."

"There's a county . . . ," said the Doctor, and then stopped to gently push Mona out of the way. "Meeker County . . ." He glanced quickly at me with a bashful, nervous expression. "It's about two hundred miles from here. The judge there is a friend of mine. And on Tuesday I say we drive over there and get married."

"Married!" I cried.

I jerked to an upright position.

The Doctor was looking at me with a timid smile. His whole big powerful shy figure seemed suddenly quite timid.

Mona stared down at the bottom of the tub with her mouth wide open.

"You'll do *anything* to get me to write this biography!" I said, laughing.

He smiled, but an embarrassed flush covered his face. I looked at him again. Great God! Was the Doctor serious? I ventured a glance at his nostrils, usually a sensitive barometer. They looked anxious as normal, but crestfallen. Heavens! What an odd position for Laetitia Snap! Not to know if a man had just proposed holy matrimony or a——book deal. Gads! Was the Doctor in love with me? Or just out for revenge against the three maggots? I was totally confounded.

"It's a solution to the problem," said the Doctor with dignity, his face clouding over, thickening across the nose, darkening, and at last turning a rich heliotrope. "You don't look so good, Tish," he said suddenly.

"Neither do you," I replied, and as I spoke blood began trickling out of his nose.

"I don't feel so well," he said in a hollow tone.

"Me either, come to think of it," I said. "I may throw up." I burped a gassy fog.

"If we can make it out of here, it may not kill us," said the Doctor. And indeed, I could barely move. "The cleansing chemicals must have gone haywire!" said the Doctor. Ready to make any sacrifice for me, he passed one arm under my bottom and another around my waist, and with a great lusty heave lifted my corpse-like figure halfway out of the water. I cannot express how enthralled I was by this heroic act. "I'll fucking sue the bastards!" he cried out, throwing back his head; and then he dropped me. It was no use. His strength was gone, alas!

His evident surprise and vexation as he——

Now here. I'm on a death scene which is a model of its kind. Two or three pages of extreme beauty, and then the biographical section. But I've a mind to go to the biographical section directly. The night is quiet. The owls and mountain lions, frogs and night-hawks are peaceful. The wild beast is only waiting to start drinking and snorting and screeching and gong-shooting with his brace of pistols. I suggest we take immediate advantage of this hush and turn back the clock to 1958, when, as you will recall, Reader, we left our stupid young protagonist and his so-called career as a sportswriter on the Eglin Air Force Base newspaper, *The Command Courier*. It is at this juncture, just as he is discharged from the Armed Forces and ready to corrupt the civilian population, that we join him in New York.

C H A P T E R
SIX

Fortune is a woman. It is necessary to beat and
coerce her.

—MACHIAVELLI

1

Hunter said, "You remember Gregory Corso, the fucking guy who
wrote 'Boom'?" I said, "Yeah." "Well," said Hunter, "he's reading
tonight at the Living Theater. Let's go." I said, "Fuckin' A!" So we
put a case of beer in two big bags and got a cab to the Living Theater. Fourteenth Street.

We sit about in the middle of the theater, and put the bags of
beer between our legs, we pop a couple, and we watch. . . . We're
both working at *Time* magazine as copy boys. The only thing
Time requires of copy boys is they have no aspirations to journalism. . . . Now the evening's entertainment is Frank O'Hara reading
his poetry and then Gregory Corso.

Kerouac is sitting in the front row. And we're there with a case
of beer between us, and we're ready to hear some fucking poetry.
All we know about Corso is he wrote "Boom." "Boom boom you
clouds, boom boom you wind. . . ." We're looking for a guy with
hobnail boots about six-six, two hundred and forty-five, solid
build to stalk down there on the stage with his lumberjack pants
and his lumberjack shirt, stick his ax into the canvas, and read his
fucking screed. That's what we're looking for.

So up comes this mincing, miserable little fag. Well, by this time
Hunter and I are pretty well fucking oiled. And one of the distrac-

tions of the evening is that when we finish a can of beer, we put it down beneath our feet, and kick it, because it's a canted floor. And once the beer can gets sideways and rolling it goes Brrrrrrr Ding Brrrrrrr Ding Brrrrrrr Ding Brrrrrrr. So every time we have a beer, it goes Brrrrrrr Ding Brrrrrrr Ding. Well, we ended up in a shouting dialogue with Corso. Hunter was convinced the rest of the audience was going to lynch us.

Corso would not go on reading. He was insulted. He said to the audience in general, these are his words, precisely: "You're all a bunch of baaaystuds." Baaaystuds. That's what he said. And he pointed at Hunter, and he said, "And *you* are a cweep!" A cweep. And he stormed off the stage.

To save the evening, Kerouac came up and read *Doctor Sax*. He was totally unintelligible. Well, *Doctor Sax* is totally unintelligible. But it was Jack Kerouac. And we all enjoyed him.

> —GENE MCGARR, close friend of HST in the fifties
> and sixties; director and producer of
> commercials; presently doing voice-overs

I went down on spring vacation and visited Hunter in New York after he'd been up to see me at Yale. He was in a very bleak apartment in Greenwich Village, with absolutely no food except a jar of peanut butter.

He smoked a pipe. Wore a long overcoat buttoned up to his neck. And he was thin. I think he was enjoying New York, from an impoverished point of view. He drove this old car and parked it with impunity wherever he wished. And wherever he parked the car he'd get a ticket. And he'd just slide that ticket into the glove compartment. At one point I think he had a hundred and twenty-two tickets. I mean the glove compartment was *jammed* with parking tickets. The car was not in his name. It might have been in his mother's name. And he couldn't care less about the parking tickets. He got a couple of tickets when I was there. And, Bang, right into the glove compartment.

He had absolutely no money. We walked around and rode in his car. It was OK. It was interesting. But to be perfectly honest, I never went back to see him again.

Maybe it's the snobbishness in me, but just as a practical matter, in that really stark and unattractive flat, without a guest room, sleeping on the couch and waking up to peanut butter and going out and this parking ticket business, and you know . . .

—GERALD TYRRELL, childhood friend of HST; retired Executive Vice President of a bank; partner of The Dickens Group, a Louisville literary agency.

His apartment on Perry Street was below ground. You walked down a rickety flight of stairs into a courtyard where people hung their clothes. You had to watch out you didn't strangle yourself on the line. Then you opened a door and immediately you were in a furnace room. And the furnace happened to have a broken door on it, so dancing flames protruded from the wall. It was like something out of *The Hairy Ape*.

So you walk along a catwalk next to the furnace where there's this thing going bahhhhhhhhhh, and the flames dancing, and just off the furnace that was Hunter's apartment. It was warm in the winter, I'll say that for it.

It was furnished with hand-me-downs of one sort or another, all cheap stuff, painted entirely black. The walls, ceiling, everything. Black. Yeah. It was a dungeon.

—GENE McGARR

The world Hunter introduced me to was so alien to anything I had ever known. Lots of artists. Everybody had coke. I'd never heard of coke. They had black jazz musicians coming and playing in the apartment and snorting coke. Coke? Coke? They were into the Wilhelm Reich orgone box. Reich was a psychologist at that time up at the New School. And they had a fucking box about six feet by six feet, you got in the box and all your orgones got taken away from you. And you sat there for an hour. And then you got out of the box and you were clean.

—PORTER BIBB, friend of HST; former publisher of *Rolling Stone*; currently Director of Corporate Finance for a major investment firm.

I was raised in Dix Hills, Long Island. It was country then with potato farms and there was a thoroughbred horse farm across the road from us. Daddy was the chairman of the board of a large insurance company. He's got a Ph.D. in economics. He taught at NYU and Columbia, and he's on the board of a lot of things. He's a gentle person, nothing aggressive or macho about him at all. He's quite a humble man while being brilliant and successful. He was a Rhodes scholar, but he couldn't accept it because he had secretly eloped with my mother.

My brother is two years younger, a doctor. I was spoiled and not very serious. I was a B student, always wanting to be an A student. And always thinking that I wasn't smart enough. My whole life was spent thinking that I wasn't smart enough.

I was into boys. I was just totally into boys. I mean it was flirt, flirt, flirt. I wore very feminine clothes, but I was very athletic. I went to a private day school until I was in seventh grade and then I went to a private boarding school for five years run by Quakers.

> —SANDRA DAWN THOMPSON TARLO, married to
> HST; with him eighteen years; still close;
> currently engaged in helping AIDS patients.

One hot night Hunter, my soon-to-be wife, Eleanor, and another young lady and I went swimming at the LeRoy Street Pool. It's a city pool. Big fence around it. So we hoisted the ladies over, it was absolutely empty, it was one o'clock in the morning, so we hoisted over, stripped down to bathing suits or underwear, and dove in the water and had a good time. Until five or six guys came over the fence.

It was an Italian neighborhood. And they started kicking our clothes in the water. Hunter and I grabbed a couple of them and beat the shit out of them. They went over the fence and escaped and we started picking up our clothing. Then ten guys came over the fence. And immediately we're into it again. Well, shit, after a few punches we beat the hell out of them, too! They went back over the fence. We finished picking up our clothing, turned, and the fence was now black with people. There must have been fifty guys.

So we hoisted the girls over the fence and told them to run like hell. As soon as Hunter and I got down they came at us. There were so damn many of them they were interfering with one another. They used bottles, sticks. It was less than a minute of heavy action. They disappeared when the cops arrived. Hunter was lying in a fetal position. They kicked the shit out of him. *Once they got him down.* But I think it's enough to say that Hunter is as brave as any man I've ever met.

The cops sent us to the hospital, where they had to use hoses. They put us in a tiled room, stripped us, and hosed us down to get the glass off. They wanted to keep Hunter, his eyes didn't look good. He had a concussion. But he refused to stay, and I was ambulatory, so we left.

—GENE MCGARR

McGarr gave Hunter a run for his money. Gene McGarr was a very influential personality himself. And he and Hunter together were the wild boys.

I arrived right after they got beaten to a pulp at the swimming pool. They were standing there bloody, and really in bad shape. McGarr had a kind of aggressive personality. I think Hunter has a penchant for finding partners who will rise to the occasion, and then create this kind of gladiator combat.

—"PETER FLANDERS," close friend of HST in the fifties, sixties, and seventies; presently a historian; does not wish his true name used

When I was twelve years old I found my mother unconscious. She had tried to commit suicide. I walked into the kitchen and the gas was on. Mom was slumped over, she had peed on the floor, and was slumped over in the chair. There was a note on the table, but I didn't see it. I was totally confused. I had no idea what it all meant. My friend Amy turned off the oven, threw open the windows and said, "You have to call somebody." And I said—which indicates how much fear I had of my mother—"No, if I made a big deal of this, Mommy would be really angry." So we ran to Amy's mother's house, which was about a half mile away.

Of course, there was suddenly panic everywhere. My mother was dragged into the back yard. And pretty soon there were a couple of ambulances, and police cars and people started hanging on the long white fence.

I ended up at Amy's. My brother and I. And at about seven o'clock that night, I remember it was still light, it was summertime, my mother and my father arrived. Totally together. Straight back, everything. Not a word, except, "Sandra, George, please get into the car."

The next day Amy came up to me and said, "Do you know what happened yesterday? Your mother tried to kill herself." It shook everything in me, totally. This was my first awakening. I was terrified from that day on for many many years that she would try again. And that I would lose her.

And then she began drinking heavily and I went to bars with her a lot. She was a fairly intimidating person. She wasn't affectionate. She never held me or kissed me that I remember. . . . She'd be really sweet, really loving. And then she would just, in a minisecond, turn around, and be vicious.

—SANDRA DAWN THOMPSON TARLO

I don't remember how long Hunter was with us at the *Middletown [New York] Daily Record*, but not long. He had a few little quirks which led to a confrontation. He kicked the candy machine and gave everybody free candy bars. And his clothing habits! He insisted on wearing sneakers. And often he would just take off his sneakers and walk around in his socks!

I don't remember any of his other sins.

—AL ROMM, editor-in-chief (retired), *Middletown Daily Record*, New York

Working on small-town papers, Jesus! Hunter and I covered meetings of various associations, there were the usual run of fires, accidents, visiting expert stories and, of course, the winners of the local beauty contest.

We drank a lot, it didn't bother us too much. We drank big bottles of Ballantine Ale, those big green bottles. And we'd sit on the floor and play records. . . . Hunter had a little tumbledown shack in a place called Cuddebackville. After he was fired from the *Record* he continued to work on his novel [*Prince Jellyfish*] out there. He had a picture of Hemingway hanging over his head when he sat at his desk.

He had a couple of records of what he called Louisville jazz. But there was another album we played a helluva lot. Oh, André

Previn, and another one was Pearl Bailey about a whorehouse or something. We were always kind of running around in cars from one place to another. Hunter drove an old Jaguar. It was a monstrous old thing. Made a helluva lot of noise. It needed shock absorbers in the back and it dragged. He bought it for some ridiculously low price. But it really had a lot of power. A down-and-dirty kind of car.

So we picked up girls here and there and deposited them here and there and sometimes stayed overnight with them here and there.

Geez, the women all went nuts over Hunter. He would pretend to listen very closely to what they had to say, holding out his pipe in his kind of chuckling way. He was quite the handsome lout. I've seen several girls turn to mush talking to Hunter. But he was a man's man too. He would get terribly indignant over the state of the world.

—ROBERT BONE, reporter with HST on the *Middletown Daily Record*; longtime friend; presently Hawaii-Pacific travel correspondent for the *Chicago Tribune*; author of *The Maverick Guide to Hawaii* and other books

The first time I met Hunter was in a bar, in the Village, on Christopher Street. I think it was called Christopher's. It's no longer there. It was Thanksgiving vacation and I was up from school. I was a senior at Goucher College in Baltimore, a girls' school, the only uneventful years of my life. Eleanor McGarr was my college roommate. She and Gene weren't married yet. They were there. It was a wild little bar scene. Music was playing, there was a jukebox, and I remember my date dancing on the table. I was in a booth. And suddenly, Hunter and I were together, sitting. In those days I wore tight skirts, just below the knee, and tight sweaters. I did have a good figure. And I wore my hair long, kind of free, not styled, and high heels. So I found myself sitting next to Hunter. He made very little impression on me.

—SANDRA DAWN THOMPSON TARLO

Hunter came over one night. I was out working. I never bothered locking my door, because anybody who wanted to climb five flights of stairs and rob from me, they were welcome to. This was a hot summer night. All the windows in the block were open.

Hunter, apparently feeling a little frisky and being bored waiting around for me and not knowing when I was coming home, went into the front room, the windows opening up on the street, took off his belt, and started whipping the wall. You know, this loud thwack! Every time he'd thwack the wall, he'd yell, "Ahgggh! Ahghhh! Aghhhh!"

Then he stopped the thwacking and in another voice would say, "Do it again. Do it again. Keep doing it." And then this thwaaaack! So apparently there were people hanging out of windows yelling, "You son of a bitch! You can't get away with that . . . !" Then Hunter put his belt back on and sat down.

Well, about five minutes later there were the thundering hoof-beats of two New York City policemen, who by the time they had climbed five flights of stairs were truly apoplectic. They banged on the fucking door.

Now Hunter sat with, you know, his cigarette in hand, beer in the other and said, "Who's there?" Two cops came in. They wanted to know what the fuck was going on. They had heard the complaints. They wanted to know, where were the bodies. They made Hunter take his shirt off. To show that he had no whip marks on him.

After the cops left, Hunter left. I came home none the wiser, until I looked in the refrigerator, saw there was beer gone, and figured who had taken it. The following day I was coming up the stairs with some groceries and my friendly Chinese neighbor who lived on the fourth floor saw me, and *flattened* himself against the wall as I passed. I got to the fifth floor and the little girl who always played in the hallway was playing there and I said, "Hi, little Katie," and her mother, who was cleaning in the kitchen, looked out the door, ran down the fucking hallway, grabbed the kid and rushed back into her apartment and slammed the door.

After a moment, the door cracked and her eyeball peeked out at me. When she saw me, she slammed the door again. Later, of course, Hunter told me the story. I was Dracula in the building. The landlord, the superintendent left me strictly alone. They didn't care what I did to that apartment. They left me fucking alone.

—GENE McGARR

But the first time I *really* saw him was in a basement apartment in the Village. Standing in the doorway. The doorway was kind of short and Hunter *loomed* in under it in his madras shorts and white alligator shirt. And he had a big thick manuscript under his arm. And he stood there in the doorway. He hadn't said a word. And I remember I was in this little alcove bed thing. Lying on the bed. The McGarrs and Peter Flanders were there and we were all being very serious. Serious beatniks. Life was very serious. And I looked at Hunter in the doorway and I was absolutely gone. My heart just *leapt* out of my body.

—SANDRA DAWN THOMPSON TARLO

I was actually going out with Sandy before Hunter. She was gorgeous. Long blond hair. Very nice body, small waist. A nice person, sensitive, a counterpoint to Hunter.

Hunter was a theater. He was a roving kind of theater. He was not just a writer at that point, he was an actor. He was creating his own subject matter. He was a strapping character. Strong. He always had a sense of his physique. And he complained about everything. His idea was that the bastards were there from the get-go.

—PETER FLANDERS

Pretty soon, whenever I'd see Peter, Hunter would be there too. I don't know how it happened. Whether Peter asked Hunter to come over or Hunter asked, I don't know, but the three of us would take walks around the East River, and then I would make dinner for all of us. I was powerfully attracted to Hunter. It never occurred to me that he could possibly want to be with *me*.

And then one very, very hot day, it must have been August, in New York, late afternoon, we had one fan, a standing fan going, and it was hot as blazes in this little apartment. It was the three of us. And Peter was sitting over by the window, and Hunter said, "Sandy, God! It's hot! Do you think you could just take this talcum powder and rub it on my back? It really helps the heat." And he got down on the floor.

He took his shirt off.

I knelt, and I touched his body. He had a beautiful build. And he knew exactly what he was doing.

—SANDRA DAWN THOMPSON TARLO

And I, in my Irish sensibility, harbored a certain, shall we say, vengeance within my soul for the belt beating. So very late one evening I went over to Hunter's apartment and sat down at the upright piano that was there. Hunter, of course, couldn't play the piano for shit. But I did. So I started on my version of "Old Kentucky Home" and sang through the window with the bars on it which was at the bottom of the air shaft in the middle of his building.

As soon as I started to play the piano and sing, gallon jugs of water started splashing against the bars. Some thrown from five floors up. People had gallon jugs ready to hurl, because Hunter had been making the most ungodly sounds in this apartment apparently for months. I played and sang everything but "Lili Marlene."

Having delivered my entire lounge act, I retreated from the premises. The following morning there came a banging on Hunter's door. And there was a policeman. Along with a deputation from the tenants and a summons. The entire building was ready to swear that Hunter was the devil incarnate and that there was no goddamned way that they could possibly live with this beast in the basement.

—GENE McGARR

Hunter called me from Viking. He was taking *Prince Jellyfish* around to publishers, and he asked to meet me for a drink. My heart just raced! It was Christmas Eve.

We met at that same bar on Christopher Street. We were both absolutely smitten. Just drinking away, getting drunker, and more and more attracted. He wanted me to come up to the cabin with him that night. But I said I had to be with my father at his new house on Long Island and help decorate the tree. I took the last train, which was at eleven. The whole way out there I was just flying on the train. I stood between the cars, outside, and I don't believe I had ever been higher in my life.

—SANDRA DAWN THOMPSON TARLO

Sandy was an exact sixties generation Xerox of Rosana Arquette.

—PORTER BIBB

Then he called me a couple of days before New Year's Eve. Three o'clock in the morning. I should have known right then! He said, "I'm coming to the city. Would you like to get together?" He came to my apartment. We just fell into each other's arms. We spent four or five days in my single bed in my teeny bedroom—we had a bottle of something, Christian Brothers or something awful, and rum or something—wrapped around each other. I was so happy. And he was so happy.

—SANDRA DAWN THOMPSON TARLO

2

I always remember Hunter as basically giving his heart to Sandy. Although he would run around with a lot of women. I mean Sandy was a terrific girl. I was sort of half in love with her myself.

After Middletown, I took a job on *The San Juan Star*. Hunter followed and went to work for *El Sportivo* [a bowling magazine]. Bill Kennedy [author of *Ironweed*], of course, was down there in Puerto Rico. He was the editor of the *Star*. They eventually became good friends.

—ROBERT BONE

Right now I'm planning to write a piece about Hunter and other matters to include in a collection of my journalism and essays that Viking will be bringing out. . . . I don't want to talk myself out on the subject, and I do want to use, in my own work, that which is most outlandish, meaningful, etc. . . .

—WILLIAM KENNEDY

We were in our little cement house with the big screen window right at the edge of the water. In the jungle. It was total jungle all around us. There were birds and little lizards.

One day I went for a walk on the beach. Hunter was swimming. And I walked down the beach and went around a bend. All of a sudden I heard screaming.

It was Hunter.

Of course I came running back, and he cried, "Don't ever do that again! Never get out of my sight again!" And threw his arms around me.

—SANDRA DAWN THOMPSON TARLO

I lived with him at the beach house in Puerto Rico. But staying with him on a day-to-day basis just was *not* possible. In the beginning he didn't yell at Sandy but he did yell at me. Every day I would go in to San Juan for him, to my job, and I would come back, and I would be the messenger. Hunter would stay at home sleeping and writing. I would have this list of things that I had to get. And if I left something off the list, or couldn't find it, he would fly off the handle.

We were both drinking, I mean, everybody gets a little crazy. And we did too. We were, I guess, out on the edge together. So that meant that we were both susceptible. Now my character is not so extroverted or so dominating, so I got tired of his jabbing me all the time.

But Hunter and Sandy were obviously deeply in love. Puerto Rico was their honeymoon.

—PETER FLANDERS

Hunter had quit *Sportivo* and was working on his novel *The Rum Diary*. He was incredibly disciplined. Every single day he would write without fail. He probably wrote six hours a day. Faithfully. Always. And nothing would interfere with that. He was driven. He was an absolutely driven man.

I typed a lot of his work. And I felt wonderful doing that because here I was working hard, involved with this great writing and this great man, and it made me feel worthwhile. . . . I didn't voice my opinion. I spoke very little. Because I was so afraid I would say something foolish and he would understand that I was not intelligent. Intelligence was such an important thing for him.

Then he'd go out and chop the coconuts, and we'd eat the coconuts and we'd have coconut rum drinks and then he'd carve them. He had this whole row on the wall of carved coconuts. They held pens and different things. And he read a lot. The people who stand out are Fitzgerald and Hemingway. Conrad, too.

And we'd make love. There was a big screen, and we were right on the ocean, the sand and the ocean, and I remember I was sitting up and we were in bed and I just thought I can't get any higher. If I were to die in the next instant I would be happy.

—SANDRA DAWN THOMPSON TARLO

I just don't believe that anything is as important as doing your work.

—HUNTER THOMPSON in a taped conversation with Robert Bone around this time

3

The three of us crewed on a sailboat from Puerto Rico to Bermuda.

Can you *imagine* being in a confined space with Hunter? And you can't go to a bar? It took seven days. And we actually had to work. Hunter was just trying to get back to New York.

—PETER FLANDERS

We weren't shy. It was full on. That's the way we were in the beginning. You know what they say. In relationships, the dessert comes first. It was two very strong, very passionate, very deep souls meeting.

But there was an incident early on. It was after we came back from Bermuda to New York. We went upstate to visit a friend of Hunter's who was a newspaper editor. He and his wife asked us for cocktails and dinner, and to spend the night. We all talked and drank and then I remember going into the kitchen and the husband was there and we got into my favorite and *only* conversation for years and years—we talked about Hunter, this amazing man.

When I came out of the kitchen, Hunter had left the living room. I went upstairs to our room. It was dark and the bed was on the floor.

I knelt down on the bed and all of a sudden, out of nowhere came this really powerful punch across my face.

I was instantly in shock. What I saw was that for reasons unknown to me, my very high and loving and wild life with this amazing man was *over*. My world had ended! That pain far superseded any physical pain. It *never* occurred to me that he was crazy or violent and that I didn't deserve it. Of course he was jealous and after a lot of sobbing and crying I "realized" it was all a "miscommunication."

—SANDRA DAWN THOMPSON TARLO

Hunter's view was a genuinely common attitude, an affliction, if you wish. Hunter felt the same way I did, which was: Number One, it's OK for me to get laid as often as I possibly can. But it's not OK for anybody else. That's position Number One. Position Number Two, I can get laid as often as I want but my wife can't get laid by anybody but me. Hunter is a complete believer in these propositions.

—GENE MCGARR

4

When we were in Big Sur I got pregnant. I had two abortions. In Mexico. The second time was about three months later. There was never any question in my mind, both times. We were very poor. We were not at all ready. There was no question. Had I had either of those children, Hunter would have had to have left me.

I was working as a maid in a motel a couple of days a week. And I'd go to San Francisco and do temporary work. Hunter was writing, sending off articles to *Argosy* and *Playboy* and maybe to Gordon Lish at *Esquire*. He was working every day, very disciplined, and sending copy off.

We were living in the servants' quarters of the big house at the Esalen property before Esalen was even conceived. On the Pacific. It was wonderful. Jo Hudson, the sculptor, was there. Dennis Murphy [the writer, author of *The Sergeant*], Michael Murphy [cofounder of Esalen], Richard Price [cofounder of Esalen]. The Murphys' grandmother, Vinnie, owned the estate, a great old dowager. Joan Baez was there. I think she had just cut her first album.

Joannie wasn't particularly fond of Hunter, I don't think. Hunter was a hunter. He started hunting in Big Sur at night with lights. To put food on the table. Joannie didn't like that night running business at all. She was very much into peaceful sorts of things and that wasn't Hunter's style.

—SANDRA DAWN THOMPSON TARLO

Hunter has always had the ability to ingratiate himself with people in such a way that they would support him. He did it with the Murphys when he lived at Big Sur. They essentially just gave him a sinecure job and a place to stay.

But he had to feed himself, which was always a pain in the ass.

I remember once, he was so flat-ass broke, when we were staying in Big Sur with him, we ended up with crowbars scraping abalones off the rocks. Have you ever gone for abalone? The waves are coming in on you and you're getting all cut up on the rocks and crap. It's sweaty, nasty, rotten work. Get them back up the hill. Then you take the sharpest, strongest knife you can find, and then you wear it dull. Getting those sons of bitches out of their shells! Then after you've worn it dull, and you sharpen the hell out of it again, then you cut away all the extraneous parts of this mollusk, and then you get nothing but this very muscular foot. It's the only edible part.

At this point you could use a hacksaw to try to cut that foot into steaks. Your arm aches after a while. Then after you cut it into steaks you get one of these hammers with the little dimples on the end, like a little pyramid? And nobody knows what it's for? I know what it's for. You hammer the shit out of the abalone with it. To tenderize it.

We were hungry as shit.

—GENE MCGARR

How it all ended at Big Sur—Hunter wasn't a great fan of gay
people at the time. And two old Southern ladies who ran the restaurant had hired Hunter to watch the baths. He wrote an article
for *Argosy* or some such and told about what he was doing, what
Big Sur was like, and in it he said that the baths were gay. Vinnie
[the Dowager] came striding across the big, circular lawn, the
grand dame, and she said, "You have to leave." We'd been there
a year.

—SANDRA DAWN THOMPSON TARLO

[Thompson, equipped with guns, would] sit in the caretaker's
shack firing away at the homosexuals who climbed the fence.

—ADAM SMITH, *Power of Mind*, Random House,
1975

5

SITUATIONS
WANTED

CORRESPONDENTS
Politics, travel, features. No hack work. Young,
good experience, contacts. Advise needs, rates.
Box 969.

—HUNTER THOMPSON, ad in
Editor and Publisher,
January 27, 1962

We had cocktails and shish kebabs with an Air Force friend of his
and his wife. We got into a conversation about blacks, and it was
heated. The guy's wife was the worst racist. It wasn't like me to
speak up for myself and say what I believe when Hunter was
around. But I did. I stated my admiration for the black race. I'd
been drinking, we'd all been drinking. And when we got in the car,
Hunter just screamed and hollered and screamed and hollered. He
tried to push me out of the car, actually while the car was moving.
I don't know if he was angry because I had spoken up—I

thought at the time that it was because he just could not tolerate that kind of thinking, you know, pro-black.

He's changed since then. He's changed on the gay issue too.

—SANDRA DAWN THOMPSON TARLO

John Clancy [an attorney and old friend of HST] and Hunter were constantly arguing about race politics. Hunter was still a good ol' boy. He was benighted, let's say of the mentality "all niggers want to fuck white women."

So Clancy said, "You're going to come with me tonight. I want you to see a lecture. There's a guy coming from the NAACP Education Fund to give a speech to the Columbia Law School." Well, that guy was Thurgood Marshall. And Hunter, apparently, sat in the audience just dumbstruck. He'd never seen a six-foot-six "gorilla" with a suit on before. And not only that; Marshall, of course, was brilliant. That was a seminal experience for Hunter. Thurgood Marshall, I think, single-handedly began to loosen him on race.

—GENE MCGARR

6

Hunter was working on getting to South America with the *National Observer*. His grandmother, Memo, died and he received fifteen hundred dollars or something like that. He bought a camera and then he bought a ticket to South America. The *Observer* promised to pay him per article.

Meanwhile I was working in Queens for a company called Nuclear Research Associates with these bright young scientists who were making speed as a little sideline.

Anyway, the idea was that Hunter would send me a story, and I would type maybe five, maybe ten copies and send them to travel sections of newspapers. He wanted the articles individually typed. But it was OK, because now I was taking lots of speed!

—SANDRA DAWN THOMPSON TARLO

Hunter arrived in Brazil and I was driving on Copacabana Beach in an open MG with a guy named Archie Dick who was one of our gang down there, and I saw Hunter sort of loping along. And we picked him up and he'd been drinking a little bit and he was really damn glad to see us. He looked like death warmed over. Just really ragged. But the thing that really struck us was the fact that he had a monkey in his pocket. And the monkey was drunk. And had thrown up in his pocket.

As Hunter explained it, he'd just come in from Bolivia. And he said, if you think this monkey is interesting, you should see this creature I've got in my room. Come and tell me what it is.

He said some people had been mistreating this little animal in Bolivia and he bought it to keep them from mistreating it. So we went back to his room and there was a furry creature. It looked like a cross between a rat and a honey bear. It looked like a rat because its tail had been chewed so badly. Hunter had rescued this animal!

The Brazilians knew what it was. They called it a coati. A coatimundi. Hunter named him Ace. Ace used the toilet. The monkey, however, subsequently committed suicide. The maid, everybody had maids, of course, the maid was all upset and crying and screaming and yelling because the monkey jumped off the balcony. Everybody figured the monkey, being an alcoholic, had the DT's.

I remember there was no talk of Sandy coming down. And all of a sudden she was there.

—ROBERT BONE

During carnival. I love music and I love to dance. And there were groups of drummers in front of our apartment building. And I was kind of in this huddle moving and dancing to the samba music and this man came up in front of me or in back of me and started kind of rubbing himself up against me, and I was so happy and I was having such a good time, I just moved away. No big deal. And the next thing I knew was Hunter, who'd been out in the city drinking, with his journalist buddies, was there and he had this guy literally by the neck. Off the ground!

And said to him, *"Tiene problemas?"*

And it was a big scene. And then, of course, Hunter took me upstairs, and you know what he did after that? He locked me in for the Carnival.

He went out. But he locked me in. I was not to go out on the street. He literally locked me in.

—SANDRA DAWN THOMPSON TARLO

You have to remember that even after Brazil, even after he was with Sandy, I saw him with plenty of other girls. Including prostitutes. That was the very accepted thing down there. Prostitution was so much a part of the scene that you never thought much about it. First of all it was safe, and second of all it was an accepted part of social life.

Mainly we'd go to the Kit Kat Club, a block and a half from Copacabana Beach. We'd stay till five or six in the morning, and we'd drink until that time or maybe sometimes pick up the women. But normally we'd just sit there and drink. Somehow or other the liquor seemed to flow a little bit more in Brazil. You didn't think twice about it. Being drunk was a kind of natural state.

The prostitutes were good and they were friendly. Very pleasant people. And clean. So a lot of the dancing that we did at these clubs and so forth was with prostitutes even if we didn't end up taking them home.

—ROBERT BONE

This was the first time he'd ever really been with heavy reporters like the *New York Times* people and the major network reporters. And it was his first time drinking with the heavies, and I would guess he loved it.

He also swam every day. Swimming for Hunter was relaxing. He liked the backstroke. The backstroke was like meditation. It just totally calmed him.

—SANDRA DAWN THOMPSON TARLO

Writers of greatest influence? Conrad, Hemingway, Twain, Faulkner, Fitzgerald—Mailer, Kerouac in the political sense—they were allies. Dos Passos, Henry Miller, Isak Dinesen, Edmund Wilson, Thomas Jefferson.

> —HUNTER THOMPSON, as quoted by William
> McKeen in *Hunter S. Thompson*, G. K. Hall &
> Co., 1991

Hunter and some guy decided they were going to go out and shoot rats in the dump in Rio. Hunter had a .357 Magnum. So they were out shooting rats and somebody called the cops, and eventually Hunter was arrested and taken to jail. But Hunter, of course, with his considerable charm, began to make friends with the police. Naturally he had gotten rid of the gun. The other guy had taken it away. So there was some doubt whether it was really Hunter shooting, and he said it wasn't him. "I wasn't shooting the rats. It must have been those other guys." And eventually he and the cops were having coffee together and so forth.

Then Hunter put his feet up on the desk and leaned back on the chair. And the .357 Magnum bullets rolled out of his pocket. They threw him back in jail and the embassy was called.

> —ROBERT BONE

7

He needed someone who was devoted and I was devoted. It was decided that I should go back to the States while Hunter traveled to other countries for the *Observer*. I lived with my mother and worked at her travel agency. Then I went to Louisville to visit Hunter's mother, and his brother Jim.

While I was there, Hunter came home. I don't know how long we intended to stay there; but one day Hunter called upstairs to me. He said, "Sandy! Put on a skirt!" I came down in a little green plaid skirt and a great big charcoal-gray sweater because I had my arm in a sling from a riding accident. And it was underneath the sweater.

And we all got in this little old white car. His brothers, Davison and Jim, were in the front seat. And Hunter and I were in the back and Hunter was holding my hand. And I said, "Where are we going?" And Hunter said, "Jeffersonville, Indiana." And I said,

"INDIANA!" I thought it was at least five hundred miles away. "Why are we going to Indiana?" I said.

And Hunter said it just like this: "Oh. To get married."

—SANDRA DAWN THOMPSON TARLO

Sandy appealed to all of us because she seemed to be so direct, so down-to-earth, and honest. Very beautiful too. I thought, "She's a *great* person for Hunter. She'll probably calm him down."

—JIM THOMPSON, HST's brother

We consummated the marriage in the back seat of that car.

—SANDRA DAWN THOMPSON TARLO

CHAPTER
SEVEN

The man who hungers for truth should expect no
mercy and give none.
                                    —HUNTER S. THOMPSON

1

God knows how many females the wild boar proposed to in between. My own astonishment as I remembered the Doctor, Mona
and me in the Hot Tub was intensified with every review of it.
That I should receive an offer of marriage from Dr. Thompson!
That I should save his life the next instant by pulling the plug and
draining the poisonous compounds! That he might have been
burning with love for me, adoring me to distraction, to the point
of idolatry——

Excuse me.

One moment.

Oh, let me sob. I'm so tired of acting indifferent.

It might interest physicians and psychiatrists who study the effects of isolation on prisoners to learn that I have just written the
monster's name (spelling out "Stockton") in blood on the icy walls
of this ghastly sewer.

We will now turn directly to the next biographical section, as I
feel a little lightheaded.

CHAPTER
EIGHT

No one thinks a dog's prick handsome.
                    —H. Spencer Ashbee

1

It is I, Tish Snap, again. Yes. Good. My life is a deplorable catastrophe.

Fine.

That nonsense in the last chapter has not given rise to slanderous speculations, I hope. To begin with, the reader probably thinks I had hysterics. Pish! I just happened to have been embarking on one of the most dangerous parts of my story, so I was a little agitated. That's all. At first I was not even going to mention the Episode of the Couch. But my conscience has now dictated otherwise. So let me warn any crass dolts who would call Tishy Snap a slut, or say that her principles are not firm, or compare her to a howler monkey in estrus——it is only my worship of Truth that impels me to describe the following incident.

To be perfectly frank, then:

After the Hot Tub, the Doctor asked me to gamahuche him.

2

His precise words were: "I want you to suck me, Miss Tishy."

Naturally, I immediately lost consciousness.

One of the last things I remember was sitting on the couch in the kitchen (after the Hot Tub) and the Doctor trying to kiss me. He was greatly worked up. "Oh! Stop!" I said, blushing. He was wearing a white terry-cloth robe and when he moved his arms forward, I could see down his hairy chest as far as his navel. Steadily, he let his lips travel between my ear and my clavicle. "Oh! Don't be nasty!" I cried. He fondled my hair. He rumpled my T-shirt. He kissed me every which way for half an hour. "Oh! I can't bear it!" I said. He forced his tongue into my mouth. "Pray! What are you doing!" I shrieked. He pulled my head back and thrust his tongue in again. His hands began to sweep all over me. I struggled. "Oh! Doctor! Do stop! I shall faint!" I said. But he held me down and worked his right hand around and into my armpit. "Oh! It's wicked!" I whispered. "You're dying for a prick," said the Doctor, flattening me down in the cushions. He slid his hand down under my rib cage and the other hand crept up over the tops of my bubbies, pausing to to to to to to to to touch the tips. "I shall die if you don't stop!" I cried. Indeed, a heat had suddenly come over me and my feet had begun to tingle. "Now, Miss Tishy, dear, I'm not raping you," said the Doctor in a deep voice, lifting my T-shirt, rolling back the straps of my pink lace $75 bra and kissing my firm, sweet, succulent, fully ripened bubbies, which are in no sense lacking in plumpness and which were heaving in a state of excitement, indeed I was in a condition bordering on insanity——forsooth, when the Doctor said, "Where is your hand," I gave it to him. "Put it here," he said. At first I thought it was a drainpipe. When I sneaked a look, what was my surprise to see it was the Doctor's toolywagger! "Oh! Pray! I'm almost dead!" I cried. "Feel it," said the Doctor.

To be utterly frank, I was curious.

Grasping it like the handle of a posthole digger, I gave it a good clomping up and down, up and down, up and down, the way I'd seen in *Caligula*. The Doctor seized me around the neck, his bald head in flames, in flames! and whispered the fatal words.

3

He revived me with two glasses of Beefeater's.

Hardly knowing where I was, reduced to a randy stupor, with his repeated urgings ringing in my ears, I was again introduced to that formidable lance wherewith the Doctor was outfitted. "Oh! I shan't!" I screeched. "Go on, Tishy, dear," he said, softly. My bubbies were at his mercy. He mauled them without letup. Indeed his big fingers seemed to put me in a state over which reason is rarely triumphant.

"Go on, dear," said the Doctor.

I bent forward, my long hair spilling all over his chest. I touched my lips to his solar plexus.

"Yes!" moaned the Doctor.

My ringlets slid across his quivering belly. "Yes! Yes!" whispered the Doctor, twisting violently.

I touched my lips lower.

"I'm so nervous!" cried the Doctor, grabbing a handful of my hair, which was tickling his belly button.

One flowing lock grazed his groin.

"I don't know what's the matter!" croaked the Doctor, jerking his pelvis upwards, "I'm so nervous!"

Curls cascaded into his crotch.

"God!" screamed the Doctor. Indeed he had grabbed my hair with both hands and for a moment I thought he would rip it from its roots. He was thrashing about like a drowning man, twitching, howling, yanking my hair, grabbing at throw pillows and kicking objects left and right off the coffee table.

I reached my dubious goal. The Titanic Rutabaga had shrunk to the size of a big wax bean. "Goddamn it!" groaned the Doctor. It was landscaped in a forest of pretty chestnut-colored fuzz and it smelled like a Chanel fritter. I had seen the operation performed twenty or thirty times in *Caligula* and *Unthinkable* and set about my task with scientific zest.

The Doctor howled.

A she-wolf could have not have licked her pup more thoroughly.

"I don't know why he's so nervous," said the Doctor after a quarter of an hour, looking down at me, and mournfully lowering his eyebrows.

"Does he have a name?" I said, lifting my head.

"No," said the Doctor sadly, taking a drink of Chivas. "I don't know what's the matter."

4

Needless to say, the next afternoon when I sobered up I obtained a reservation on the next plane out of Aspen. In the coming biographical section, incidentally, our Hero, who yearly grows balder, uglier, and more and more peevish and insufferable, is assaulted by the blows of fate in San Francisco. It is not a chapter for the squeamish. As I said, I was not going to mention the Episode of the Couch, but it has been eating away at me.

CHAPTER
NINE

We see the value set on animals even by the barbarians of Tierra del Fuego, by their killing and devouring their old women, in times of dearth, as of less value than their dogs.

—CHARLES DARWIN

1

[Interview conducted with prisoner 82740-011, Federal Correction Institution, Phoenix]

Hunter wrote an article about us in *The Nation*. It wasn't a bad article. The guy is a hell of a writer. He's very descriptive and knows how to put his verse together. He's one of the greatest writers I've ever read. That doesn't mean I like him personally. At any rate, he asked if he could write a book about us. So we took a vote on it and said, "Yes." The cost was a keg of beer at completion of the book. To this date we've never gotten the keg of beer.

The guy beat us for a keg of beer! He's a no-good, lousy—as long as he owes it he's a lousy, backstabbing whatever you want to call him. We got burned bad. We got burned for one hundred percent of the deal. We gave him everything he wanted for a lousy keg of beer, plus our friendship. And then he turned around and stuck us for it.

—RALPH "SONNY" BARGER president, Hell's Angels, Oakland Chapter

Was he an alcoholic at the time he was writing *Hell's Angels*? I don't know. He'd been drinking for a long time. I don't know when he started, fourteen or something like that. He never went a day without alcohol. Me either. The alcohol dulled the pain. And then what the speed would do for him was to sharpen his mind again so he could write, so he could think. And then the alcohol would take the edge off again. It was an incredible formula for years and years.

My first recollection of Hunter taking acid was with the Jefferson Airplane.

It happened at our apartment on Parnassus Street in San Francisco. In the Haight. They gave it to Hunter and left. He began to act very strangely. Juan [the Thompsons' son] was asleep in his crib. I was terrified. I didn't know whether Hunter was going to kill our son, or kill me, or what was going to happen. Everything I had ever read about acid scared me to death. I thought that people just went crazy. My feeling about it was that you could just totally lose it and mutilate your own child.

Hunter and I were sitting on the bed which was also the couch. And he was *out* there. He was saying things to me that made no sense whatsoever. About animals, about God, about I didn't know what. And it was scaring me. Then he said, "Where are my guns?"

And I said, "Your guns? I don't think that's a good idea, your guns."

He said, "Where are they?"

I said, "That's OK, I'll take care of them."

Then he went on to something else and I got his guns and hid them. Then about an hour later he said, "Where are the guns?"

And I said, "I've taken care of them, they're fine."

And so this went on. About every hour he would remember the guns, and finally he said, "I want the guns." It was totally paranoid. It was "I WANT THE GUNS!" He didn't want to do anything with them, he just wanted them so nobody else could do something with them.

And so I said, "I cannot give you the guns."

And he said, "If you don't give me the guns, I'm going to throw this boot through that window." . . . There were bay windows across the back that overlooked Kezar Stadium. . . . "I cannot give you the guns," I said. And he took the boot and he threw it through the bay window, shattering glass everywhere.

I went into shock.

And there was some kind of box on the floor, and I got up on that box, and Hunter was standing there, and I got up on the box and I just scraped my nails down his face, and I drew blood, actually. I was so scared and so angry. I just clawed him. All that had to happen was for him to throw that boot and it went crash and I went wild.

Then he decided that he was going to get on his motorcycle and go see our friends in Sonoma, Bob and Terry Geiger. They lived fifty miles away.

—SANDRA DAWN THOMPSON TARLO

Dr. ——— was a good friend of Hunter's. He was a physician and an artist. Dr. ———'s the one who gave Hunter his speed all those years. Later Hunter seduced Dr. ———'s daughter and that ended the friendship.

—CALIFORNIA ACQUAINTANCE, name withheld by request

2

Billy and I moved to San Francisco to be near Sandy and Hunter. Sandy worshiped, *worshiped* Hunter. Some people thought, "Poor Sandy, how could she . . ." But in fact, she was the only person who could control Hunter.

She had a darling figure. Sexy. She had nice bosoms and a tiny waist. She was very soft-spoken and had this soft sense of humor and this beautiful long hair and this beautiful brown baby and this wild creative husband.

She was the perfect sort of straight man for Hunter. He could go ranting around and carrying on and she'd say, "Sheeesh! Oh, Hunter . . ." and he would just stop. He adored her. In front of other people, except maybe people that were very close to him, he would treat her like some sort of servant. But if you knew him, he would say things like, "Don't tell Sandra"—he called her Sandra— "Don't tell Sandra this or that. She'll kill me." He was afraid of her.

He did not like her in short skirts, he'd have a fit. It was so funny. She would come in wearing a miniskirt and then they'd have a big fight. And he'd ignore her birthday, their anniversary, whatever; but just out of the blue he would come home with some wonderful present, like a super ring one time. And a beautiful— you know those hippie coats that people wore that had lamb wool on the inside and leather on the outside with embroidery?—he got her one of those, just out of the blue. But he was *not* going to be forced into giving regular birthday presents.

> —ANNE WILLIS NOONAN, longtime friend of the
> Thompsons; artist

At any rate, he wanted to write a book, and I thought I could put up with him.

I didn't think he was no more odd than any of us. He ran around with us for a year. He wore a plaid-type wool shirt and a pair of jeans and one of those knit-type caps sometimes. And those brown lace-up type boots that you might wear on a camping trip or something like that. He dressed like a hunter. He didn't ride and live a Hell's Angel's life. He would come around sort of on week-ends. And when we went somewhere, he went out and made a few notes.

He always liked to pack a big Magnum gun and he liked to shoot it off. One time when we went to Bass Lake, there was some kind of big scene about they didn't want us at the lake. Anyway, the police had created some kind of vigilante committee. And all the cops formed a line. And we were advancing towards the cops, towards the line, and Hunter jumped in the trunk of his car and closed it.

> —RALPH "SONNY" BARGER

What was that old car he had? A Nash or whatever that thing was—a Rambler?

He shot it with his .44 Magnum. What happened was we stopped. We used to carry beer in front of the radiator, and then when we were driving, it kept cool. Well, we had stopped some-where up north of Big Sur. One of those mountain roads that look down to the ocean, and we stopped for more beer and the car stalled and wouldn't start again. So Hunter shot the fucking thing, shot it with the .44. Then we pushed it over the side. It was a good fall.

We took the beer out before he shot it. And then we hitchhiked back to town.

—MICHAEL SOLHEIM, longtime close friend of HST; now in real estate in Aspen

Well, Hunter wasn't working and there was the baby, and before he started writing *Hell's Angels* they had no money, they had no rent, I mean, it was a constant struggle. Oh, it was constant, I tell you. Sandy and Juan and I went into the grocery store and stole meat so that they could eat. We put big steaks under our coats. I don't like to admit it, but we had to steal food.

And Hunter, meanwhile, was ordering, I'll never forget this, was ordering Pendleton shirts by mail, and Juan didn't have any milk.

—ANNE WILLIS NOONAN

I decided, "Fuck journalism," and I went back to writing novels. I tried driving a cab in San Francisco, I tried every kind of thing. I used to go down at five o'clock every morning and line up with the winos on Mission Street, looking for work handing out grocery store circulars and shit like that. . . . I never got picked out of the lineup. . . . [Then] I got a letter from Carey McWilliams, the editor of *The Nation*, and it said, "Can you do an article on the Hell's Angels for us for $100?" I said, "Of course. I'll do *anything* for $100."

—HUNTER THOMPSON, *Playboy*, "Playboy Interview" conducted by Craig Vetter, November 1974

I was an editor at Ballantine. I was reading *The Nation* and I said, Gee, this is great stuff. So I wrote Hunter Thompson a letter and I said, "I think there's a book in this. And if you're willing to try it, I'm ready to offer you six thousand dollars to do it." A *lot* of people thought of him doing a book. They'd all written him letters, but nobody made him an offer.

Well, he accepted. And he started turning in the material in chapters, three, four, five thousand words, and it was wonderful. It soon occurred to me that this was more than a paperback book, which was what we were doing at Ballantine. So I called up my friend Jim Silberman at Random House. I think I showed him maybe a third of the book. So Jim Silberman thought it was wonderful, and then an arrangement was made for Random House to publish the hardback. And Silberman took over the editing at that point.

And then Hunter got beat up by the Angels for writing it. He showed me a picture of what he looked like afterwards. I mean he had lumps all over him. He was lucky to get away with his life.

—BERNARD SHIR-CLIFF, former editor, presently an authors' agent

Well, the place where they lived in the Haight was a nice old two-family house, and one time Hunter went away, and Sandy and I thought we'd paint the kitchen pink. Well, he came back and I mean, smoke was coming out of his ears! The kitchen looked darling. But he didn't like anything with a feminine touch. Feathering the nest—he didn't like that. He liked to do it with his own things. He had a lampshade that was supposedly made out of human skin. He had a lamp base that had three elk legs on it, fur rugs and all this crazy stuff. That was fine. But let Sandy put in one little lacy curtain or paint the kitchen pink—he was so mad about that kitchen!

—ANNE WILLS NOONAN

3

Before Hunter got beat up, he took me to Sonny Barger's birthday party. I felt so out of my own element I could hardly drink my beer. I guess I was trying not to meet anyone's eyes. It was like being in a room full of Hunter Thompsons.

Hunter held his own until the last scene, where they nearly killed him. But he probably enjoyed the physical danger. He was strong enough to defend himself in a fight. He was a good fighter.

—**"Peter Flanders,"** close friend of HST in the fifties, sixties and seventies; presently a historian, does not wish his true name used

Juan was two years old and was into everything. And he reached into the refrigerator one day and he got some aluminum foil. And he came out and he was looking at me with this big smile on his face. And I looked and I realized there was acid in the foil. Pills that Hunter had put in the back of the refrigerator. Juan was just looking at me and I shook him and I said, "Did you take these?" He was too little to know what that meant. I opened the foil and the pills were all there. That was a fright.

—**Sandra Dawn Thompson Tarlo**

It seemed to me that Hunter was sort of becoming a para-Angel. I mean he was *really* into it. He was as inside as any outsider can get.

I wanted to keep my distance from those guys because I didn't want to get stomped. They were a menacing bunch. They were the kind of people that Hitler recruited for the Brownshirts. Guys who like to party and drink beer and stomp on people. They were a dangerous pack. They had a pack mentality. Hunter showed them his Magnum. He blew a hole through the wall of his apartment. But they stomped him anyway.

—**Bill Murray,** journalist; wrote about the Hell's Angels for *The Saturday Evening Post*; presently a staff writer for *The New Yorker*

I don't think we affected Hunter's philosophy at all. He had his Magnums before he met us. I saw him shoot his guns out the window of his house in San Francisco. He had his whiskey and his speed. He had a motorcycle before he met us. He was a wide-open rider. That means he got on, turned it open, would go till it stopped and then he got off it. He didn't have control. He was sitting way up in the air to begin with. A BSA doesn't sit like a

Harley. So you don't look like you're sitting on a Harley when you're stting on a BSA. The bottom line is I bought my wife a BSA for her first bike. After two months she traded it for a Harley. She sold the BSA to an attorney.

—RALPH "SONNY" BARGER

4

I remember his calling me late at night and saying, "Listen. I'm in the hospital. I'm OK. I've been beaten up by the Angels, but I'm OK." And when he got home he looked *awful.* His face was all swollen and blue and black. He couldn't walk very well. He was in lots of pain and stayed in for days and days recovering. It never occurred to me that his ego would have been hurt. Because for me, Hunter was God. And God's ego doesn't get hurt. He was absolutely God.

—SANDRA DAWN THOMPSON TARLO

On Labor Day 1966, I pushed my luck a little too far and got badly stomped by four or five Angels who seemed to feel I was taking advantage of them. A minor disagreement suddenly became very serious.

. . . The first blow was launched with no hint of warning and I thought for a moment that it was just one of those drunken accidents that a man has to live with in this league. But within seconds I was clubbed from behind by the Angel I'd been talking to just a moment earlier. Then I was swarmed in a general flail. . . .

—HUNTER THOMPSON, the famous Postscript, *Hell's Angels,* Random House, 1966

And then he went and wrote the book and I guess he made his deadline and he was happy. So he showed up and wanted to go on the Squaw Creek run with us. And personally, I believe he planned this whole scene in advance.

While we were at Squaw Creek, George Zahn, who was Junkie George, happened to get in an argument with his girlfriend and he slapped her. Now that was George's girlfriend and not Hunter's, and he slapped her. Then George's dog, Bruno, bit him, and George kicked the dog.

Then Hunter jumped up out of the clear blue sky and said, "Only punks slap their old ladies and kick their dogs."

And George said, "Now it's your turn."

I believe Hunter provoked George so he could say he was beaten up.

And George sort of beat him up a little bit. The whole time Hunter was yelling, "Sonny, Tiny, help me!" He never threw a punch. George just knocked him down and kicked him a little. He might have kicked him in the head, I don't recall. Hunter rolled up in a little ball.

We picked him up and put him in his car and told him, "Hunter, split. If he sees you around here, he's really going to beat you up." Then Hunter drove off. Probably the happiest guy in the world with the cover of his book stating: "I met, I rode with and I was almost killed by the Hell's Angels."

—Ralph "Sonny" Barger

I said my bike was faster than his, which it was ... and all of a sudden, I got it right in the face, a terrific whack ... then the *other* guy cracked *me* on the side of the head—and then I knew I was in trouble. That's the Angels' motto: "One on all, all on one" ... So here I was suddenly rolling around on the rocks of that Godforsaken beach in a swarm of stoned, crazy-drunk bikers. I had this guy who'd hit me in a death grip by now, and there were people kicking me in the chest and one of the bastards was trying to bash my head in with a tremendous rock.

—Hunter Thompson, "Playboy Interview"

I was at Squaw Rock, a run site by Cloverdale, California, I would say sixty, seventy miles north of San Francisco. And our camping area wasn't too far from Highway 101. And I remember it was night. And we were all standing around the fire. And one of our members at the time, his name was George Zahn. And he got in an argument with his old lady and he, and this was right by the campfire too, he punched his old lady. And Hunter looked at

George and he said, "Any man that will hit a woman is a punk." I mean first of all nobody calls us a punk. If I get in a beef with— I don't like to see members getting beefed with their old ladies and smack them and stuff but that's their business, it's none of our business, you know. And George Zahn kicked the shit out of Hunter. It was just George Zahn who beat the fuck out of him.

It wasn't a whole bunch of Hell's Angels like the book said. Maybe it felt like it was a bunch to Hunter but I mean I was standing there looking, watching. He fell on the ground and rolled in a little ball like a baby and George was kicking him.

—ELLIOT "CISCO" VALDERRAMA, Hell's Angel,
currently active in the Oakland Chapter

I was showing [the Angels] the cover and it said $4.95 . . . and the Angels said, "Jesus, $4.95! What's our share? We should get half." And I said, "Come on," I was getting careless, see. I said, "It takes a long time to write a book. Nothing—that's your share." The next thing I knew, I was waking up in the back seat of a car, and my nose looked like putty. My head was the size of yours and mine put together. It was morning, and a cop was looking in the window. He said, "My God, what happened to you?" And I said, "I went to a Hell's Angels party last night."

—HUNTER THOMPSON, Rolling Stone, interview
with P. J. O'Rourke, December 10, 1987

And George Zahn wasn't that big. I would say George Zahn was probably five-foot, ten. And he weighed probably a hundred sixty, a hundred sixty-five pounds. George Zahn was real fast and he was tough. Half of his life he spent in the penitentiary. You know. He's dead now. I think he OD'd.

Of course if George was losing, it probably would have been all of us. If two members in the club fight each other it's one on one regardless. Now if a member is fighting a citizen that ain't in the club and the member is winning, we're going to let him win. But if he starts to lose, we're going to jump in. We ain't going to let no member get hurt. Whether it takes one of us or twenty of us, we ain't going to let one of our guys get hurt.

But Hunter got punched by George, got knocked down and got

George's boots put to him, you know. George never needed our help. Tiny was there, watching, and I'm almost positive Sonny was there.

The reason I could remember this so well, see, because Hunter Thompson, I mean I met him, the name didn't mean anything to me, you know. I'm not, you know, really a person that reads a lot of books and knows a bunch of authors and all that stuff, but I do remember Hunter Thompson mainly on account of that incident there. I had just gotten in the club, I wasn't in the club that long when that happened. And after George beat up Hunter and put the boots to him, Hunter got up and he ran. The last I seen him he was running down Highway 101 screaming like some chick that was being raped, man. And that was the last I saw Hunter Thompson.

—ELLIOT "CISCO" VALDERRAMA

C H A P T E R
TEN

Reader, I married him.
—CHARLOTTE BRONTË

1

I loved him, oyster-sucking, coke-snorting, pill-popping, grass-smoking, whiskey-drinking, acid-eating, gun-toting, stink-fingering, fast-driving man tho' he was. Forsooth. A male poem! How I trembled in Chappy's Restaurant when I saw the Doctor rip an oyster from its shell, drag it through the Tabasco sauce, the green sauce, the tomato sauce and carry the whole mess to his mouth, followed with a fistful of crackers!

When a good song came on the Doctor would shout for the restaurant manager to turn it up. The manager would turn it down and yell, "What, Hunter?" And the Doctor would shout joyfully, "Turn it up! Turn it up!"

It was our Engagement Dinner.

Had the Doctor sprinkled mescaline on my grapefruit? Was I mentally disturbed? Had I not been preparing to flee Owl Farm after the Episode of the Couch? When, pray, did this hideous *new* adoration for the Doctor begin?

Reader, it came upon me so piecemeal, I can hardly tell when it started. But I believe I can date it from my first glance at the Doctor's beautiful Royalty Statement.

It was on the kitchen counter. I was waiting for a cab to take me to the airport and looking around for something to disgust me with the Doctor forever. I glanced at the top page. Saw it was a list of books and total six-month net sales for each book and——Did my senses play me false? Or were all the books written by the Doctor! If the evidence of sight could be trusted——I seized the next sheet——Egads! the Doctor had written more books than the Brontë sisters put together! And every one of them selling like hotcakes! Of course, after I calmed down and tried to *read* one of the nasty things, I had second thoughts. Indeed, I could not even find a decent edition of *Fear and Loathing in Las Vegas* in the house. I had to settle for one all covered with ink splotches.

But if I had had to hold it with a pair of tongs, Reader, I would have! Needless to say, my bags were unpacked, my plane reservation canceled and a beautiful Spanish omelet awaited the Doctor when, an hour later, he got out of bed and shambled into the kitchen.

2

My Fiancé had seen fit to shod himself for our Engagement Dinner in a pair of elegant leather shoes which earlier in the evening he had wedged, whispering under his breath, "Fuck the shoehorn! Fuck the shoehorn!", onto his fat sockless feet, driving his meatball-sized toes every inch of the way in, till he nearly shoved the skin back to his knees. I myself was wearing nothing but black stockings, black pumps, and a gold-fringed, red satin cook's apron with a bib embossed with a black-gloved hand holding a burning cigarette, an outfit selected personally by the Doctor. He was, however, not quite satisfied with the lay of my bubbies under the red satin bib. "I had it pictured differently," said the Doctor.

"Hands to yourself!" I screeched.

"I wanted them sort of *falling* out the sides so I could see them."

"My bubbies never *fall*!" I said.

Indeed, the Doctor did not stop fondling and titillating me the whole Engagement Dinner, whereas I only let go of my knife and fork at short intervals, and more and more feebly, to slap his face.

The manager of the restaurant, the waitress and the cook's assistant, a barefoot slattern, appeared at our table to drink our happiness.

"When's the wedding?" said the manager happily.

"Tuesday," said the Doctor.

Though he had mentioned the date before, my modesty was so great as to overleap the bounds of decorum.

"Tuesday!" I screamed out, accidentally kicking the manager in the femur. Today was Sunday.

"After a honeymoon in Phoenix, my bride will be writing my biography," said the Doctor, "for which I am now negotiating a record-breaking advance."

"Delightful! Wonderful!" said the manager.

"And *I* shall continue to work, to create, to save my soul," said the Doctor.

The cook's assistant touched the Doctor's sleeve.

"The cook has a wedding present for you," she whispered softly.

"What is it?" said the Doctor, raising one eyebrow.

"A bottle of acid," whispered the cook's assistant.

3

"You're in love! You're lucky! You're driving to Meeker! A beautiful drive! Beautiful lives! Beautiful people! You're the two most beautiful people in the world!" cried the cook's assistant as the Doctor lunged into the kitchen; indeed, there was no holding him at the table, and as a matter of fact,

C H A P T E R
ELEVEN

A Drunkard can ruin the State.
—PLATO

1

Hippies May
Elect Sheriff

Aspen, Colo—He was a little shaky, Hunter Thompson
admitted. He had just tripped all night on mescaline and
now he stood on Mill Street, ever present beer can in his
hand, sun hat covering his bald head. . . .

"It was really horrible," he said, referring to the long
night. "I thought I was going to have a little time to be
crazy, but all I could think about was this f——— race."

—LEROY F. AARONS, *The
Washington Post,*
October 18, 1970

I was in such a nasty mood, Reader, after recalling the Doctor saying he was "negotiating a record-breaking advance," I could not go on. But then I said, Go on, Tishy!
Go on! And so now we rejoin our hideous hero as he shaves his head and creates
panic across the country by running for public office; and may the Reader continue
to show Tishy Snap indulgence for the appalling details which she must now relate.

Then *Hell's Angels* came out and things began to change. We went to a party in Aspen. And all of a sudden for the first time I was at a party where people were all very sophisticated and well-to-do and I wasn't feeling sophisticated. I was a little country kind of girl. And they were all dressed to the hilt with very exotic expensive clothes which I don't know about at all. I was still shopping secondhand, still in my cute little numbers. So I felt threatened at this party. I was uncomfortable. I felt little. I felt stupid. I felt out of it. It was this la-di-da house. They all seemed very, very aristocratic.

And I went into this room and saw a woman on Hunter's lap. And Hunter's arm was around her somehow. And little Sandy came in the room, and even though it was the very, very beginning, this was my first taste of fame. I didn't like it at all. I was scared to death. And I just flipped. And I went outside and ran.

And Hunter came out, ran after me, and caught me, of course. He always came running after me. I ran all the time. For years and years and years and years. I would run away scared, and he would always run after me. He would always get me and always bring me back.

—SANDRA DAWN THOMPSON TARLO

Hunter's *still* making money off that book about us. It's required reading in English 101 in California.

—RALPH "SONNY" BARGER, president, Hell's Angels, Oakland Chapter

He was pleased to get the book out. But he was just dreadful on the *Today* show. He sat there frozen in his seat. Hugh Downs would ask him a question and Hunter would go, "Yeah, raurrrrr, muuuuuullllll ahhhhhh-huh . . ." It was an embarrassing performance. But Downs liked the book so he carried Hunter through the interview.

I think to get up the courage to go on the program, Hunter had been up all night gorging himself with whatever he could get his hands on.

—GENE MCGARR, close friend of HST in the fifties and sixties; directed and produced commercials; presently doing voice-overs.

Hunter and Sandy came to Aspen to be in our wedding. Hunter was Billy's best man. Hunter walked into the church for rehearsal and put his cigarette out in the holy water fountain. My mother just—she just swooned away.

> —ANNE WILLIS NOONAN, longtime friend of the Thompsons; artist

We stayed a month and then we moved into a beautiful house, no, not Owl Farm, another house way out on Woody Creek. I was pregnant again and ecstatic. Juan was two and a half and it was perfect. I would get pregnant every single time I went off the Pill. I mean I was *instantly* pregnant. I was very fertile and Hunter was very potent.

Then Hunter started going by a house, a log cabin kind of place on the road, and it looked empty. So a couple of times he just went into the house. It had a great big fireplace and great big picture windows, and he'd go in and build himself a fire, and sit there alone, in this house.

So I contacted George Stranahan, a physicist, who owned it. The rent was a hundred and twenty-five dollars a month for the big house, the little cabin next door and a hundred and thirty acres. So we moved in. And Billy and Annie moved next door.

> —SANDRA DAWN THOMPSON TARLO

Then Hunter and some of his friends proceeded to steal stuff from all over the valley to furnish it.

> —CALIFORNIA ACQUAINTANCE, name withheld by request

This little, skinny guy came to the door looking for Hunter. He had on little glasses and had a little bowl haircut, and a plaid shirt, and I thought he was creepy. And I said, "Well, no. Actually Hunter Thompson lives next door, and you'll have to go over there."

It turned out it was John Denver. He had just written "Rocky Mountain High" and won a song contest at Snowmass and he was looking for Hunter, who had some notoriety by then.

> —ANNE WILLIS NOONAN

Why did *I* call it Owl Farm? That's like why did I call Juan, Juan.
Hunter named it Owl Farm because he had a fetish about owls.
He had owls everywhere. And "Juan" comes from the fact that we
lived in Brazil before Juan was born and Hunter wanted to give
him a Portuguese name. So he went with Juan. And I love it. And
Juan does too. His middle name is Fitzgerald for F. Scott Fitzgerald.

—SANDRA DAWN THOMPSON TARLO

But the thing about Hunter was that he never got up until three
o'clock in the afternoon. I mean you *tiptoed* around the house until three. With baby Juan and, you know, God forbid you should
wake up Hunter! A couple of times a week Sandy and I would go
into town together, have a sauna, go shopping, visit Peggy
Clifford's bookstore; but always at quarter of three it was like a
bomb fell.

You could not keep the girl in town! Hunter would get so mad
if she was not there when he woke up. I think she was on a tight
string. I think she was tightly wound inside. Because she just knew
there were certain things that had to be on schedule, like hurrying
home to fix breakfast at three in the afternoon. She was walking
on eggs a lot. You know, you couldn't turn on the record player,
or if people came over before he got up—"Shhhhhh, Hunter's
asleep!"

—ANNE WILLIS NOONAN

2

He had speakers specially made so you could hear every note of
every instrument and you could have it *blaring*. Hunter liked
haunting things like "Mr. Tambourine Man." That was romantic
for him. Romantic and haunting. The sound took up the whole
house and the whole front yard. There was a lot of the "White
Rabbit," a lot of the Jefferson Airplane, there was the Grateful
Dead.

Then he went through a fire extinguisher period. He sprayed
people with fire extinguishers. And he used to give people emetics

[substances that induce vomiting]. They're not very nice things. Usually the object was just to scare the person. So it was not so funny—the idea that somebody was totally paralyzed with fear.

—SANDRA DAWN THOMPSON TARLO

I never saw him spank Juan. Oh, never. Never! The cruelest thing Hunter did to Juan was a joke. He said to Juan one day, when Juan was about five, he said, "Now, Juan. I've changed your name. Your name is now going to be Dirt Bag." And little Juan thought this was the truth. And he came over to the cabin crying to me.

But Hunter made us promise that we would tell his son that his name was now Dirt Bag. And I said, "Oh, Juan, honey, what's wrong?" And Juan said—he always called his parents Hunter and Sandy. Never, never, never, never Mom and Dad. Always Hunter and Sandy. Juan said, "Hunter says my name is Dirt Bag."

And I said, "Well, Juan," and I'd been sworn not to tell him the truth. I said, "That's all right. It's an OK name." The onus was lifted by his father about a week later. And poor Juan for this whole week was just completely devastated.

—ANNE WILLIS NOONAN

When Hunter got bored in hotels he used to get on the phone and harass the guests. He'd call up some unattractive female and say, Hello? Is this Mrs. McKinney? Oh, good! I saw you in the dining room, Mrs. McKinney! I read your name tag and got your room number from the desk. I was thinking I would come over. And you and I could get acquainted. No need to start screaming, Mrs. McKinney! I'm just being neighborly, you fat, rib-sucking bitch!

—NAME WITHHELD

I didn't want to be the little wife who badgered Hunter. I was afraid he'd be angry. And he would have been. Hunter had a terrible temper. If I had asked him something like "Where were you?" or "How come you had to stay out so late?" he would have said, "Goddamn it, Sandy! That's just some kind of crazy jealousy and it makes me feel caged and controlled and I don't like it!"

It was the same when he wanted dinner. I would make wonderful dinners and would keep them in the oven for him. Waiting for him to come home. He finally just said to me, "You know, I appreciate what you're doing. But I don't want you to keep doing it because it makes me feel guilty. Because when I'm at the bar, I know you've got this food in the oven, and I don't like feeling guilty. I don't like feeling the pressure. So just forget making meals for me." I loved making meals for him, you know? But I just stopped.

—SANDRA DAWN THOMPSON TARLO

Then Hunter would call the same room again and say, Hello? Oh! Mr. McKinney? This is Detective Squane—Squane was one of Hunter's favorite names. This is Detective Squane with Hotel Safety. I have a report here—what are you talking about, Mr. McKinney? Where? When? Well, Mr. McKinney, I'll look into your wife; but I'm calling for another reason. It's about that racket you've been making. What do you mean *what* racket, Mr. McKinney? I'm the hotel detective! I was up there. The racket nearly deafened me! And it's my job to make damn well certain that fucking racket stops, if I have to come up there and break your fucking legs, McKinney. I don't care *who* you call, McKinney, your fucking ass is doomed!

—NAME WITHHELD

In 1969 I wrote Hunter a letter about my being gay. I worked on that letter for days. I tried to make everything just right. I soft-pedaled everything. I was very diplomatic and appealed to his sense of—to his good nature. He never responded. Nor has he *ever* responded. I never heard any comment. It has never been discussed. *Never* been discussed.

—JIM THOMPSON, HST's youngest brother

Greetings, Mr. McKinney? This is the Hotel Manager. Pardon me? I don't know *who* you just talked to. *I'm* the manager, Mr. McKinney. And I'm just calling to apologize for any crank calls you may have received and ask you not to leave the hotel. We will give you a night free, Mr. McKinney—with a twenty-four-hour bodyguard. . . .

—NAME WITHHELD

In 1969 I was pregnant again. I had lost two babies before this. At six months and four months. Then this child. Nothing was going wrong. The cat was pregnant. Benji, our Doberman, was pregnant. Benji and Darwin [the Thompsons' male Doberman], right?—they were husband and wife. And it was beautiful at Owl Farm. It was summertime and there were lots of flowers. Everything just could not have been happier or more fertile and growing. Hunter was happy and Juan was just this little tiger of a kid in a cowboy hat and cowboy boots and he wore a little pistol.

I went into the Aspen Valley Hospital. I don't remember my labor pains. I remember it was a beautiful day. Hunter was in the delivery room. And then she was born. And then I remember silence. And then there was hushed talk. I was lying there and I did not open my eyes. I did not open my eyes because I didn't want to see trouble.

They rolled me into another room. I was right next to a big window looking out onto the grass. Hunter told me she was as big as a football player. I was hopeful. I was very, very hopeful. Then the doctor walked in the door. And the minute I saw his face I knew she had died. It was like an incredible iron gate had been slammed in my face. It was excruciating. It was so painful I couldn't handle it. I wouldn't accept it. I couldn't accept it.

And I looked out onto the grass and there were little different-colored flowers on the lawn and then I looked at Hunter and I said, "I could just walk out of here. Just walk out there and then nothing is real. And if that's not real, then my baby didn't die either." I really seriously considered going insane.

And then Hunter looked at me. And he said, "Sandy, if you need to do that, then you do that. If you need to go away, then you do that. But I just want you to know that Juan and I need you and that we'll be glad when you come back."

And I just switched. And I came back. And to me that was one of the most beautiful things Hunter has ever done for me.

—SANDRA DAWN THOMPSON TARLO

Hunter went into one of his rages and said he would not allow the hospital to "dispose" of his daughter.

He and Billy went to the hospital and basically stole this little baby girl. And Hunter came out and he was crying and he put his head down on the hood of my car and just wept.

They took the little baby and buried her on the land that Billy and I had bought on the Roaring Fork. They dug a little grave down by the river. And no one ever knew about it.

—ANNE WILLIS NOONAN

You're leaving, Mr. McKinney? At what time? Right this moment? Wait! You're not going to the airport are you? Good God! When? *Now?* I must warn you, Mr. McKinney, as a friend, our airport, according to statistics, is the most dangerous place in the country. The ticket counters, the parking lot, the rest rooms, the waiting lobbies, the bars, even the better restaurants, are prey to rampaging gangs of black drug addicts. Why, every hour, McKinney, some poor bastard is thrown up against the wall at the baggage claim and has an eye gouged out, or at the very least, he is beaten unconscious. Every thirteen minutes someone is robbed. A female is raped every seventy-seven minutes. The situation is so critical, for instance, whenever I leave town, I take the bus, or if I'm *forced* to take a plane I buy a ticket in advance, and then, wearing a bulletproof vest, I run like a bastard from the curb to the boarding gate. . . .

—NAME WITHHELD

3

I want to talk a little bit about my near nervous breakdown in the summer of 1970 after I flunked out of college. I was smoking pot every single day. It was ninety-five degrees, ninety-five humidity in Louisville, and I started to lose it.

My mother thought I was going to kill myself. I would wander over to the park every day and sit there and smoke pot. Very unhappy. No job, completely lost. And my mother apparently made a secret phone call to Hunter and asked him to please help me and bring me out to Colorado for a little R and R. They worked this out behind the scenes. Hunter probably paid for it, I don't know, but he consented to have me come out for ten days.

But I vow that visit was hell on earth! Hell on earth! I got there and everybody in the house was stoned on acid. I kid you not. Including Oscar Acosta [Thompson's sidekick in *Fear and Loathing in Las Vegas*] and two young children.

All these people were out in the front yard; a volleyball game was going on. They offered me some acid. They had some sort of punch or something going. I wasn't prepared to take acid on my first visit to Owl Farm. So Sandy took me by the hand and led me downstairs to the guest bedroom, and I just holed up down there. My mother had the best intentions, but Owl Farm was almost enough to push me right over the edge!

But when Hunter was asleep I actually had a pretty good time. I got up into the mountains and explored the area on my own and touched "nature" for the first time ever. But at night I would lie awake plotting to escape. And one day I actually got up, my room was downstairs, I got up and went upstairs, and the dogs started barking. And, of course, it blew my cover and I dashed back downstairs. But I thought if I could figure out a way to get out of that house without those dogs barking then I was going to hitch-hike down to Glenwood Springs, and catch the next California Zephyr to San Francisco!

I used to dread Hunter getting up in the afternoon—three or four o'clock in the afternoon, and immediately he would be grouchy, very sleepy and very domineering from then on.

He had his routine. You know, his grapefruit, his Bloody Mary, he would oftentimes be just in his underwear, and he would go out on the porch and sit out there and read his newspapers, smoking, drinking. I don't think any of us were happy to see him up. I think we were all sort of saying, "OK, fun's over. Hunter's up!" Sandy would then start cooking.

Wonderful, beautiful breakfasts, great meals, everything was perfectly cooked and beautifully served. Outside on the deck. She just waited on him hand and foot. Being very pleasant. Even if he were to say, "SCRAMBLED EGGS! GODDAMN IT! I'M SICK OF SCRAMBLED EGGS!" and throw them out in the yard, she would go in and cook some fried eggs. I saw him rave about something she had just cooked for him, saying, "I don't want this Jello-O," or whatever it was, and he threw it off the porch.

And she'd go back and put it together again. I never once saw anyone give him any guff. Oscar was there. A rough-looking character, very Latin, dressed in kind of a Latin style, short and stocky. I remember reading about him afterwards, and saying, "That was *the* Oscar Acosta?"

And people would show up for this volleyball game, which was a very male-oriented, male bonding kind of macho competition thing. Scared me to death, intimidated me. I'd never played volleyball before and I didn't want to get out there with all these *men*, and struggle to participate. I didn't want to be a part of it. So I said, I don't want to participate. Hunter said, "WHAT! YOU'RE GONNA JUST SIT HERE AND READ!" That's how he would talk to me. "YOU'RE JUST GONNA BE A LITTLE WIMP!"

But that's how I felt. Which was just exactly what I was trying to get away from. That sense of being a wimp. Being just a weakling. A pathetic little nobody.

All those crazy drunk people, I was just intimidated by the whole situation. Drugs, and big men and Hunter, of course, this towering figure of strength, masculinity and adoration on my part, I just didn't want to get in there and make a mistake. What if I made a mistake? What if I swung and missed the ball? I really thought about things like that.

Because sometimes Hunter would make you feel bad if you fucked up. He'd point it out. One time he had me do some chores around the house, hammering the screens onto the windows. And I fucked it up. And he came out and he said, "You put 'em in backwards! JESUS CHRIST!"

Hunter was distant the whole time, but right when he was taking me to the airport he said something to the effect: "This suicide business, you're not serious about that, are you?" This was pulling into the parking lot at the Aspen Airport. And I said, "No." I was horribly embarrassed. "Suicide?" I said, "No, Mummy's just worried." I downplayed it completely. I didn't want to look bad in his eyes. Because he indicated that that was a pretty pathetic thing to do.

—JIM THOMPSON

When you talk to Hunter, tell him I'm keeping the bed warm for him here.

—RALPH "SONNY" BARGER, from the Federal
Correction Institution, Phoenix

4

Freak Power Candidate May Be Winner in Sheriff's Race

"I'd really prefer not to win. In the end, I may make my program so outrageous, I won't get any votes."

—HUNTER S. THOMPSON, quoted by
Jerry Cohen, *The Los Angeles
Times*, October 7, 1970

Billy and I had gone home for my sister's wedding, and it happened to be at Derby time, and Hunter called up and said he was doing this story for—was it *Rolling Stone?* No. *Scanlan's.* He said he was doing a story on the Derby for *Scanlan's* and could he come and we said fine. I checked it out with my dad, and we had some empty seats in our box.

So this poor Ralph Steadman [the artist who illustrated *Fear and Loathing in Las Vegas, Fear and Loathing: on the Campaign Trail '72* and *The Curse of Lono,* among many other Thompson writings]— Imagine, he flew to the States, flew to New York, then flew to Kentucky. He never met anybody until he got off the plane in Louisville. And there was *Hunter.* They came back to my parents' house. And it was Billy and Hunter, Billy's brother Jimmy, and his wife, and Ralph and myself, and Ralph was darling. And everybody got drunk, especially Ralph, who was probably very nervous. And he was sitting there and started drawing caricatures of people in the room.

And he drew this caricature of this little wife of Jimmy's, who was a darling girl. I think her name was Bonnie. And she burst into tears when she saw this sort of gargoyle portrait of herself. And she was a beautiful girl. And she burst into tears. I mean, he absolutely frightened the life out of her.

So Ralph was the absolutely and completely *perfect* match for Hunter. He was very Irish, very, very, very typically English or

Welsh or Irish, or whatever he was, and astounded by what he had fallen into.

—Anne Willis Noonan

You can't get anything out of me. You don't know what a terrible tongue-lashing I'd get from him. He can be pretty brutal when he wants to be. I won't. I can't. I won't talk to you. I'm sorry. It's just ridiculous. All I'd get is bloody hideous abuse. I can't take any more. I'm really sorry I have to be like this. My apologies.

—Ralph Steadman

Hunter's such an amazingly brutish physical specimen. I couldn't believe his stamina. I remember he tore apart his hotel room in New Hampshire when he was covering Jean-Claude Killy. It was a fucking mess. He tore it apart, physically, tore it apart. I mean just demolished it. Everything. I said, "I'm getting outta here. I'm the editor of *The Boston Globe Magazine*. The police are going to be here any minute." You know, his violence always scared me. I was fat when I was a kid and I was shot. That was the end of my gangster period. So Hunter's violence always scared me.

Then he wrote the Kentucky Derby piece for *Scanlan's*. And I sent him a letter. I said, "I don't know what the fuck you're doing, but you've changed everything. It's totally gonzo."

I think the word comes from the French Canadian. It's a corruption of g-o-n-z-e-a-u-x. Which is French Canadian for "shining path."

—Bill Cardoso, close friend of HST during the
seventies; writer

The journalist . . . reaches over to open the door on the passenger's side and shoves the Englishman out, snarling, "Bug off, you worthless faggot! You twisted pigfucker! [Crazed Laughter.] If I weren't sick I'd kick your ass all the way to Bowling Green—you

scumsucking foreign geek. Mace is too good for you ... We can
do without your kind in Kentucky."

—HUNTER THOMPSON, "The Kentucky Derby Is
Decadent and Depraved," *Scanlan's Monthly,*
June 1970

Hunter was working on the Kentucky Derby piece for *Scanlan's.*
And he could not meet the deadline, which seems to me was a
first. He tried and he couldn't do it. And he said to Warren
Hinkle, the editor, "Look, all I've got are notes." And Warren
said, "Well, send the notes." And Hunter said, "I can't, it's gibberish." And Warren said, "Well, send them anyway." And Hunter
said, "I can't do that. They're just crazy." And Warren said,
"That's OK, just *send* them." And he did. Hunter was mortified.

—SANDRA DAWN THOMPSON TARLO

Finally, I just began to tear the pages out of my notebooks ...
When I first sent one down with the copy boy, I thought the phone
was going to ring any minute with some torrent of abuse from
whoever was editing the thing in the New York office. I just sort
of sat back and watched TV.

I was waiting for the shit to hit the fan ... but almost immediately the copy boy was back and wanted more.... So I just began to tear the fucking things out. But I was full of grief and
shame. I thought this was the end. It was the worst hole I had ever
gotten into.

They printed it word for word even with the pauses, thoughts
and jagged stuff like that ... and I slunk back to Colorado and
said, oh fuck, when it comes out I'm going to take a tremendous
beating from a lot of people.

But exactly the opposite happened ... I started getting calls
and letters. People were calling it a tremendous breakthrough in
journalism, a stroke of genius. And I thought, *What in the shit?*

—HUNTER THOMPSON, in an interview with Ron
Rosenbaum in *High Times,* September 1977

I was pregnant five times between 1967 and 1972. Years later I
was with Hunter and another person and I said something about

"my" losing children. And Hunter looked at me and very gently he said, "Sandy, they were my children, too."

—SANDRA DAWN THOMPSON TARLO

5

My wife Alixe and I owned a beautiful old schooner, the *Maya*. It belongs to Ted Kennedy now. So when Hunter, who was a friend of ours, got an advance from *Scanlan's* to write about the America's Cup, of which he knew absolutely nothing, he covered it from the *Maya*.

He arrived in Newport [a few days before officially entering the sheriff's race—Ed.] in a Cadillac hearse with a group called David Peel and the Lower East Side. Their hit songs at that time were "Up Against the Wall Mother Fucker" and "Have Some Marijuana." And Ralph Steadman came too. They all descended on Newport one evening with Hunter wearing—I called it "the coat of many colors." He had gone to Abercrombie & Fitch and bought a corduroy and canvas patchwork-quilt affair with these big squares of russet, brown, green and tan on it. I think it was his idea of what a yachtsman would wear. On his head he had an upside-down Navy hat. He pushed his fist through so it came down over his head like a rubber. That was his costume.

The first night we went to a place called the Candy Store and got kicked out of there. Hunter had at least a couple hundred hits of mescaline with him and we all went back to the *Maya* —there must have been twenty boats tied up behind us. They had conga drums. After the first night we were asked to leave the harbor by the Harbor Master.

The next day, at the race, David Peel, egged on by Hunter, poured orange dye into the water. It's a dye-marker for a man overboard that can be seen from airplanes. So you had all these yachts out there watching the race with white topsides and here came this ugly orange splash dye.

After a couple of days, Hunter got bored and kind of pissed off at the Newport scene, the boaters, the blue blazers and the red pants. So at about three in the morning, he hopped in the dinghy, got Ralph and a couple of cans of spray paint. Ralph was pissed. He didn't want to get in the dinghy and row at four o'clock in the morning. He was an artist. And here he was heading into Newport Shipyard, where the American racing boat was, and on which Hunter planned to paint "FUCK THE POPE."

—JEFFREY HUGRET, old friend of HST; ship broker

I was campaign manager for Hunter's sheriff's race.

What we had hoped to do was get a guy named Ned Vare into office as a county commissioner. Ned was a quiet and conservative-seeming person, who in fact had a lot of undercurrents, and our concern was that the opposition, the old status-quo guys, the guys who wanted to let the development happen as quick as they could, that they would get the scent of what Ned was all about and make sure he failed.

So Hunter decided to be a lightning rod. We opened our headquarters at the Hotel Jerome, in Parlor B up on the second floor, and announced a platform.

—MICHAEL SOLHEIM, close friend of HST; currently in Aspen real estate

Sheriff Candidate Hunter Thompson Discusses Law and Order

1. Sod the streets at once.
2. Change the name "Aspen," by public referendum, to "Fat City."
3. ... Install, on the courthouse lawn, a bastinado platform and a set of stocks—in order to punish dishonest dope dealers in a proper public fashion. ...

—*THE ASPEN TIMES,* political ad, September 17, 1970

Let's see, what else? Hunter, as sheriff, was going to insist that he have an unnamed number of days off for psychedelic experience. Whenever the mood hit him, in other words.

In fact, a guy sold us a bunch of bad dope on the night of the elections, for heaven's sake! He would have been put in the stocks. It was bad mescaline. Basically the mescaline that you generally find on the streets, and this has pretty much always been true and I'm sure it still is, it's really diluted acid.

Well, it was a pretty exciting platform. There was an enormous uproar in the town.

—MICHAEL SOLHEIM

National Press Gawks at Local Race

National newsmen, like the craven crowd around the geek at a circus side-show, are gawking at the independent candidacy of writer Hunter S. Thompson for Pitkin County sheriff.

And among eternally law-abiding local citizens there are those who, silent-majority mouths agape, fear Thompson is a half-mad cross between a hermit and a wolverine.

—B. R., THE ASPEN TIMES,
October 8, 1970

"Well, right from the start we had our troubles. First of all, those aerosol cans have these steel ball bearings in there to stir up the paint, and they clatter when you shake the can up to get it operative. . . . Well, as soon as Ralph shook the can, things began to happen. . . . all the lights went on. . . . time for a diversion. I set off a parachute flare . . . *whoosh* . . . [it] popped open above the *Gretel* [the Australian boat]. It lit up the whole scene. . . . We had to pull out. [Ralph] was very badly upset—the frustrated artist.

—HUNTER THOMPSON, talking to George Plimpton,
Shadow Box by George Plimpton, Putnam, 1977

'Cause we really went right at the establishment! Right at their teeth! We weren't thinking of our effect nationally. In a way our reasons were kind of selfish. In the sense that we wanted to keep our town the way it was. We had no idea, we didn't see it as a national movement. But when you look back on it—well, the enthusiasm was coming from all over the country for our Freak Power Ticket! God almighty!

—MICHAEL SOLHEIM

We were fucked. . . . Steadman was raving incoherently as we rowed back to our boat. . . .

. . . [We] chartered a small plane to Boston. Ralph was barefooted, out of his mind, and his only refuge was New York. I called down there and found out that *Scanlan's* had folded, but a friend of Steadman's would meet him at the airport. I said, "Now look, you *have* to meet him, because he's in terrible condition . . . I have to be back in Colorado today in order to file to run for sheriff."

—HUNTER THOMPSON, introduction to Ralph
Steadman's *America*, Straight Arrow Press, 1974

Well, there was a group of right-wingers who were opposed to us and there were rumors rampant that things were going to happen. So in order to try and calm things down, the local sheriff, Carrol Whitmire, who was running against Hunter, called the Colorado Bureau of Investigation. The CBI. And he asked them to come up and look into these rumors. And so this monkey came up here in his gray suit, and he said that he had just had a meeting with some of these folks and that tensions were much higher than he had estimated, and that his advice to us was that we should close down our headquarters in the Hotel Jerome, go somewhere and arm ourselves.

Well, that really got our attention. *What?* Was he kidding? The CBI was advising citizens to *arm themselves* and go somewhere? What the hell did *that* mean?

So we did. We closed down the Jerome, and brought Sandy and Juan in to stay at my house in town. And then all the rest of us went out to Hunter's and armed ourselves. There were about thirty of us.

Dave Meggyesy [the football player] was there, John Clancy [attorney and close friend of HST] was there, Bill Kennedy [author of *Ironweed*] was there. Bill Kennedy was on the floor. He would *not* get up off the floor to look out the windows. And Oscar was there.

And we all damn well had guns! I had my deer rifle. Three-0-eight Savage, I believe it was. And then a car pulled up, an old Chevy or whatever it was, with about six guys in it. And it stopped in front of Hunter's driveway. The gate was closed. But it's just a swing gate, you know, not any problem. And these guys stopped there and they turned their lights off, the motor was running, and there was mumbling, you know, they were talking among themselves in there.

And Teddy from Wisconsin said to them, "If you guys are thinkin' about comin' into Hunter's, you'd better think again and just turn that car around and get out of here." And it was like the bushes were talking to them. He said, "There's a lot of us here." And the car started up, went farther up the road, turned around, came back and split.

Now that could have come to some serious gun fighting. It could have been, you know, a terrible mess.

—MICHAEL SOLHEIM

Besides I told [Steadman] with great sincerity that many New Yorkers went barefoot in the summer, no one would notice when he got there, even in the evening, if he wanted to go out to the theater, or the Empire Room at the Plaza. It was quite common to see guys who were shoeless. How would he know? He was English. I told him the fastidious ones wore black socks.

—HUNTER THOMPSON, quoted by George Plimpton in *Shadow Box*

The night before the election, there were six of us carrying rifles at two o'clock in the morning patrolling Hunter's house. There was a wild rumor that the yahoos from the valley were going to come up Woody Creek and burn Hunter's house down. So we're out there guarding the premises all amped up. At one point I was thinking, "Christ, we're all so damn paranoid, one of us could get shot."

You can't put the campaign in the context of any "normal" political campaign. It was being done from a sense of outrage, to outrage. To expose the terrible truths of what was in store for Aspen, and indeed the rest of the country, as we were soon to find out. The point was to take the valley back from the greed-heads. I took it seriously. At the time I thought if Hunter was elected, it would be fucking incredible.

—DAVE MEGGYESY, friend of HST, former line backer for the St. Louis Cardinals; author of *Out of Their League;* presently National Football League Players Association western director

'Freak Power' Candidate May Be The Next Sheriff In Placid Aspen, Colo.

The fact is that Hunter Thompson's bizarre campaign, probably the most bizarre on the American scene today, may well make him the next sheriff of Pitkin County. . . .

—ANTHONY RIPLEY, *The New York Times,* October 19, 1970

The night of the election Hunter had the flag wrapped around him and the blond wig on. He had shaved his head because there were a series of debates scheduled between him and the standing sheriff, Carrol Whitmire. Whitmire was a crew cut-wearing sheriff of the old school. This guy had a good half-inch of hair on his head. And most of the guys on his staff all wore crew cuts. Well, Hunter shaved his head for the first debate so that he could refer to Whitmire as "my long-haired opponent."

We had meetings all over town, like open houses, in lodges, hotels, any place that would hold a crowd. Question-and-answer things. Big crowds of people would show up.

Billy Noonan ran for coroner. Oh, yeah, we had to have Billy in there, because through some odd loophole in Colorado law, if the sheriff is deemed to be unmanageable or unable to run his office then the coroner takes over. Can you believe that? So we had to cover that base.

The population of Pitkin County was, let me see, I'm not guessing, I do know it. I'm trying to think of the population versus the number of registered voters. Somewhere in the six thousand mark, I believe. Registered voters was something in the twenty-five hundred to three thousand. Somewhere in there. And, well, the returns began to come in. We were up in the office there. Up in Parlor B. And we had a blackboard there that showed the breakdown, you know, the precincts and all the rest of the stuff, with the opponents' names and Hunter's name, just like a real headquarters. And they started coming in and we were doing pretty well. In fact we were leading in a number of the precincts, including downtown Aspen. We thought, "What is this?" It looked like we were going to damn well do it!

—MICHAEL SOLHEIM

Will Aspen's Hippies Elect A Sheriff?

If Mr. Thompson is indeed elected sheriff, his techniques are likely to be copied by young people elsewhere.

... The real-estate developers and other business men are in something of a state of terror at this point.... But the business community hates Hunter Thompson even more.

—EDWIN A. ROBERTS, JR., *The National Observer,* November 2, 1970

Nobody met [Steadman]. He had no shoes, no money, he didn't know anything about New York. People in the hotel *Scanlan's* used remembered this strange, wild-eyed Britisher pacing around the lobby, kicking the walls with his bare feet and cursing everybody who came near him. . . .

—HUNTER THOMPSON, introduction to Ralph
Steadman's *America*, Straight Arrow Press, 1974

It was very close. And we would have won it if we had taken the thing a drop more seriously. You have to remember that originally, this thing was a—what do you call it? A stalking dog? A stalking horse. It was something just to pull attention away from Ned.

Then we got caught up in the idea that we were going to be the law enforcement of the town. God knows how that would have been. Can you *imagine?* Jesus!

—MICHAEL SOLHEIM

ELECTION RESULTS

SHERIFF
Glen Ricks..171
Carrol Whitmer..1533
Hunter Thompson..1065

CORONER
Dr. Charles Williams...1836
William Noonan 910

COMMISSIONER
Dr. J. Baxter...1372
Sam Caudill..233
Ned Vare..1175

—*THE ASPEN TIMES,* November 5, 1970

Aspen Rejects Bid of Hippy Candidate For Sheriff's Office

"If we can't win in Aspen, we can't win anywhere."

—HUNTER THOMPSON, quoted in *The New York Times*, November 5, 1970

C H A P T E R
TWELVE

Dostoyevsky told me he had molested a little girl in a bath. "Why are you telling me this!" I demanded. "Because I despise you," said Dostoyevsky.
—IVAN TURGENEV

1

DUTIES OF THE BRIDE:

1. *GAMAHUCHE THE GROOM*
2. *SNORT COCAINE WITH THE GROOM*
3. *TAKE ACID WITH THE GROOM*
4. *PLAY IN THE HOT TUB WITH THE GROOM*
5. *WATCH PORNOGRAPHIC MOVIES WITH THE GROOM*
6. *RIDE IN THE SHARK WITH THE GROOM*

Numbers One and Six, Reader, I combined by chance on the way home from Chappy's Restaurant at two in the morning, when, frightened by the Doctor's 112-mile-an-hour speed, I flung myself on the seat——my mouth open in terror——and tangled ignominiously with the Doctor's crotch. The effects caused his foot to immediately jump off the accelerator and shoot to the side under the heater. I found this operation to be useful whenever the Doctor exceeded the speed limit. Which, indeed, was whenever he got behind the wheel. Number Two——and here let the profane and licentious Reader pause, and not go around thoughtlessly saying that the Doctor was *always* pressing cocaine on innocent people, or that his morals were not strong. Indeed, I only saw the Doctor actually *force* cocaine on one person, and that person was an ex-addict, so we can hardly count that.

It happened, as a matter of fact, at Chappy's in Basalt, the evening of our Romantic Engagement Dinner. It was about one a.m. We were the only patrons in the restaurant, and at the end of the meal when the waitress said, "Coffee?" the Doctor answered yes, and then, in the most attractive fashion imaginable, after asking for two more margaritas, he offered the waitress his little black grinder full of cocaine.

"Oh!" cried the waitress, coloring violently. "Thank you, but no."

"Go ahead," said the Doctor, gallantly.

The waitress shook her head. "No, Hunter."

The Doctor put the grinder on the table, and with an amiable grin, pushed it toward her.

She took a step backwards.

"I won't be offended by your offering," she said, smiling affectedly and twisting her hands together, "if you won't be offended by my refusal."

"Right," said the generous Doctor, pushing the grinder closer to her. "Here."

"It's not good for me," said the provoking creature, taking another step backwards. Really! You'd think she'd be more considerate of the Doctor's feelings!

The Doctor stared at her affably by the light of the candles.

"Just a little," he said.

"I *can't*," said the waitress rudely. "It's not good for me."

"What's the matter with you?" said the Doctor, surprised.

"She doesn't want any, Dr. Thompson!" I said, pulling the grinder back, endeavoring to spare his feelings.

"Just a little," said the Doctor, gently slipping the bean-shooter into her hand.

"I can't," said the waitress, putting it on the table and hiding her hands behind her back.

"I insist," said the Doctor.

"No, please."

"Come on."

"Please, no."

"*Jesus!*" said the Doctor, finally, in a pique. "Don't be so uptight."

Dr. Hunter S. Thompson, the Greatest Degenerate of the Twentieth Century. (© *Louisville Courier-Journal*)

HST's childhood
home in Louisville,
Kentucky.
(John Cougar,
Courtesy of Janet
Cook Hollamon)

HST (left) and his brothers, James (center) and Davison.
(Courtesy of James G. Thompson)

HST begins his journalistic career at age 10 as a reporter for *The Southern Star*. He is the author of the lead story, "War !"
(Courtesy of Walter Kaegi)

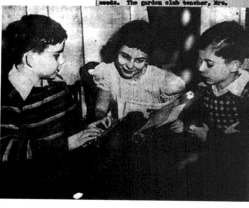

Walter Kaegi (left), HST's first editor.
(© *Louisville Courier-Journal*)

Owing to the fact that he is in the Jefferson County Jail after being arrested for theft, HST does not graduate from high school. He is released on condition he join the armed forces. He is inducted into the Air Force and becomes Sports Editor on the Eglin *Command Courier*. (Courtesy of the J.A.W. Collection)

THE
COMMAND COURIER
OFFICE OF
INFORMATION SERVICES

Sandra Dawn Conklin,
the future
Mrs. Hunter Thompson.
(© Robert W. Bone)

HST and Sandra Thompson in the Owl Farm kitchen during the Sheriff's campaign.
(© David Hiser—Photographers / Aspen)

Election night. Wigs have long been a Thompson beauty aid.
(© David Hiser—Photographers / Aspen)

(© David Hiser—Photographers/Aspen)

Overleaf: The future of American politics.
(© David Hiser—Photographers/Aspen)

The waitress rocked backwards on her heels.

"OK," she said, quickly leaning forward. "Just a little."

All that tizzy over a little cocaine! Really! The Doctor had taught me how to ram the bean-shooter up my nostril and snort cocaine earlier in the evening. Aside from making my food taste like a package of mentholated Tampax, swelling my nose to twice its normal size and bringing on a catatonic state the next day, I found it quite pleasant.

Number Four I complied with, no problem.

Number Three ditto.

Number Five.

Now Number Five was fine until, forty-two hours before our wedding, the Doctor decided he was going to run for the U.S. Senate on "The Woman's Ticket." He said he was anxious to jump back into politics and thought he could help his country. When I asked how he planned to conceal his plethora of vices and aberrations from the Republicans, the Doctor smiled and referred mysteriously to his "ace in the hole."

"What's that?" I said.

"Ahhhh," said the Doctor.

2

"I'll show you," he said, fumbling through his videotapes, and indeed, perpetrating a massacre throughout the length and breadth of the kitchen counter. He found what he was looking for at last and put it into the VCR. We sat down on the stools. Up on the big TV flashed a picture of a naked girl in the Doctor's Hot Tub.

"Yoicks!" I screamed.

"Now, wait, Miss Tishy," said the Doctor, lighting his marijuana pipe, "you'll see."

She was a pale dark-haired puny little thing with a pair of enormous eyeglasses. The water was up to her neck. She stared into the camera, not moving.

"Very charming!" I said.

"Just watch," said the Doctor.

Then all of a sudden my heart missed a beat as the Doctor shambled onscreen wearing one of his stupid robes, carrying——Reader! Are you sitting down?——a bowl of strawberries, a bottle of Chartreuse and a plate of Dove Bars. He put them down on the make-out couch and shambled out again.

Then he shambled in again with a Dunhill in his mouth and a plate of fettuccine Alfredo. He put *that* down on the make-out couch and shambled out again.

O! Reader! I nearly toppled from my kitchen stool. For several moments I could not get my breath. I gripped the edge of the Doctor's IBM Selectric and nearly pulled the space bar off. Had I not had a six-pack of Heineken out on the porch while I was sunning myself that afternoon, I would have clawed the Doctor's back till the blood ran down his heels.

"Now, now, Miss Tishy," said the Doctor, glancing at me. "Let's think of my Senate race."

Onscreen he shambled his raggedy carcass past the camera again, TarGard and Dunhill tilted confidently, sat down on the side of the tub, and heaved his big calves and fat feet into the water. The girl clung to his leg like a barnacle on a ship's hull.

"I'm divorcing you immediately!" I screamed.

"Watch," said the Doctor.

On screen he opened his robe.

3

On the screen the Doctor opened his robe, shook a marshmallow-sized pile of cocaine onto his doodlebanger, and the girl, who had removed her glasses, with no improvement, and was watching him like a seal eyeing the sardine bucket at Sea World, scarfed her nose upon the Doctor——a suckfish cleaning a river bottom would not have been so exhaustive; and then, Reader, my hand on the Holy Bible, she began to gamahuche the Doctor!

I swayed, tottered, grew faint, but held on to the counter and managed not to collapse on my face.

"Who is she?" I whispered.

Indeed, I planned to strangle her.

On the screen the Doctor had put out his cigarette and was sitting, looking off toward the camera, wrapping the trollop's hair around in his hands and molding her boyish shoulders. Then he moved slightly to the right and shifted the unflagging fellatrix also in the same direction so as to get a profile of the operation.

"*Who is she?*" I screeched, yanking on one of the Doctor's earlobes.

"Ouch! A Republican speechwriter!" said the Doctor, crooking his neck.

A Republican! Huh! I am from Indiana. I know all about Republicans. I was surprised she wasn't entertaining him with a rim job.

"But why are you filming this?" I said. "Consider to what impertinence you may expose yourself. You can not *show* this to anyone. You are too principled. You are too honorable."

The Doctor smiled.

"No, *I* wouldn't show anyone," said the Doctor. "But I've sent copies to all my lawyers."

4

And so ended the happy preparations for my wedding. And as another delicious day at Owl Farm drew to a close, little did my Fiancé or I suspect that a horrifying disturbance was about to take place which would throw our bright bliss into chaos. But it is time now for the next biographical section. Yes, hark back, Attractive Reader, to the early 1970's, the unfortunate years the twisted legend of Dr. Hunter S. Thompson was born and blazed across this luckless country.

> **Note**
>
> No, it is not known how many women the Doctor has on videotape. But help is available. Feminine Reader, if you suspect *you* might be one of them, please contact VICTIMS OF OWL FARM: 1-900-923-5484.

CHAPTER
THIRTEEN

Don't run, Odysseus, they'd like an excuse to shoot you!

—HOMER

1

You worthless, acid-sucking piece of illiterate <u>shit</u>! Don't ever send this kind of revolting brain-damaged swill in here again! If I had the time, I'd come out there and drive a fucking wooden stake through your forehead! Why don't you get a job, wino? Like maybe as a night watchman, or delivering the Shopping News. You ——— cocksuckers are all alike—just like those dope-addled dingbats at Rolling Stone. I could kill those bedwetting bastards for sending me this tedious and embarrassing tissue of delusions . . . and I wouldn't mind killing you, too. Stick this manuscript where it belongs: up your ass.
                                        Cordially,
                                        Yail Bloor
                                        Minister of Manuscripts

—REJECTION LETTER, *Rolling Stone*, circa 1972

He is violent. He is violent. I've seen him yell at people till they burst into tears and that's violence. I think he sees the world as violent. He reduced every editor that ever worked for him on *Rolling Stone* to tears at some point, including myself. I mean, you just got so tired—see, the way it worked when you edited his pieces was, he gave you a paragraph every hour over the Mojo [an early version of the fax, so called by HST]. And your job was just to keep him giving you those paragraphs.

But Hunter was on his chemicals, so he could stay up for three days. And you had to stay up for three days with him to make sure he kept getting that stuff on the Mojo and to make sure that the paragraph you got this hour had anything to do with the paragraph you got the last hour. And if it didn't, then after three days when he crashed, you had to stay up for another three days while he was sleeping to put together those paragraphs in some kind of sense, do a little rewriting and that sort of thing. So by the end of the week you had had no sleep at all. And that was when Hunter threw the tantrum and that was when you broke into tears and said, "No one has to put up with this!" You would start to feel sorry for yourself. For good reason.

> —DAVID FELTON, friend of HST; former editor and
> writer at *Rolling Stone;* presently a writer and
> consultant for the Editorial Department of MTV

Rolling Stone was about sex. Everybody was sleeping with everybody. Men and women, men and men, women and women. It was like college in the sixties. Everybody slept with each other 'cause it was a friendly thing to do. ——— was sleeping with ——— and ———. His wife was sleeping with ———. ——— and ——— had a big thing. I was sleeping with ——— and ——— and ———. ——— was sleeping with ———. ——— slept with everybody in the whole place. Ummmm, who else? Of course we were all doing drugs. You know, so who'd remember, right? It was like a soap opera. And *none* of this goes in the book, at least not from my mouth.

> —*ROLLING STONE* STAFFER

One night with Hunter and Oscar [Acosta] we were just driving around and Hunter was having some argument with Jann over expenses. So we were driving around in an area where Jann lived. Maybe I was driving.

And Hunter said, "Stop the car." He had the key to Jann's

house. And he knew Jann was out. And he said, "Just wait a minute." And he walked in and he came out with Jann's stereo amplifier in his arms and he said, "OK, I guess that takes care of business." And he just took it.

And Jann loved that. He loved it when Hunter did stuff like that. He just thought it was the greatest joke.

—DAVID FELTON

. . . As you know, I am a fan of your work and we have been delighted to publish some of it in the past.

However, at Hunter's very strong request, I must decline being interviewed at this time for your biography. I am sure you understand that I am absolutely duty-bound to respect his wishes in this matter.

Sincerely,

Jann (signature)
Editor & Publisher

JSW/mm
cc: Hunter S. Thompson

—— I haven't told *anybody* "You can't talk to her."

—— Well, you told Jann Wenner and Terry McDonnel that.

—— No, I didn't.

—— Yes, you did.

—— I've said nice things about you. I tell people when they get here that you're an old friend and I was going to marry you.

—HUNTER THOMPSON interview

Hunter wrote *Fear and Loathing in Las Vegas* downstairs in the basement of Owl Farm. It was a giant room with a huge stone fireplace and a door that went outside—you came up through the woodpile. It had redwood walls and a beautiful deep plush red rug. It was a very elegant room, a sanctuary. A beautiful cave. He would have a fire and we'd make love down there. I'd have my

drink and he'd have his drink and we'd make love on the carpet.
He used a door desk on sawhorses. He wrote with Dexedrine and
bourbon. I think *Fear and Loathing in Las Vegas* was written to
J. J. Cale. Cale is kind of country-jazz, a real moving kind of music. It just rolled. Similar to Dire Straits. And Hunter would just
play it over and over and over and over and over again. He liked
mournful songs. He liked sad songs. The song about the poor little
girl who was left out in the snow, Hunter used to love that.

We made love in the snow too. We'd be on acid. Three o'clock
in the morning, we were on acid, it was not cold outside, it was
just bliss!

—Sandra Dawn Thompson Tarlo

The book began as a 250 word caption for *Sports Illustrated* . . .
about a motorcycle race [in Las Vegas].

—Hunter Thompson, "Jacket Copy for Fear and
Loathing in Las Vegas: A Savage Journey to the
Heart of the American Dream," *The Great Shark
Hunt,* Summit Books, 1979

Yes. Hunter tied me up. But it was with my permission. I did *not*
like it. So he didn't ask to do it anymore.

—Sandra Dawn Thompson Tarlo

I'll tell you what it was. There were girls who fucked Hunter. It
was not that Hunter was so attractive to them. But Hunter would
give them access to celebrity. Being involved with Hunter was
great pointage. It would elevate the woman in Jann's eyes. It was
the groupie factor. You know? Hunter. He was everything men
wanted to be. *Everything.* I think women got tired of him. They
got tired of those high jinks—coming in the office in the morning
and having the typewriters thrown out the windows, and having
to stay up all night getting stuff on the Mojo. It got old real quick.

—*Rolling Stone* staffer

So *Fear and Loathing in Las Vegas* was written in that den. It was a very sensual place. Hunter liked that sensual quality, like the hot tub, the red light, the peacock feathers and the J. J. Cale.

He would get up when he was writing *Vegas*, take a long shower till the hot water ran out—Hunter was incredibly clean. He really had a thing about cleanliness. He was one of the very first people to start flossing. He did it every single day, in a very sort of religious way. He was never sloppy or scraggly. He always had a thing about clean clothes. Clean underwear, clean socks. And he was always ordering Converse All Star shoes. You know, he must have bought hundreds and hundreds and hundreds of those things.

Then he would have his orange juice, maybe grapefruit. He loved grapefruit. About six cups of coffee. And then, I'm trying to think. OK. One thing that he loved. You take tuna fish out of the can, right? And then you smash it into the plate with mayonnaise, pickles, onions and celery. Then you slice tomatoes really thin and put them all on top of this mashed tuna salad thing. Then you fry bacon strips and put four on the top. He loved that. That was one of his favorite dishes. He came up with that himself.

So that was one. Another one was peanut butter, mayonnaise, garlic, pepper, salt and lettuce. He made that one up, too. He loved scrambled eggs with hot sauce and cheese and chilies. With toast. Always. He loved toast. And he also liked things like jam and orange marmalade. He would eat breakfast in the living room by the fire or, in the summertime, always outside on the porch.

—SANDRA DAWN THOMPSON TARLO

Hunter, Annie [Leibovitz, the photographer] and I were stopped by the cops, and Hunter talked his way out of a drunk-driving arrest not by being nice but by being belligerent. And I realized, "Oh, here's a different way of doing things." When we got back to the hotel, and there was no firewood, Hunter just decided that he had every right to smash the furniture and burn that. He knew it would be taken care of, and we wouldn't suffer for it. *Because after a few experiences you realize Hunter gets away with it.*

—DAVID FELTON

———— was sleeping with Hunter and ———— wanted to sleep with Hunter. ———— was sleeping with Mick Jagger and ———— wanted to sleep with Mick Jagger.

—*ROLLING STONE* STAFFER

OK, fine. I want to introduce you to the office coke dealer. His name was Owl Henry. Have you heard of him?

Well, he was a very sinister guy. A dark nihilist and wastrel. Among other things, he was a writer groupie. Personally, I found him to be something like a black hole of intelligence collapsed in on itself. I have rarely been in the presence of anybody more fundamentally warped than he was.

He was originally, I believe, Hunter's pal. I'm not sure how they met. But before he became, or perhaps during the time that he became a coke dealer, Owl Henry had been a merchant seaman. And that's how he began smuggling drugs.

Then he was introduced to Jann, and this was during Jann's first coke addiction. Owl Henry supplied virtually everybody in the office with coke, and if it was a writer that he liked the coke was free. So it was free to Jann. It was free to Hunter. And if you fell within, you know, the beneficence of this guy, he'd keep you supplied. I mean he was a big-time dealer. A dangerous creep.

And he systematically seduced—drug-seduced, I should say—he systematically seduced almost everybody on the masthead.

I was going up to interview Lee Marvin, the actor, on location, in Oregon. And Owl said, "Oh, you're going to see old Lee, huh? Well, he's one of my favorite actors." And he gave me a huge package of coke to take to Lee. Eventually I gave it to some needy junkie at the office, if I recall.

—GROVER LEWIS, *Rolling Stone* editor; presently a free-lance journalist

He would count on me to get him up. And I'd go in, and in this little, little voice, I'd kneel next to the bed and say, "Hunter"— This big huge bed was on the floor. And I'd say, "Hunter, it's time to get up." And he'd go, "Ohhh, mmmmmMMMmmm-ooooohhhhh half an hour more." And then I'd go back out in the kitchen and I'd do whatever, and then I'd return and I'd say,

"Hunter, it's time to get up." And he'd say, "Ohhhh mmmm-MMmmm give me another hour." And I'd go back to the kitchen. So I couldn't go anywhere. Of course, I *could,* but I wouldn't. And when he got up, already the adrenaline had started to pump seriously in me. It was like, "The War has begun!"

I would have gone down and gotten his newspapers, but I wouldn't talk to him. It was quiet. No. No. The TV would never be on. If somebody telephoned at that point, I would say, "Hunter's in the shower." Breakfast, as I think of it, was a sacred time for him.

And after breakfast he would go down in the basement, taking a beer with him. And he'd pretty much stay down there. Six hours, something like that. Down there in the envelope of sensuality, the alcohol, the J. J. Cale and the smoke.

—SANDRA DAWN THOMPSON TARLO

One time at Jann's house, he was just fooling around and took one of those fire extinguishers and blasted Jann's dog with it, you know, which made Jann hysterical. I also remember one time taking, I don't know what it was, whether it was a gram of cocaine or an ounce. But making it into a swastika on a mirror and then just doing the whole thing in one sitting.

—DAVID FELTON

Gonzo Journalism . . . is a style of reporting based on William Faulkner's idea that the best fiction is far more *true* than any kind of journalism . . . *Fear and Loathing in Las Vegas* is a *failed experiment* in Gonzo Journalism. My idea was to buy a fat notebook and record the whole thing, *as it happened,* then send in the notebook for publication—without editing . . .

—HUNTER THOMPSON, "Jacket Copy for Fear and Loathing in Las Vegas"

I was supposed to transcribe a tape. These two guys I had never heard of go to Las Vegas and one of them had some sort of Hispanic accent, and then the other was Mummblblublblublblbub, I couldn't understand anything. So I had the little things in my ears and a foot pedal and my little sandals and short cutoff jeans and granny glasses, and I was sitting there listening to this tape. In the particular scene I was supposed to transcribe, the two guys I couldn't understand were in some kind of Las Vegas fast-food joint. And the woman at the fast-food place couldn't understand them either and they couldn't understand her, and it was going on and on and on. So I transcribed away, and after a while, I just said, "Well, it sounds to me like they're saying this," so I would type it in. I had my own punctuation, like dot dot dot, dash dash, and sometimes I'd capitalize this, sometimes I'd lower-case that, and when it was printed in the article, it was exact. Exact. Word for word.

I mean, it was exact! And half of it I really felt like I had made up! As I was transcribing, I thought, well, this guy I can't understand will probably go through it and change it. But Hunter didn't change a thing. He took it verbatim. I was amazed. I couldn't believe it.

> —SARAH LAZIN; began her career at *Rolling Stone*, went on to run Rolling Stone Press; now a well-known literary agent

It lifts you out of your seat when you're reading it. It's out of control, but it's out of control in an exhilarating, hallucinatory way. His prose style reads like he's careening down a mountain highway at 110 miles an hour, steering with his knees.

> —TOM ROBBINS, author of *Even Cowgirls Get the Blues, Another Roadside Attraction, Jitterbug Perfume, Still Life With Woodpecker, Skinny Legs & All*

Hunter was surrounded by acolytes, suck-asses, sycophants, brown-noses and people who had something to gain from association with him. His gonzo approach tended to infect the other writers, the lesser writers at *Rolling Stone*. Joe Eszterhas being a conspicuous example. Joe was a kind of tenth-rate talent, but ravenous with ambition.

> —GROVER LEWIS

Was he exercising freedom or repression? A classic example. One time I visited Hunter in San Clemente. As I approached him at the hotel, he had a leer on his face and he was just slamming the door to his apartment as hard as he could, over and over again. Until it practically came off the hinges. He would slam it and then he would smile and open it; and he'd slam it again. It was because the guy upstairs complained about the noise. And Hunter's theory on those things, which he's done many times, is that if somebody complains about the noise you turn it up, not down, and they'll stop complaining eventually.

—DAVID FELTON

It was pure carny to watch Hunter and Jann. I mean they were both carnies in a sense. Hunter was constantly vying for money and influence with Jann. Hunter was just a guy from the sticks. He had no dough. He had talent. He did not have the backup of rich profits from the magazine. Jann had all that and so Hunter was constantly trying to con him out of it.

One evening at Jann's house Hunter ran an outrageous bloody con. He was wearing, you know, his usual dishabille, whatever it was at the time—some kind of rotten tennis shoes and shorts and a bloody T-shirt, bloody around the navel, also he had an enormous hypodermic needle, the kind used by veterinarians. And he pretended—to Jann's wide-eyed wonder—to be going in the next room, or in the bathroom, and injecting himself in the navel with tequila. Then he would come back out feigning a high to end all highs. It was hilarious. But I could see the O-eyed Wenner just lapping it up as a real happening. Hunter shooting up in the belly button. He had some piece of bloody meat or something hidden in the next room and he would go in and smear himself with blood and come back out bloody.

—GROVER LEWIS

I haven't thought about whether Hunter's books will live on. I guess I'm more interested in physical immortality. I just assume his books will die, and *he* will go on living into the next centuries.

—TOM ROBBINS

The happiest I've ever seen Hunter was the very first moment I met him. He arrived at my door. I had been assigned to work with him on a piece that he was doing on Ruben Salazar, the Chicago journalist who was killed, who I knew because I worked at the *L.A. Times*. And Hunter had just come back from Las Vegas and he had just written his first like eight or nine pages or fifteen pages of *Fear and Loathing in Las Vegas*.

And you know, practically before he said hello, I'd never met him before, he just said, "You gotta read this!"

—DAVID FELTON

True Gonzo reporting needs the talents of a master journalist, the eye of an artist/photographer and the heavy balls of an actor.

American print media are not ready for this kind of thing, yet. *Rolling Stone* was probably the only magazine in America where I could get the Vegas book published.

—HUNTER THOMPSON, "Jacket Copy for Fear and Loathing in Las Vegas"

He has so deeply impressed so many readers that he has infiltrated the culture. Gonzo. Fear and Loathing. He's all over the place. Can you imagine Vladimir Nabokov in *Doonesbury*?

By the way, I saw something in the paper that alcohol reverses the ionization in the brain and to a certain extent allows you to think better. For most people it would be just the first half beer.

—JEROME KLINKOWITZ, literary and cultural critic, author of *Literary Disruptions: The Making of a Post-Contemporary American Fiction; Structuring the Void: The Struggle for Subject in Contemporary American Fiction;* and *The New American Novel of Manners,* among others

It's going to be interesting to see, a hundred years from now, how history judges these times. I think that the sixties are going to get a lot more attention than they do now. And Hunter will have guessed correctly on that one. Hunter and William Burroughs are about the only two journalists who have openly, without reservation, talked about the situation of drugs that every other journalist has pretended wasn't there. I think drugs will turn out to be the Achilles' heel of this country.

—DAVID FELTON

I warped a few things, but it was a pretty accurate picture. It was an incredible feat of balance more than literature. That's why I called it *Fear and Loathing*. It's as good as *The Great Gatsby* and better than *The Sun Also Rises*.

—HUNTER THOMPSON, quoted by William McKeen
in *Hunter S. Thompson*, G. K. Hall & Co., 1991

When the flash went off, one senses, Hunter S. Thompson, Doctor of Gonzo Journalism, was standing at ground zero.

—MICHAEL MATZA, *Boston Phoenix*, August 21,
1979

I'm on the corner of Third and Brannon Street. It's an Italian restaurant. Well, all of a sudden, *Rolling Stone* moved across the street from the joint. I think Paul Scanlon and Grover Lewis started coming in here, the next to fall in line was Joe Eszterhas, then of course, Tim Cahill came, and Sarah Lazin, Ben Fong-Torres, Tim Ferris, Charlie Perry, and it just developed. The Simon and Garfunkel guy. Lots of celebrities they brought in here.

I fell in love with little Theresa Brewer. I'm trying to think of the famous guy that plays guitar—yeah! Keith Richards. He was here all the time.

I have a Ralph Steadman at home that he autographed for me that's probably worth a pile these days. Once in a while Jann would come in in the evening when he had to tell those guys something when he knew they weren't coming back. 'Cause there's no getting around it. Those guys were heavy-duties. They did a number. I lost a bundle when *Rolling Stone* moved to New York.

You know Jann drove a little Mercedes 280 SL. And he'd park it in the wrong direction. And he'd come in and Jann, you know, never drank the same drink. You never knew what the hell he wanted to drink. It was either a Tom Collins or a Bloody Mary, next time it was bourbon and Seven-Up. Next time it was scotch and water. He was just a kid. He didn't know how to drink.

Mr. Thompson we would stick in the back room. He could rant and rave and do anything he wanted. The instructions from the company were to give Hunter Thompson anything he wanted. Yeah, and then just send *Rolling Stone* the bill. Hunter used to come in and get completely shitfaced. If need be they used to put him up in a hotel way out by the beach, the Seal Rock Inn. He'd stay goofy for two or three days. It was hard for my regulars to get used to him.

Yeah, now people come in here and ask about all the famous celebrities. They used to ask about Hunter and Jann. But I have to be honest, now everybody asks about Joe Eszterhas. God! He got that three-million-dollar advance on that movie! So they're not saying too much about Hunter Thompson anymore. I can honestly say that the last few months it's been nothing but Joe Eszterhas.

—JERRY FRANCESCHI, owner, with his brother, of Jerry's Inn, San Francisco, hangout of the *Rolling Stone* staff before the magazine moved to New York

2

What is this guy? A drug dealer?

—RAKISH, Indian astrologer who had never heard of Hunter Thompson, after looking at his astrological chart for three or four seconds

He turned up on the campaign trail rather early on. When no one else was following me. I was told by [Frank] Mankiewicz or Gary Hart who he was, that he wrote for *Rolling Stone* and that he was an eccentric, unique reporter who would probably be sympathetic to my world-view and certainly to my opposition to the war. I'd heard the stories about his drug involvement and his candidacy for sheriff. I knew he was a somewhat offbeat character. So I kept an eye out for him. But he wasn't a big figure in my game plan. He was just another reporter who I was told to be alert for.

But Hunter *did* stand out. He was an intense guy. He had been writing columns out of New Hampshire when I had *five percent* of the polls saying I might go all the way.

—GEORGE MCGOVERN, friend of HST; Democratic nominee for President, 1972; former U.S. senator from South Dakota

Going to Washington? It was a really exciting prospect. We were ready to leave Woody Creek for a while and go to the Big Leagues. Go to Washington!

Rolling Stone paid all the expenses. We rented—for us it was a fancy house. A nice neighborhood, right across from Rock Creek Park, a nice two-story brick house, squarish, European, with proper furniture. I was pregnant again. This was going to be the last shot. I asked the doctor what my odds were. He said, about twenty-five percent. I said, OK. I'm willing to do it. I wanted a child mostly because I wanted another Hunter. I wanted more of that energy on this planet.

—SANDRA DAWN THOMPSON TARLO

[Wenner's] contract with Thompson for the 1972 campaign year called for the writer to receive a retainer of $1000 per month, an incredibly modest sum given Thompson's worth to the magazine, plus expenses, which would later be taken out of Thompson's book royalties. As it turned out, Thompson's share of the paperback rights for *Fear and Loathing: on the Campaign Trail* amounted to approximately $33,500, of which all but $2,000 went back to Wenner for expenses.

—ROBERT SAM ANSON, *Gone Crazy and Back Again,* Doubleday, 1981 (A slightly different version by Anson appeared in *New Times,* December 10, 1976)

Hunter was gone a lot. And then when he was home, he was wild. He was either working frantically or sleeping. It was totally different. It was not a peaceful, happy time at all. I remember myself smoking—I had taken up smoking!—and drinking a lot. Here I am pregnant, right? The doctor gave me a prescription for Valium.

Hunter was just so much in his own thing, in his own world, that he wasn't aware until I got really outrageous. He didn't know that every single night I was drunk. He didn't know that.

—SANDRA DAWN THOMPSON TARLO

I knew how incredibly in love with Sandy he was. I knew how protective of her he was. And for some reason that you can only allow yourself to believe when you're twenty-two or twenty-three, I believed that my affair with him only strengthened their marriage. I mean it was—"*Hunter loved Sandy.*" It would never have occurred to me to think that they would divorce or separate. I would do anything to protect her. I thought she was wonderful. I thought they were wonderful. I loved him, but I loved her too.

He and I never talked about being in love. But one time he did. He turned around and he had that hat on, sort of like almost *Casablanca,* he turned around and mouthed the words "I love you." And the snow was coming down at the airfield, and he got on one of those little propeller planes, and I stood on the tarmac just heart breaking in ecstasy.

—BARBARA (last name withheld); a prominent labor activist

He had one section in the book where he listed things that might have changed his life if he had done them. And one of them was spending a weekend in Bermuda with Eleanor McGovern. And I said to him, feigning indignation over this, "How can you write that! Stop ruining reputations like that!" Then he said, "You hypocritical bastard! You're just as immoral as I am in every way!" [Laughing.]

—SENATOR GEORGE MCGOVERN

My impression on meeting Hunter was the same as all impressions since. He was a rather staid, straightforward, quiet, understated fellow. Very courteous. Not Southern, but a gentleman. He waited to be spoken to. He was a counter-puncher. I figured Hunter for absolutely straight. Hair was cut very close. I've always said [*Fear and Loathing: on the Campaign Trail '72*] was the most accurate and the least factual book about the Seventy-two campaign that I ever read.

> —FRANK MANKIEWICZ, friend of HST; former Press
> Secretary to Robert Kennedy; political director of
> McGovern's campaign; presently vice-president of
> Hill & Knowlton

I was sports editor at the *Washington Star*. And Hunter came down to see me. Just to hang out. Of course by then he was publishing in *Rolling Stone* and all the copy boys and everybody were just gaga. I mean Robert Redford could have walked in and it wouldn't have made a difference. Hunter had driven down in his new Volvo.

About three days later he called me up and he wanted to know where his car was. And I said, "Your car? I don't know where your car is. Where'd you leave it?" And he said, "Well, I was at the *Star*. And I said, "Jesus, Hunter, that was *three* days ago." And he said, "My dogs are in it."

> —DAVID BURGIN, friend of HST; currently editor-in-
> chief, Alameda Newspaper Group

He was very perceptive. It was a very accurate portrayal of my character. He saw the human situation clearly. He couldn't avoid it. So there was a certain amount of sadness about him. Hunter was a patriot. But he thought in universal terms. He was not a jingoist. He hated that war in Vietnam with a passion. And he hated the hypocrisy of the establishment. Basically, I think he wanted to see this country live up to his ideals. And he wanted us to do better. There is no doubt that what he wrote in 1972 was the most valuable book on the campaign.

> —SENATOR GEORGE McGOVERN

Well, he came down to the office and we went looking for his car. He told me he thought he parked it next to a big wall, which turned out to be the freeway. And we found it—and there were three or four little black kids standing there watching the scene.

And there the dogs were inside the car. A terrible sight! They were all right, but they had chewed the shit out of everything.

—DAVID BURGIN

Sandy and Hunter rented a house in a place called Juniper Street, in Washington, all the way out Sixteenth Street almost to Silver Spring. It was in a neighborhood of really old people. It was a brick house, two-story brick house, next to Rock Creek Park. They had two Dobermans. Benji and Darwin, just bunny rabbits. In the entrance I remember was a coat rack, and hanging from the top was a white pith helmet. And written across the front it said "Raoul Duke."

And I asked Sandy about it, and she said, "Raoul Duke has always been one of Hunter's fantasy personalities."

There were regular kind of middle-class furnishings inside. Mexican rugs on the walls and hanging Mexican-type things. You walked in, on the left there was a living room with a big couch. There was a dining room with Hunter's junk all over. Sandy was very pretty and she was God knows how many months pregnant.

—TOBY THOMPSON, journalist; author of *The Sixties Report, Saloon,* among others

I liked Sandy a lot. Of course, a lot of people said, "How the hell does she put up with Hunter?" I just found her a wonderful person. If one were to hope to find a good mate, she seemed to be that kind of person. I mean this, of course, from the point of view of an egocentric, self-centered writer as opposed to a normal person. She was a kind of "I see you with love." She was strong. Hunter was a rather difficult adult. I sort of had the feeling that she just kept him together. She was extremely sexy and attractive. I certainly had the impression that she loved him mightily. I remember many of us saying, "This guy doesn't appreciate what a wonderful wife he has."

—NICHOLAS VON HOFFMAN, friend of HST; journalist; television commentator; author of *Citizen Cohn, Capitalist Fools,* among others.

We weren't at Owl Farm. There was a lot of madness. There were lots of people. There was a lot of action. Tim Crouse [author of *The Boys on the Bus;* Wenner had assigned Crouse to assist Thompson] was there. The energy had begun to get very intense. Physical. Hunter had begun to get angrier. A lot angrier. You know? And more violent. His language was more violent. He was louder. He was tenser. His muscles were tenser. He was in a whole different ball game.

He was dealing with The Heavies. He was playing with The Players. And he was even winning. But it was taking its toll. He didn't come home to have fun. He came home either to write or to crash. He was taking a lot of speed. I don't remember any fun. The Fun Factor didn't happen on Juniper Street. That's why Hunter dedicated the book to me. He knew how hard it was.

There was no *relief.* It was just boom, boom, boom, boom. He was wired. He didn't have recovery time. It was really hard on Tim [Crouse]. It was hard for his ego. To be yelled and screamed at. There was a lot of noise. Shouting down at Tim or myself to get something, or bring something up.

—SANDRA DAWN THOMPSON TARLO

He's maybe the twentieth century's greatest political journalist, if you want to change the definition of journalism. What Hunter did was to expose how unconscionably wimpy political journalism was, and still is.

If people had just one ounce of Hunter's attitude they would rise up! They wouldn't take this miserable farce of a government we have!

—DAVID FELTON

(Hunter, at a New Hampshire Exeter Inn men's room urinal, to Senator George McGovern, also at a urinal):
  "Say . . . ah . . . I hate to mention this . . ."

—*Fear and Loathing: on the Campaign Trail '72,*
Straight Arrow Books, 1973.

3

About the second or third day out on the Zoo Plane [McGovern's campaign press plane], Hunter came up in this incredibly gentle, shy, almost high school kind of way and he said, "Would you go out on a date with me?" Having read *Fear and Loathing in Las Vegas*, I looked at him, and said, "Well, ———" I can't remember actually where this was. I think it was in Grand Rapids, Michigan. I think it was the day that McGovern told the guy, right in the general election, to kiss his ass.

So we agreed that we would go out on our date, whatever that meant. And he said, "Well, why don't you come to my room?" We all stayed in the same hotel, and I thought, "Barbara, why are you doing this? This has got to be the *craziest* thing, going out on a date with Hunter Thompson." I knocked on the door of his hotel room. He answered wearing a towel on his head. I think he was shaving. And he had on either short shorts or underwear. I was too confused by the whole scene to know which.

There was music playing. And I walked in and he said, "I have to rearrange the room!" And he moved the beds around, moved the television around. So I sat there very nervous, thinking, I'm going out on a date with Hunter Thompson, on the edge of the bed, and I watched him walk around, rearrange the lamps, move from one direction to another direction, walk into the bathroom, say "Excuse me," come back out of the bathroom with all the towels and hang them over the lamps. So the lights were all very diffused, and I thought, "I probably shouldn't be here. I should probably get out of here very quickly!"

Then he walked back into the bathroom and came out again, and he opened up his hand. He had all different kinds of capsules. And he said, "Would you like some drugs?" And I said, "Uhhhh. No, thank you." And he opened a beer, put them in his mouth and swallowed them all! Different colors. Different shapes.

And I thought, "Oh, God! *I've got to get out of here now!*" I had never taken any drugs. I had marijuana one time when I was in college. I had no idea. I didn't know if he was going to fall down and faint, or what. I had no idea what was going to happen. And I kept saying, "Well, I think we oughtta leave now, I think we oughtta go now. I think we oughtta leave now."

—Barbara

He sure gave Sandy a hard time. One night we were in Washington and he had rented a Dodge Charger. I was in the back seat, Sandy was in the shotgun seat and Hunter was driving. And he went over the Connecticut Avenue Bridge in Northwest Washington at a hundred miles an hour. Nobody's ever done that. Sandy was hysterical. I just assumed I was dead.

—David Burgin

I always thought that Hunter was a very vulnerable, sweet, gentle, kind person. He always was to me. There was something soft about him. And gentle. Underneath all that craziness. He was never anything but absolutely polite with me. Completely polite, and he had wonderful manners. Yes, he had beautiful manners. That's the side of him—I loved the zany, the outrageous and everything else, and I thought that was amusing. But what really appealed to me about Hunter was that he was a gentleman. I always thought he was—vulnerable, sad, too. Melancholy.

—Sally Quinn, friend of HST; newspaper and
television journalist and novelist

4

The Seventy-two convention in Miami was incredibly secured. It was surrounded by a huge fence and you walked across a kind of war zone between the fence and the convention hall. The idea was to keep the crowd so far away that they couldn't even throw things. And then once you got in that, every day you had your daily credentials, and you had to have those credentials around your neck, and they checked everything as you went in. Well, one day, I was standing there in line and I looked to my left and there was Hunter standing there. And we all had our tags around our necks, and Hunter was holding a jacket over his right shoulder with his finger, and the guards were going through everything that he had hanging around his neck, which included binoculars and camera, and I think maybe even a lens. So I observed this with great interest. They were going through *everything*. They were opening up the cameras, looking through the binoculars, and Hunter was standing there quiet and silent.

And a little later, I walked into the convention hall, and standing there underneath the bleachers in the darkness was Hunter drinking an exotic bottle of foreign beer. Very exotic. It was from Denmark. And I went up to him, and I said, "Goddamn it, Hunter, where did you get that great beer?" And he said, "Oh, I had a six-pack in my jacket over my shoulder."

—JUDITH ROBINSON, biographer, *The Hearsts*

I was covering the campaign for the *Village Voice* and had infiltrated the Nixon Youth at the Convention in Miami. I think I might have been wearing a straw boater to hide my face and I was looking down and mingling with the Nixon Youth and suddenly I saw Hunter! He was sitting down against the wall with either a hat over his eyes or something like that trying to be inconspicuous and I was trying to be inconspicuous. And I can't remember whether he kicked me or I kicked him and we were both sort of worried that each of us would blow the other's cover. But we managed to march in with the Nixon Youth at the convention amidst a shower of balloons.

—RON ROSENBAUM, journalist, contributing editor
 to *Vanity Fair*; author of *Manhattan Passions:
 True Tales of Power, Wealth and Excess; Travels
 with Doctor Death and Other Unusual
 Investigations*, among others

... All three network TV cameras looking down on their spontaneous Nixon Youth demonstration and zeroing in ... on a weird-looking 35-year-old speed freak with half his hair burned off from overindulgence, wearing a big blue McGovern button on his chest, carrying a tall cup of "Old Milwaukee" and shaking his fist at John Chancellor up in the NBC booth—screaming: "You dirty bastard! You'll *pay* for this, by God! We'll rip your goddamn teeth out! KILL! KILL!"

—HUNTER THOMPSON, *Fear and Loathing: on the
 Campaign Trail '72*

Hunter Thompson? He's dead or something.

—JOHN CHANCELLOR, NBC News

Hunter was a walking, living rebut to people like that. But they all loved him. He was allowed to tell the truth and they weren't, so they all were fans of his. Hunter was the most widely read, and, in some ways, the most respected correspondent on that campaign.

—RON ROSENBAUM

5

When our baby was born, he looked really good. Which was amazing for all my drinking. He had to have a blood transfusion. And then he immediately developed a premature disease. The Hyaline Membrane Disease, it's called, which is what Jackie Kennedy's baby had. It's now curable. And those two things together killed him.

He lived for almost twenty-four hours. I actually looked at that baby. I didn't hold him, but I looked at him.

When I was ready to come home, I called Hunter and told him that he didn't need to come and get me, because it was like eleven o'clock in the morning, which would have been too early and he would have to get out of bed. It was an hour-and-a-half drive from Washington. And I told him I could take a taxi. And for years after that, I was hurt and angry that he had not said to me, "No, no, no. Don't take a taxi."

—SANDRA DAWN THOMPSON TARLO

But when I came home, he did something better. He took me out on the campaign trail with him. It was a train ride with McGovern across Iowa, Kansas. And he was absolutely right. It was the best thing. He was very tender with me.

—SANDRA DAWN THOMPSON TARLO

We were all sitting together on one of the train trips and drinking beer and were being jostled by this foreign, I think they were Italian, camera crew. They were completely obnoxious and pushing us. Hunter finally turned on them and pulled a knife out of his pocket and said he was prepared to sever their technical connection. He also mumbled something about cutting their fucking hearts out. The guys fled the car.

—Curtis Wilkie, friend of HST; political reporter for *The Boston Globe*

I persuaded him at last to leave his hotel room. We went to a Holiday Inn-ish type piano bar where the press was hanging out.

And we sat down and all I kept thinking about was, "I wonder when those drugs are going to take hold. I wonder when those drugs are going to take hold."

So I said something like, "I have to leave soon," and he said, "No, no, you have to stay." He ordered me more drinks and I decided, "Uh-oh. I've got to get out of here." And I just got up and left. I didn't say goodbye to him. I slipped out. So the next day when I got on the airplane about eight o'clock in the morning, he came rolling up the aisle, with his sunglasses on, with a Bloody Mary, and said, "You wretched bitch! You left me alone!"

—Barbara

He was pretty good at capturing the spirit of the times. He knew what was in people's heads. He might have been a pretty good politician. He was thinking of running for the Senate, you know.

—Senator George McGovern

The next days were frantic in the campaign. It was towards the end. And he said, "Would you like to try another date?" And I said, "Yes." And we arranged to meet in the evening on the campaign trail. It got very sweet after that. We saw each other for years afterward.

—Barbara

We broke the lease. We *had* to get back to Woody Creek. On Christmas Eve Hunter went out and bought two presents. A Siamese kitten for Juan and a mynah bird for me. Edward. Edward would say, "Hi! I'm Edward. Birds can't talk. What's going on? I love you." He was a beautiful black bird, half the size of a crow, from India. Well, Hunter went bonkers over Edward. He used to take a shower with him. Edward loved the shower. He would sing in the shower. And we all went back to Owl Farm. It always felt good going back. Always. Always.

—SANDRA DAWN THOMPSON TARLO

Hunter called me after the campaign one day. I was in my office. He was supposed to have come by at two-thirty or three, and about a quarter to six he called me and said he was sorry he was running a little late. And then he said, "I'm drunk. Do you still want me to come?" And I said, "Well, it's all right with me." So he arrived carrying a six-pack. He fumbled around with his tape recorder. He smacked it down a few times, sort of mumbling and scowling at it, saying, "This filthy thing! Filthy piece of equipment!"

He said he was late because a girl had come by his room. They had a drink, and he couldn't get this woman to go home. Well, [laughs] I had nothing else to do. Now that the election was over.

—SENATOR GEORGE MCGOVERN

CHAPTER
FOURTEEN

I'm still not married; but I've not bought a revolver and
don't keep a diary.

—ANTON CHEKHOV

1

The wedding was postponed. The Doctor's Japanese translator
and editor were coming. "GODDAMN IT!" shouted the Doctor
to Deborah, his secretary. "You've upset Miss Tishy! Why did you
wait till the last fucking minute?"

"I told you about the fucking Japanese last week!" shouted
Deborah.

"Read me their fucking letter," yelled the Doctor.

Deborah put on her glasses, and as she read, I clung to the Doctor's bathrobe sleeve, and every now and then, with tears, lifted up
my eyes, murmuring, "Why? Why?"

"You know what Japs like?" said Martin, the Doctor's Drug
Dealer. He happened to be visiting.

The Doctor was sitting at the kitchen counter in front of his
typewriter. He turned and looked at Martin with his index finger
hooked over the top of his cigarette holder and scowled.

"They love golf!" said Martin.

The Doctor's cheeks jumped.

"Yeah!" cried the Doctor, "Japs love fucking golf!"

"It costs a Jap a *million* fucking bucks to join a golf club outside Tokyo," said Martin, a sporty, jolly fellow.

"It does!" said the Doctor, throwing an old TarGard at the wastebasket and missing ("Just to keep things interesting").

Truth being excusable in a Biographer, I trust the Reader will forgive me if I quickly mention here *what* Martin, the Drug Dealer, said of me when I was out in the yard measuring the tail coverts of the peacocks. He said: "Have you ever seen an ass of such splendor?"

"Of course, we'll bring the Japs *here!*" said the Doctor, swiveling completely around in his chair, "and let them play all the fucking golf they want!"

"Man! They'll go crazy!" cried Martin.

"Of course, we'll need a green," said the Doctor. "And a flag."

"Hell, yes!" said Martin.

"Where can we steal one?" said the Doctor.

"I can get one off the eighteenth hole tonight," said Martin.

"Pray, what else are you going to steal?" I scrupled not, with some warmth, to inquire.

The Doctor was thrashing happily about his papers looking for his bean-shooter.

"What else do we *need?*" said the Doctor.

2

The Famous Writer! The Gonzo King with the Rosy Royalty Statement! The Fiancé of the afflicted Miss Tishy! The monster never mentioned a new Wedding date! "Meeker" never again passed his sausage lips! But still, don't be frightened, Reader. True, I had gamahuched the groom till I had disgraced human nature, but my chastity was yet inviolate. So lest I forgot myself and was saucy, to avoid a scene, I went to the bathroom, locked myself in, sank down in a rage and, grabbing the magazine stand, fainted against the toilet.

But let me draw a veil over a scene too brutal for a heart so affectionately delicate as yours, Reader. I cannot for both our sakes be too concise about my agony over the canceled nuptials. I shall only say that after combing my bangs, I returned to the kitchen as the Doctor was saying, "Of course, we'll need guns."

"Jesus, Japs *love* guns!" said Martin.

"Are you writing this down!" shouted the Doctor, swiveling toward Deborah.

She was. In a big black artist's notebook. The Reader perhaps wonders about Deborah. She was a Hoosier; consequently, it was impossible not to feel one's self automatically drawn to her——honey blond, handsome, divorced, with a red chest got from her hobby of glass-blowing, and continually shouting at the Doctor, heaping abuse upon him and always on the point of quitting. In short, an exalted female specimen.

"OK. Miss Tishy picks the Japs up at the hotel," said the Doctor, taking a swig off the Chartreuse. "In the Chevy. Top *down.*"

"That's the ammo, the guns, the golf clubs, the tees, the golf hats, the flag, and the Chevy," said Deborah, reading off her list. After we married, I planned to keep Deborah.

"You're driving along," said the Doctor, "you're pointing out the sights, and suddenly!"——he assumed a solemn expression, which, however, made him look absolutely ridiculous——"I'll appear in *another* red convertible! With a shotgun! Wearing my black wig with pantyhose over my face, dressed as a bull fruit. I'll shoot over your heads. You'll barely escape. Either that, or—— Yeah! I'll shoot Miss Tishy right in front of the Japs' eyes!"

"Yeah!" shouted Martin.

"You'll be wearing one of those blood sacks, Miss Tishy, that spurts!" said the Doctor.

I said nothing out of a sense of my own dignity.

"Man," cried Martin, "those poor Japs!"

"Jesus! I forgot the bomb!" said the Doctor.

3

"Now, here's the plan. You pull right in front of the garage. OK?" He threw one of his big arms around my shoulders. "The Japs reel out of the car. The first thing they hear is the mad dog. (Needless to say, the Doctor had a tape.) Then Deborah will set off the pig-squealer. Then *I* appear from around the corner, with a shotgun. I have my black duster on, and *that's* when I shoot you, Miss Tishy!"

"Why must you always shoot *me?*"

The Doctor shrugged.

"OK. I run over Mona with the car. OK. Anyway, the Japs are in front of the garage and the beating tape is going. [A lunatic in an asylum being beaten and flagellated.] Then you take them on the porch and they see the guns! And just at the point when they're going to turn and run like rats, *then* I come out as myself! Of course, we pick them up an hour *early* so they are totally unprepared."

"The Japs are gonna *love* this!" cried Martin.

4

After a midnight dinner at the Woody Creek Tavern where the Doctor made a refined appearance in his hat of "unborn wolf——an entire litter" (see picture section for the loathsome reality——observe it! observe it, Reader! *This* is the man whose biography I am being compelled to write!) and a whole night spent in frenzied faxing all over the country ("I'll be bigger than the Beatles in Japan!"), I was subjected to yet another of my barbarian conqueror's monstrous pre-marital love orgies——suffice to say, he picked me up, carried me into the bedroom, and hurled me upon the bed, where I was obliged to undergo the uncouth meanderings of his fingers, the recital of which would only serve to arouse the emotion and perplex the attention of the Reader.

In short, my pajamas were ripped from my body, my bubbies sucked, my legs pried apart, my buttocks clasped, my thighs flung over his shoulders, and a Gonzo tongue was applied to my aperture, an action which caused me to beat upon the Doctor's bald head like a gong, and ask at short intervals, and more and more excitedly, when the date for our wedding was, till suddenly, my body was seized by such violent rhythmic convulsions that even an hour later my eyeballs had not returned to normal position. Indeed, it was apparent that if I ever did marry the Doctor, I would go completely blind in a week.

Yes, and many, many times, when I used to read to the Doctor out of *The Curse of Lono,* he would rock back and forth and say, "That's true. That's all true. That's just what happened. I'm not making this up."

5

At five o'clock p.m. the Japanese were to be picked up at the——I can't remember the name of the hotel. It was not the Jerome. At four o'clock p.m. the Doctor was loping through the house, his delicate nostrils swelled up like cauliflowers, belching and flatulating ("All that acid," said the Doctor), collecting guns from his safe, his file cabinet, his drawers, his closets, indeed, I believe the Doctor was better outfitted than the Colorado National Guard with a .357, a .44 Magnum, several little pistols, a revolver, a Thompson submachine gun, an AK47, an elegant lady's shotgun, several Browning automatics, identical Weatherby rifles with infrared spotting scopes, and a dozen or so firearms which I could not identify, strange-looking, brutal weapons, some with engraved maxims on the barrel or butt, "When the going gets weird, the weird turn professional," for instance, whatever *that* idiotic expression means.

Then he collected the ammunition boxes, an operation which took the better part of an hour because he decided to clean house at the same time——i.e., whenever his bloodshot eye fell upon an object which was out of place, he heaved it out the front door.

"What *is* this fucking junk?" he would scream, and then he would throw it out the front door, or if he was in the kitchen, he would yell with the sweat splashing off his forehead, "I can't live this way!" and stagger past the refrigerator and throw the offending object, whatever it was, a bottle, pan, picture, book, glass tray, the cat dish, the cat, down the basement stairs.

Finally, when all was in order, and half his possessions had been thrown out of the house, and Deborah had tried to persuade him to eat something ("I don't have *time* to fucking eat! The fucking Japs are coming!") and change into his wig and pantyhose ("I wish these fucking Japs weren't coming!") and we were about to leave for town to pick them up, the Doctor, his neck now very red and tense, suddenly asked where Mona's sister was. Now, Mona herself had been hauled up the mountainside by Handsome Ron, the Doctor's mechanic, and was perched on a fence overlooking the bombsite.

"You gave Mona's sister away," said Deborah.

The Doctor seized his secretary by the shoulders and searched her face in anguished disbelief.

"I didn't give her away!" he whispered.

Big beads of perspiration rolled down in front of his maroon ears. For a moment it looked as if he had put on earrings.

"You did," said Deborah. "I can't remember to who."

The Doctor stared at her in wonder for several moments; then his hands dropped to his sides. Breathing hard, he sat down on his stool.

"I *couldn't* have!" he said and almost burst into tears. "Those goddamned Japs!"

"We have to go pick them up now, Hunter," said Deborah. Indeed, the shooting range was ready, the golf green and flag were in place, the pantry was crammed with sake, the porch cooler was stuffed with French champagne, German beer, Scandinavian mineral waters and Caribbean fruit juices; the roses and lilies were arranged, the cars, motorcycles and tractor were polished, and the bomb had been set to detonate.

"Well, don't bring them back *here!*" said the Doctor, attempting to cool his suffering bulk with a snow cone of Chivas.

"We'll drive them around Aspen," said Deborah.

"Yeah."

"Then we'll bring them here."

"Jesus!" cried the Doctor, miserably. "Well, call me first from the drugstore!"

As we left he was dragging everything out of the cupboards, searching for the beating and flagellating tape. Would the Doctor pull himself together and shoot me as agreed? Or would his recent hysterics lead him to load the gun with live bullets and mow down the Japanese? And when was our wedding? Upon these questions and other matters I shall have occasion to speak more at large in future, but now we must turn to a distressing biographical section in which the Doctor proves himself as great a villain as ever lived, indeed, I believe it will be the longest section of the book what with all his Crimes and Cruelties, so I would just hint to the Generous Reader, as I have stayed up all week preparing it, the least you could do is stay up all night reading it.

CHAPTER
FIFTEEN

> I had been the first to recommend the use of cocaine
> . . . and this recommendation had brought serious
> reproaches down on me.
>
> —SIGMUND FREUD

1

> You're a goddamn nightmare to travel with.
>
> —YAIL BLOOR to Hunter Thompson, *The Great
> Shark Hunt,* in *Playboy,* December 1974

Then two major changes occurred with Hunter.

One of them was when he started to use cocaine. I would say it was perhaps around seventy-three or seventy-four. What had happened was he was given the assignment to review [Freud's] *The Cocaine Papers.* It had just come out. Hunter was told to review it. Up to that time, Hunter had never done cocaine. In fact he had no respect for it. He thought it was just a jive drug. He called me up and he said, "This stuff—" In order to review the book he'd had to try the drug. He said, "This drug is really totally hyped. You tell me the effects," and I said, "Well, it's sort of like speed, you get a rush, but it's not the same, and . . ."

He said, "See! You can't describe it any better than anybody else. It's all psychological. Because it's expensive. The dealers are running a scam. It's just the drug of the idle rich."

And then he said, "Still, I guess I might as well finish the rest of this off, you know, there's no point in letting it go."

The second thing that got in his way was the celebrity.

> —DAVID FELTON, friend of HST; former writer and editor at *Rolling Stone;* presently writer and consultant for the Editorial Department of MTV

It was a hot, nearly blazing day in Washington, and I was coming down the steps of the Supreme Court . . . and all of a sudden I saw a crowd of people and I heard them saying, "Uncle Duke." I heard the words *Duke, Uncle;* it didn't seem to make any sense. I looked around, and I recognized people who were total strangers pointing at me and laughing. I had no idea what the fuck they were talking about . . . and I thought, Why am I being mocked by a gang of strangers and friends on the steps of the Supreme Court? Then I must have asked someone, and they told me that Uncle Duke had appeared in the *Post* that morning.

> —HUNTER THOMPSON, in an interview with Ron Rosenbaum, *High Times,* September 1977 (Uncle Duke first appeared in Garry Trudeau's comic strip *Doonesbury* in late 1974)

I didn't know about Hunter's escapades. People would say to me, "Oh, he's so faithful. It's just amazing he's so faithful." Well, Hunter was in Cozumel doing the [*Great Shark Hunt*] for *Playboy* and Lucian Truscott sent Hunter a tape. I opened a lot of Hunter's business things and stacked them up. I would not have opened a personal letter. But somehow this was in a package and I opened it and the letter said, "It may not be a good idea to let Sandy listen to this tape." Well, of course, I had to listen to the tape. And the only odd thing on the tape was Hunter and a woman in the car and she was saying something like, "Shall I get some Wild Turkey?" And that was it. But that was enough. I immediately knew.

> —SANDRA DAWN THOMPSON TARLO

Hunter and I went out and actually caught a shark in Cozumel. Yeah, we did. Hunter was deathly afraid of the damn thing by the time it surfaced. Jesus. I mean, you know, try shark hunting at night on acid.

—MICHAEL SOLHEIM, close friend of HST,
accompanied him on the *Playboy* story; presently
in Aspen real estate

Sandy found out. I was in the car with Lucian Truscott the Fourth and Hunter in New York. And my voice was on a tape which she then heard. So she knew there was a woman. And actually that was the beginning of a sort of slowing down in the amount of times I would see Hunter. Our code name was Mankiewicz. I was Frank Mankiewicz. Then I got to be other people. I'd see Hunter two or three times a month, and then I would see him two times a month, and then I'd see him once a month, and then I'd see him every two months, and then I'd see him every six months. I don't know that there was ever a last time.

—BARBARA (last name withheld); a prominent labor
activist

First I went to Oscar. He was sleeping in a sort of boarding house, in a little tiny room, and he was all rumpled up and hung over, and I said, "Oscar, Oscar, I'm going to kill myself unless you tell me the truth about this woman on the tape." Oscar honestly didn't know.

And then I called Lucian. And I said, "Lucian, I have to know about this. Otherwise I am going to kill myself." And Lucian was saying, "I can't . . . I can't . . . I can't." And finally, after I carried on with all these threats, he finally said, "Look, it was nothing."

—SANDRA DAWN THOMPSON TARLO

Meanwhile Hunter and I were going to try and eat all the drugs we had before we departed Cozumel. Oh, Christ, we had a pocketful of reds, we had a lot of cocaine, there was still some MDA. We ended up eating all of it. We sure did. Then we got to Customs in Texas and I noticed before we got off the plane I still had a bunch of reds in my pocket. I thought we'd taken everything and, Oh, my God, look at this! Here's about fifteen or twenty reds!

Well, Hunter didn't want to get rid of those. So he put them in his shoes, this was real good thinking, this will give you an idea of how sharp we were.

—MICHAEL SOLHEIM

I'm the Most Famous Drunkard. At any airport in the world at any given time, it'd be a good bet that I would be the most famous person and the easiest busted at the airport. Right?

—HUNTER THOMPSON interview

At the end of three or four days on Cozumel we monitored our guests' bills because we were paying for their food and everything. The publicity man came to me with Hunter's bill and said, "Herb, you won't believe the figures!" I said, "Do me a favor and get this guy on his way." His bill was three or four times higher than anyone else's.

—HERB PHILLIPS, former head of Striker Yachts,
host of the international fishing tournament
which HST covered for *Playboy*; current
president of Herb Phillips Boats

Hunter put [the reds] in his tennis shoes. But on the *outside,* just under the laces. So that they looked like a design. And as he walked, well—there was a trail of them behind him, on the marble floor in that Customs shed. The guy at the Customs counter looked at us. And I'm sure he said to himself, "Well, obviously these guys have eaten everything they had."

—MICHAEL SOLHEIM

2
The Moving Finger

Dr. Hunter S. Thompson, the famed gonzo journalist of
Rolling Stone magazine, is making news on his college

lecture tour, all of it bad so far. At Duke, he showed up drunk, hurled a few objects and epithets at the audience, and never did get around to his speech. As a result, several other colleges have canceled him....

—AP NEWS RELEASE, November 22, 1974

He sat with me during the flight [to Zaire for the George Foreman–Muhammad Ali fight]. He said he was trying to recover from a humiliating evening back in the States a few nights before when, lecturing at Duke University, he had been given the hook for being outlandishly drunk on Wild Turkey bourbon and making a fool of himself in front of a large and muttering audience.

... He asked me if I thought he was going to get paid.

"I don't know," I said. I asked how long had he been out there on the stage before the hook arrived. He couldn't remember. "Did I say it was Duke?" he asked.

"Yes," I said.

"Well, I *think* it was Duke."

He said that after his removal he had gone out into the parking lot and had talked to a circle of students ... but he wondered if that was sufficient representation of his role as a lecturer.

—GEORGE PLIMPTON, *Shadow Box*, Putnam, 1977

In Kinshasa I was signing everything "Don King." By the time Hunter showed up I had claret stains on my shirt. We were drinking St.-Émilion every night from President Mobutu's personal stash. I taught Hunter to address all the black citizens as "Mundele." I said it would bring him enormous respect. He nearly killed me afterwards. It means "white man."

I recall him swimming in the pool. I remember saying to him, "Hey, man. You better get ready. The fight's tonight. We're leaving." And he said, "Yeah." And he just kept swimming. He missed a good fight. Ali-Foreman. It was very dramatic.

—BILL CARDOSO, friend of HST during the seventies; coiner of the description "gonzo journalism"; journalist

Hunter was always finding plots in Zaire. He kept asking me to help him. For what? To get him a private audience with Mobutu, he said. The great plot he discovered was, of course, the big torpedo that was being built in the northern Congo. Things like that. And when the fight was over, he came running in and said, "What was it like?" He wasn't even there! He was lying in the swimming pool on a bed of hashish.

He wants to write what Hunter Thompson readers want to know, which has nothing to do with the event. I think what happens when he can't write is, he can't find out what it is his readers want to hear. He wrote *Fear and Loathing in Las Vegas*, as I recall, on an assignment to write about the Mint 400 for *Sports Illustrated*. And something else interested him. Obviously he wasn't writing for *Sports Illustrated* readers.

I think if you don't know what your own constituency is you're left in a type of Bedlam. Hunter lives in a weird sort of Bedlam. He has no attachments to anything. He's adrift. If you read all those writers that we've had [in *The Paris Review*] you see what a difficult thing it is to write. People think that it's easy. It's not. One of the troubles with Hunter is he seems to be constantly afflicted with a type of writer's block.

So, is it easier to go and write something about the fight or not about the fight? The fact of the matter is, Hunter didn't write about either. Nor did he in New Orleans [Ali-Spinks], so that's not taking the risk, is it? I think he's popular because he is Hunter Thompson. He is a persona writer. He's a writer like Norman [Mailer] and Hemingway and those people who are huge public personalities.

If people don't know much about writing, Hunter's probably the most popular American writer.

> —GEORGE PLIMPTON, friend of HST; editor of *The
> Paris Review*; author of *Paper Lion, Shadow
> Box, The Curious Case of Sidd Finch*; co-author
> of *Edie*

He didn't write anything after he came back from Zaire, he didn't write anything after he came back from New Orleans. He didn't write anything after he came back from Nixon's resignation. He refused to turn in the piece when he came back from Vietnam.

I don't think anybody has a right to say that anybody should live up to their potential. You know, it's their decision. But I think you do have a right to be disappointed. And I think it's a disappointment not only not to have his writing, but more than that, he's capable of being a tremendous self-promoter, wheeler-dealer, that sort of thing.

And he's done very well. So there, you can't really say he's failed. But maybe he should have won the sheriff's election. He should have gone into politics. Then he could have drunk as much as he wanted and still gotten elected.

—DAVID FELTON

"We're lucky to be alive," said Steadman. "Zaire was a narrow escape. Quite naturally when we get off the plane and walk into Brown's [in London] at nine in the morning, Hunter orders three Bloody Marys, a dozen beers, a bottle of scotch, a bottle of Wild Turkey, and the number of the nearest brothel. . . . Last night he was accused of trying to rape one of the maids and of shooting pigeons on the window ledge with a Magnum .44. This morning I find him in bed with a girl. At some point in the night he had drawn a swastika on her ass in indelible ink."

—JON BRADSHAW, "Hunter Thompson on a Bat:
Fear and Loathing in Mayfair," *The Village
Voice*, May 19, 1975; Bradshaw, a respected
British journalist, is now deceased

He couldn't write. I mean this was what he'd always done. This was what he lived for. And all of a sudden he couldn't do it. He would go down in the basement. But it just wasn't happening. He was taking a lot of drugs. He was just getting really crazy, more violent. The tension in the house was getting unbelievable.

The fact is that I was going down right along with him. I did coke with him for, I'm guessing it was about a year. Maybe longer. I did a lot of cocaine with him. . . . I remember one time we were so horribly high on cocaine that it was really really jangly coming down. And I said, "Is this the time when there's only two ways to go? And that's more cocaine or take Thorazine? Is this it?" And Hunter said, "That's it. That's where we are." That's when I stopped doing cocaine. It's a nasty, nasty drug. Cocaine is not a holy drug at all.

—SANDRA DAWN THOMPSON TARLO

"Are there any girls in town?" he asked when Steadman had gone. "I want to rape someone. I need about 113 orgasms before I can do any serious work tonight." He looked out the window. "What's the penalty for rape in Berkeley Square?" he asked.

—JON BRADSHAW, "Hunter Thompson on a Bat"

In the beginning Hunter would just say he had blocks. This is when the cocaine hit. There was a lot of it being consumed at the Jerome bar. A lot. He would drink there till three or four o'clock in the morning.

And he sometimes didn't get up till six p.m. It was just getting later and later. And then after breakfast, he'd go down to the Jerome and usually stay till four in the morning.

I myself could easily drink half a bottle of bourbon a day. I could drink a bottle and a half of wine. I could drink a lot. I was scared and fragile. . . . Then as I got crazier and crazier and weaker and stranger and more and more out of balance, every time I'd cry, *every time I cried,* Hunter would come to me. Every time I'd cry. He would just dissolve when I'd cry. He would take care of me. He would hold me and soothe me. And I could count on him.

. . . But I remember one night he said, "Sandy, if you don't get it together—" It was the first time he had ever said this. I mean I was just driveling and scared and lost. Pathetic.

—SANDRA DAWN THOMPSON TARLO

We set off for the tailor's. In the back room of the tailor shop, the proprietor listened patiently. "Listen," said Gonzo, sipping beer, "it's ridiculously simple. I need two suits, one maybe in white and one in black. You can put in some stripes if you like, or some polka dots, but nothing fashionable. They have to be boss gambler suits. That's the main thing. I use them on my lec-

ture tours. They have to create an immediate effect, you understand."

—JON BRADSHAW, "Hunter Thompson on a Bat"

—— Why don't you just run a tape recorder twenty-four hours a
day, have two people transcribing around the clock, read it, cut it,
and you have a novel?

—— It's been suggested.

—— Then all you have to do, Hunter, is go along and live your
life.

—— (*Huffy*) Well, what do you think I've been doing?

—— But you have to reconstruct it.

—— That's right. And it's hard.

—HUNTER THOMPSON interview

We finished off the bottles of malt whiskey and Wild Turkey in his
room at the hotel and arranged with an escort agency for five girls
to meet us at midnight.

—JON BRADSHAW, "Hunter Thompson on a Bat"

Do you know what a burden—a terrible burden would fall on me
if I was recognized as being the Great American Writer? It would
be a burden, I'll tell you.

—HUNTER THOMPSON interview

Gonzo produced his coke and passed it round on the end of a
switchblade. For about five minutes it was peaceful. But Gonzo,
now into his third Scotch, suddenly asked the girl if she would like
to be raped. "You'll like it," he said. "You have that look about
you. I always recognize it immediately. You can see it in the eyes.
It's a fearful look."

The girl giggled but declined. "Why use violence?" she purred.
"Can't we just fuck normally?"

"Normally?" he shouted. "What the hell does that mean? Are

you some sort of weird freak? I want to rip off your clothes, rape you, tear you limb from limb, and throw you into the street. You'll like it. Believe me, goddamn it. I'm an expert. I *know* what I'm doing."

—JON BRADSHAW, "Hunter Thompson on a Bat"

Then the Duke University thing happened. And he got thrown off the stage. Then he went to Africa and he was going to be gone for a month and I decided to go into therapy. I did not tell him because I knew he absolutely would not allow me to. Because Hunter didn't believe in therapy. He didn't believe in psychiatrists because he said we could handle everything ourselves. He said it was hogwash. They were all quacks.

—SANDRA DAWN THOMPSON TARLO

"Shit," he screamed. . . . "I can't get anything done in this town. There's nothing left to drink in the whole country, the hotel is repressed, the streets are filled with bands of armed masturbators. . . . There's only one thing to do. Go home. I'll never work otherwise. Great creeping Jesus, it must have cost *Rolling Stone* $10,000 already on this story. I'll have to give them something. . . ."

He banged the telephone receiver up and down. "This is Dr. Gonzo," he said. "I want you to get me on the first plane out to Woody Creek, Colorado. Lean on those fuckers at the airport. Get heavy. Offer bribes. Just get me on anything going west. And be quick about it, goddamn it. I've got a deadline to meet."

—JON BRADSHAW, "Hunter Thompson on a Bat"

And then one day I came back from the health club and there was a car parked right up on the cement next to the porch and I walked in and there was a body on the couch in the kitchen and it was Hunter. And he was *out!* He didn't come to for days. He woke up once and gave Juan and me presents—two huge ivory tusks.

—SANDRA DAWN THOMPSON TARLO

3

I was scheduled to go to Cleveland to cover David Bowie's tour for ·Rolling Stone. Just before heading for the airport I had a meeting with Jann, at which he told me as I was now doing nothing for the magazine except writing, they couldn't afford to keep me on. I asked what he intended to pay in the way of severance. Jann said it was the magazine's policy to pay no severance. I didn't think this was an entirely appropriate reward for my having worked hard as the magazine's New York bureau chief.

Anyway, I took a cab to the airport and hit the road with David Bowie. When we got to Memphis I called Hunter at Woody Creek. Sandy answered. She told me Hunter was in Washington at the Watergate Hotel. She said that she was sure I could reach him right away in his room because they had just gotten off the phone a few moments before. I asked her how things were going, and she said, "Fine, except that we're a bit worried about money. We have only four hundred dollars left in our bank account. After that's spent we don't know where any money is going to come from. That's what Hunter and I were talking about just now—our money problems."

Sandy and I chatted for a few more minutes, and then we said goodbye and I called Hunter in Washington. "How are you?" he said. "Well, not so great," I said. "I got fired, and Jann doesn't want to give me severance pay."

Hunter immediately said, "Do you need any money? I could let you have four hundred dollars."

—TIMOTHY FERRIS, friend of HST; former *Rolling Stone* Editor; professor of journalism, UC Berkeley; author of *The Mind's Sky, Coming of Age in the Milky Way, Galaxies,* etc.; writer and presenter of the PBS television special "The Creation of the Universe."

4

I had been a correspondent for *Esquire* in Vietnam and Jann was sending Hunter over. And Hunter called me in his usual nervous voice and wanted to know how to go about doing it. His main thing was he was worried how to get accredited to the American Army. I said, "Well, you just show a letter from *Rolling Stone* and you get your press credentials." And he said, "Yeah, but what about being from *Rolling Stone?*" I didn't even understand what he was talking about. He said, "You know, when they find out that I'm from *Rolling Stone,* they might not talk to me." He was worried about what would happen when he was in the field. "You know," he said, *"Rolling Stone* is against the war."

I said: "Hunter, you're going to tell them that you're from *Rolling Stone* and they're going to talk to you about rock and roll. They're not going to know its editorial position. They are going to look at you with your fascist haircut and they're going to think you're pro-Army."

> —JOHN SACK, friend of HST; only person, dead or alive, who was a correspondent in all of America's wars since World War II; author of *M: The Butcher; Report from Practically Nowhere; Lieutenant Calley: His Own Story,* among others

Phil Caputo and I took Hunter on his first Vietnam combat mission. Hunter had been bugging us for several days, "Take me out, take me out." And finally we said, "All right, Hunter, listen. We'll take you out, but there's no screwing around. No madcap zany bullshit. This is serious business. If you want to go with us, we're going to leave at six o'clock. Not at six-o-one. If you're there at six-o-one, we're going to be gone."

So at six o'clock the next morning, we're getting ready to go out the front door and all of a sudden here came Hunter.

And it was a sight. He was wearing Bermuda shorts. Sneakers with no socks. Hawaiian shirt. A baseball cap. Shades. A cigarette holder with a smoke in it. And he had two room boys carrying his chest of ice and beer.

Hunter Thompson. Ready to go to war. He was talking into this little hand-held tape recorder. "I'm walking down the stairs . . . I'm getting in the Jeep . . ."

I thought, "Jesus Christ!" Caputo and I were wearing helmets and flak jackets.

So we got into the car and off we went—Hunter talking all the time into his tape recorder, drinking beer from the chest and popping some sort of pills, maybe speed, I don't know what they were. He was washing them down with the beer. He was popping one pill every fifteen minutes. And he was talking into his tape recorder. I looked over, and noticed that there was no tape in it.

Then we ran into a huge operation. It was the South Vietnamese airborne going in for its last-stand defense at Xuan Loc. Xuan Loc was the one place where the South Vietnamese stood and fought. And got their asses kicked.

I mean it was a huge field with massed troops on it. And all these helicopters were coming back from Xuan Loc with casualties, and unloading litters with injured and dead on them. And as they cleared out, fresh troops would get on and be airlifted up.

> —NICHOLAS PROFFITT, friend of HST; sergeant in the U.S. Infantry and a *Newsweek* bureau chief in Vietnam; author of *Gardens of Stone, The Embassy House,* and *Edge of Eden*

Then a flight of South Vietnamese fighter-bombers passed overhead on a close air-support mission. They couldn't have been more than five, six hundred feet overhead. And they just came roaring by. A thunderous roar. And quite suddenly, Hunter let out a blood-curdling yell. I mean it was just chilling. And the driver, in fact, jerked the Jeep off the road into a culvert. We thought Hunter had been hit by a sniper.

The Jeep stopped. I looked at Hunter and I said, "Are you all right?" And then Nick turned around. Hunter said, "Man! Did you see those pterodactyls go overhead?"

Nick, I think, nearly strangled him. He reached over the back seat and grabbed him by the collar and said, "You son of a bitch!"

> —PHILIP CAPUTO, friend of HST, winner of the 1977 National Book Award for *A Rumor of War;* first in Vietnam with the Marines, later with the *Chicago Tribune*

I looked at Caputo and said, "Bag this. Let's go talk to these guys." So we jumped out of the Jeep. And we went over, got our notes, talked to a few people, and this and that and then we looked around—no Hunter.

Looked in the car—no Hunter. We looked down the highway and there was Hunter, I mean, a mile down the damn road. Walking along. Talking into his tape recorder. Heading right toward where the troops were, the last South Vietnamese presence on the highway.

Well, first of all, we debated whether to let the son of a bitch get himself killed. Then we jumped in the Jeep and I sort of had to beat the driver about the head and shoulders to get him to go down the road. We pulled up alongside Hunter and grabbed him and threw him in the car. I'd say we were no more than five hundred meters from the first North Vietnamese outpost.

—NICK PROFFITT

The paper in my notebook is limp and the blue and white tiles of my floor are so slick with humidity that not even white canvas, rubber-soled basketball shoes can provide enough real traction for me to pace back and forth in the classic, high-speed style of a man caving in to The Fear.

—HUNTER THOMPSON, from a two-page dispatch to *Rolling Stone*, April 20, 1975 (publication date: May 22, 1975)

A bunch of us set up an opium den in a room in the Continental Palace Hotel in Saigon. We took out the furniture, had mats on the floor and a little stack of sarongs, so if you wanted to, you could take off your clothes and just wrap up. It was sort of a communal thing for, oh, I guess, ten people. Mr. Vung was our opium man. You came in, there was music, mats and pillows all over the place, and you lay down and waited your turn. Mr. Vung would fix your pipes for you—twirl the opium over the flame, pack the pipe, well, you know, it ended up on a stick as a little gummy ball. Mr. Vung would roll it into sort of a black gummy ball and he would put it into the hole in the bottom of your pipe and hold it over the flame for you. Then you would sort of grab the stem and suck it down.

Hunter, of course, partook.

I remember the first time he came. It was relaxed, nobody got terribly screwed up—except Hunter. He came in and the old hands told him, "Now Hunter, the trick is to take it all in at once, in sort of a long sustained gurgle. If you're doing it right, the sound is like sucking up the last vestiges of a milkshake through a straw."

So he was doing that, and you usually have three or four pipes. Hunter had his share and more. And then at the end it was time to go downstairs and eat and there was a little ball of opium left. So Hunter popped it into his mouth and chewed it like chewing gum.

And then somebody had some buddha grass. It was in the form of about a twenty-dollar cigar and Hunter smoked that down, too.

And then we all went back to our rooms and were supposed to meet downstairs for dinner in the sort of inner central garden restaurant.

—NICK PROFFITT

Hunter was staggering around. I mean he was weaving. He was tacking like a sailboat. Of course, he does have an odd gait. The place where the Vietnamese waiters and busboys stood was under an awning made of corrugated tin. It was held up by bamboo uprights.

Everybody was eating. And all of a sudden there was a thunderous noise. And the awning came crashing down. And people were ducking. Somebody yelled "Incoming!" And people started diving.

And there was Hunter lying still, just his sneakers showing, and the rest of him buried under this awning.

Somebody said, "Jesus Christ, is he dead?"

And Proffitt said, "I hope the fuck so."

—PHILIP CAPUTO

There was some old whore—that's what Hunter was doing up in his room. There was this old mama. I'd known her for years and years and years and years. And she had been really beautiful. And she was still good-looking, but, you know, in a sort of fiftyish, washed-up sort of way. And she sort of latched onto Hunter, this really hocked-out old whore, or Hunter latched onto her. Well, he was making a show of having this woman in his room.

—NICK PROFFITT

If Hunter liked any Vietnamese hookers, he was the only one. One of the biggest complaints of the soldiers about Vietnam was how awful the hookers were. Oh, they were terrible. They were jokes among the soldiers. Somebody said he was screwing a girl and she had her arms up around his neck and he wondered what she was doing, and he rolled over and he looked up and she was reading a comic book.

—JOHN SACK

I took Hunter to American Legion Post 34 in Saigon. You would have sworn you were in some sort of joint out in the Middle West. Except the bartender was Vietnamese and there were maybe half a dozen Vietnamese bar girls.

Now, with the departure of the American Army, the women in this profession had had some lean times. Well, we walked in there and they descended on Hunter and me like Dust Bowl crows on a road kill.

I mean they fairly leaped off the stools. They got a big yuk out of Hunter because he was so big. I remember one of them grabbing him by the forearms and biceps and saying, "Oh, you so big! You so strong!"

We were literally swatting them off.

—PHILIP CAPUTO

Hunter had an abiding fear of missing the evacuation. He wanted to make sure he knew what was going on. So he went to Hong Kong to get some sophisticated electronics gear. Supposedly so he could listen in on the Embassy. Of course, he missed the evacuation.

—NICK PROFFITT

Rolling Stone paid for me to go to Hong Kong. We stayed at the Repulse Bay Hotel. I brought some mescaline in my makeup box. Hunter met me at the airport. We just immediately took the mescaline. And at the hotel we played in the bathtub, and then I went to sleep and when I woke up I saw Hunter was at the desk writing again. And I remember lying in bed, looking over and thinking, Hallelujah! He was writing again! It had been so long since I'd really seen him writing. And I had a lot of hope.

—SANDRA DAWN THOMPSON TARLO

5

I use speed as fuel, a necessary evil. Adrenalin is much smoother and much more dangerous if you fuck up. I fucked up one time in a motel in Austin, Texas. I was very careless, and I just whacked the needle into my leg without thinking. I'd forgotten the vein thing, and after I pulled the little spike out, I noticed something was wrong. In the bathroom the tile was white, the curtain was white, but in the corner of my eye in the mirror I looked down and saw a hell of a lot of red. Here was this little tiny puncture, like a leak in a high powered hose. . . . It was going straight from my leg and hitting the shower curtain at about thigh level, and the whole bottom of the curtain was turning red.

I thought, oh Jesus Christ, what now? And I just went in and lay down on the bed and told the people in the room to get out without telling them why; then I waited 20 minutes and all I could think of was these horrible Janis Joplin stories; you know, OD-ing in a motel. . . . Jim Morrison . . . Jimi Hendrix . . . needles. And I thought, oh God, it's going to come all at once. It's a delayed thing, like those acid flashbacks they've been promising all these years.

—HUNTER THOMPSON, in an interview with Ron
Rosenbaum for *High Times*, September 1977

Hunter and I used to go to the same doctor, Bob Morgan. He doesn't live here anymore. I used to go to Morgan and Morgan would say, "Well, how's he doing?" And I said, "Well, he seems fine." And Morgan said, "He's not fine. He's been dead for two years."

Morgan would continually question Hunter about his lifestyle. This was in the mid-seventies. Morgan had already told him that his liver was a mess and this was a mess and that was a mess.

—MICHAEL SOLHEIM

But his mother, who still lives in Louisville, says she visited Thompson in Colorado in October and "he did very little work. Sandy . . . says he has a bad case of writer's block."

His health may also be a factor. His mother described him as looking "terrible. He looks so much older now, and he's losing his hair. He went to the doctor while I was there. I'm surprised he kept the appointment.

"He said the doctor said he is 'maintaining.' I asked what that's supposed to mean. He said, 'I'm staying on a level.' He was supposed to go back for some tests, but never did."

> —JOHN CHRISTENSEN, quoting Virginia Thompson,
> HST's mother, *Scene, Louisville Courier-Journal*,
> January 22, 1977

Sometimes the *lack* of Adrenalin is almost like a drug itself.

> —HUNTER THOMPSON interview

I have never seen anyone who can take so much crap into his system at so great a rate and not die from it. If I lived my life one day the way that Hunter does, I would be in the hospital. If I did it for three days, I would be dead. And he does it over and over. He comes out of something that has yet to be measured. Of all the writers we talk about, I probably understand Hunter the least, because of the prodigious capacity he has. The man is a legend in successful self-abuse.

> —NORMAN MAILER, quoted by Peter Whitmer,
> *Aquarius Revisited*, Macmillan, 1987

At the Pittsburgh-Minnesota Super Bowl in New Orleans, Hunter and I had a bet. At the end of three quarters, when Pittsburgh was ahead 9–0, I paid him. The main thing I remember is I had a sore throat and I had cough drops with me, and I offered him a cough drop. He said, "Oh, thank you. I can really use that. Here, let me give you some acid."

> —DICK SCHAAP, television journalist; sportswriter;
> editor of the Dick Schaap Sports Series, Penguin
> Books

While at Northwestern University—a very straitlaced place, very collegiate—I was on the Student Activities Committee. The more

mischievous of us thought that it would be really funny to invite
Hunter [to speak]. It was the drug stuff that really attracted us.
Rather than the political stuff.

I think what we really wanted was a reason why it was great to
take drugs and have adventures. Because we all wanted to. But we
were also really bourgeois and stuck on being successful. . . . And
through a series of mishaps, I ended up having to meet Hunter at
the airport.

I had a tiny car. I was not a good driver. To this day, and probably because of Hunter Thompson, I'm still a very skittish driver.

Well, I met him. I thought he was going to be a madman, crazy
guy—but nice, you know? And he didn't say a word. I mean, he
didn't say a word! Barely. I don't know if he said hello. He did not
say a word!

> —LAURA ROSS, director of advertising and
> promotion for a major New York publishing
> house

He was totally wack-a-doo. I never saw a guy consume frigging
drugs like Hunter. I was getting married and I'll never forget this
as long as I live, Hunter and Dick Goodwin had this huge red limousine and Hunter put on an Arab headdress, and this was the
time of the Arab oil thing, you know, and he stood up through the
sunroof of the limousine and handed out dollar bills on Fifth Avenue. It was wild, the cops came. He had a stack of dollar bills
and was handing them out like an Arab potentate.

> —BOB ARUM, friend of HST; lawyer, sports events
> and fight promoter.

It was rush-hour Chicago traffic.

I get the feeling in retrospect that maybe Hunter was nervous.

> —LAURA ROSS

My new wife hated him. Hunter ate the roses for the wedding at the
Carlyle. Later at the fight in New Orleans he came into my suite
with a gun, and that's when my wife—I'm not married to her anymore . . .

> —BOB ARUM

The basic crux of it was that people wanted to know if the stuff in the books was really true, or if he was exaggerating. And I think that they came away feeling like it's probably not even the whole truth. *It was probably worse than that.*

—LAURA ROSS

6

He was just a pain. Everybody thought he was brilliant and wonderful and a great journalist and all that. A great writer. But he just made life unbearable for everybody working on any article. He never made his deadlines. You couldn't get through to him. You couldn't find out where he was.

It would mean that everybody involved from the editors to the fact-checkers would have to be simply hanging out at the magazine, waiting for Hunter's stuff to come in. It would completely throw all our personal lives into total disarray. Every time one of his pieces came in, it was going to be torture. We knew it would be wonderful, but we also knew the process of getting it into the magazine would be punishing.

It was a real tribute to his talent that people were willing to put up with something they wouldn't put up with from anybody else.

On the phone Hunter's wife was very apologetic and very nice. She would say, "Hunter can't come to the phone. He's sitting in the bathtub. He's feeling very cross right now."

—VICKI SUFIAN, former *Rolling Stone* fact-checker and researcher; presently a free-lance television news producer

About half the time I was the guy who sat up all night with the damn Xerox telecopier [the Mojo machine] with this horrible greasy thermofax paper. And Hunter would be at the other end. And there would be no organization of the story at all. And it would come in as inserts. Insert A. Insert Q. And then we'd have all these inserts. And I'd Xerox them so that Jann didn't have to handle the paper. It was all an insert. There was no beginning and no end. Every thing he wrote was like a lead.

—CHARLES PERRY, *Rolling Stone* editor and staff writer; presently the food critic of the *L.A. Times*; author of *The Haight-Ashbury: A History*

Luckily, there was enough supply of young, energetic people coming through that as various mortals burned out, there was always somebody else to send into the arena.

Hunter could wear you out.

He made a lot of noises. He used to do that *res ipsa loquitur*. Supposedly it means, "And so it is said." His translation was "Don't fuck with this."

When Nixon resigned, Ralph [Steadman] had done a wonderful cover. But Hunter didn't file. We ended up sitting in the conference room on Brannon Street with bound volumes of *Rolling Stone* literally cutting little paragraphs and articles and pieces of pieces and pasting them up. It was ridiculous. There were eight editors sitting at the conference table patching together snippets of things that Hunter had written over the last year and a half.

—HARRIET FIER, former managing editor of *Rolling Stone*; currently president of FM Productions (TV and documentaries)

One time it was "Insert CAZART."

—CHARLES PERRY

INTER-OFFICE MEMORANDUM

To: Jann
From: Sarah
Re: Hunter S. Thompson and other risks
Date: 10 May 1975

I researched the article by HST last issue as well as I could, but there were several items I could not check given the lateness of the hour. In fact several changes I did point out were not made, due also to the lateness of the hour and the temperament of the writer. Hunter does make mistakes, and Gonzo journalism is no blanket for covering up wrong facts.

The Research Department cannot take responsibility for this kind of material when it arrives so late and in such bad condition. We'll try to fact-check as much as we can with what resources we have. But we cannot check quotes and figures when we get no research packet, when businesses are closed and when we're not even able to talk with the writer. And if there's any legal problem, there is not even enough time to send the piece over to the lawyers.

Just for the record.

> —SARAH LAZIN, began her career at *Rolling Stone*, went on to head up the Research Department and to run Rolling Stone Press; now a well-known literary agent

Oscar threatened legal action and almost stopped publication of [*Fear and Loathing in Las Vegas*]. He felt he deserved some credit as a "coauthor," and in a purely gonzo sense, he may have been right. Unfortunately, this led to a desire to write and ultimately to his destruction. It may or may not have led to Hunter's. . . .

Around 1974, Hunter and Oscar, having patched up their friendship, met at the Seal Rock Inn in San Francisco. Oscar, broke and desperate, asked Hunter to finance an "illegal business operation." Hunter refused, saying the plan had the "smell of doom" to it. They parted amicably. Oscar was never heard from again. Rumors soon started circulating that he'd been killed on the high seas in a dope-smuggling venture.

Then, during the next few years, a curious thing happened. Hunter found it almost impossible to keep writing.

> —DAVID FELTON, "When the Weird Turn Pro," *Rolling Stone*, May 29, 1980

Fear And Loathing
At Rolling Stone

Hunter S. Thompson, *Rolling Stone* magazine's peripatetic, self-styled "gonzo" journalist, has asked that his name be removed from the masthead of the popular bi-weekly tabloid....

"It's a toss-up," he said, "whether I was fired or whether I quit."

Rolling Stone watchers confirm that editor Wenner and correspondent Thompson are often at sharp odds with each other. One said yesterday, "It's a marvelous situation—the world's worst employee working for the world's worst boss."

—SANDY ROVNER, *The Washington Post*, May 30, 1975

Wenner folded Straight Arrow [Books] at a time when they owed me $75,0000.... It had been an advance for *Shark Hunt*. I wrote a seriously vicious letter.... While in Saigon, I found I'd been fired when Wenner flew into a rage upon receiving the letter. Getting fired didn't mean much to me ... except that I lost health insurance. Here I was in a war zone, and no health insurance....

... I vowed not to work for them. It was the end of our working relationship except for special circumstances. About that time, they moved to New York.

Essentially, the fun factor had gone out of *Rolling Stone*.

—HUNTER THOMPSON, "Rolling Stone: Abandon All Hope Ye Who Enter Here," *Songs of the Doomed*, Summit Books, 1990

After *Rolling Stone* moved to New York, at that point Hunter was hanging out with people like Bill Murray, Belushi and Aykroyd and a bunch of the guys. No women at all. The women would just be hired. He had them provided. But I got a sense even at that time that things were moving on, but Hunter wasn't. And what happened was, it was just a matter of degree, but we got thrown out of a restaurant, a good one, good enough to throw us out.

But the reason we were thrown out is because when John Walsh [former managing editor of *Rolling Stone*] walked into the room, we were all sitting around this table, and Walsh walked in late and Hunter reacted—a very Hunter-type thing—took his steak and threw it on the floor and went, "Woof Woof." The waiter just said, "Well, that's enough." And threw us all out. Belushi might have been there. The thing is, it just didn't get the laugh it was supposed to get. It just sort of shocked everybody. And the reason it didn't work then and it did work ten years earlier, was because we were ten years older.

—DAVID FELTON

7

There were beatings. Maybe six after the first heavy wallop when we were first together. Except for the last time when I had not had a drink in six months, I was always drunk. And when I'd get really drunk I could say things I'd never say sober. It was not pretty, not sweet, and very ugly. Hunter would have been drinking too, of course, but not necessarily drunk. My behavior clearly triggered some very deep part of him and he would lash out with hands, fists to whatever part of my body. I would whine and roll up into some pathetic little ball, making him even angrier.

—SANDRA DAWN THOMPSON TARLO

My marriage had broken up. I was brokenhearted and crazy. And he invited me to come to Colorado and cool out. He put me in the cellar of Owl Farm. It was like being in a penitentiary. It was a tiny little room, a penitent's cell. I had to go through a trapdoor. Then down a ladder. And then Hunter would bolt the trapdoor. And lock me down there and not allow me up until he left the house. I'm telling you the truth. He had to lower a bottle of scotch on a rope in the morning. Then Sandy would unlatch the trapdoor and I would come up and I would drink scotch with her.

Then in the evening we would go to the Hotel Jerome bar and meet Hunter.

—BILL CARDOSO

I was going to the health club and I did not want the other women to see that I had been beaten. The reason being that I didn't want them to know that Hunter had done this.

So, I was protecting Hunter. It wasn't a matter of how I looked, that I was the kind of person who could be beaten. It wasn't that. It was that I was protecting Hunter.

—SANDRA DAWN THOMPSON TARLO

He had the world's fastest motorcycle. It was in Hollywood. He asked me to drive him to Orange County. It was night. He had to pick up the bike. It was Japanese. It was supposed to be the fastest bike in the world. He checked everything out. Got on, and that was the end of him. He roared off to hell.

—BILL CARDOSO

One of those times I hit him back. Yeah, good. Except I just got hit a little harder. I was not much of a match.

—SANDRA DAWN THOMPSON TARLO

For Hunter to wreck that marriage took a lot of work. I always had the feeling though that after a certain point, people kept telling him he was impossible, and like many of us, he got trapped in his own reputation, and had to start living up to being impossible.

Being Hunter was a career and a half.

—NICHOLAS VON HOFFMAN, friend of HST;
journalist, television commentator, author of
Capitalist Fools, Citizen Cohn, etc.

Hunter beat me. OK. Not good. OK. Next chapter.

—SANDRA DAWN THOMPSON TARLO

He kind of admires old-fashioned values. And I think he's secretly envious of people who are happily married, I don't know, it's just a thought that came to me. But he's too strenuous to take for long stretches. I just really don't know how a woman can handle him. How someone could handle him for more than a weekend. Do you suppose he's a great lover?

—SENATOR GEORGE MCGOVERN

8

I was asked to speak to a class in New Journalism at UCLA, which was studying me. I found that the best way to explain New Journalism was to say something about Hunter. The story I told was true. I was twenty-two years old and I was a war correspondent for *Stars and Stripes* in Korea. There was an ammunition shortage there. Everyone knew about it. I mean, I was out in a tank and it ran out of ammunition and it had to come back.

I was at a briefing and the pilots were told that they couldn't call in artillery on one Chinese, on two Chinese, on three Chinese, there had to be at least fifteen Chinese on top of Old Baldy because there was an ammunition shortage. All of us correspondents knew this.

The Secretary of the Army came to Korea to see if there was an ammunition shortage. He went around all of Korea. And then he had a press conference. And the Secretary of the Army and General Maxwell Taylor, Four-Star General Taylor got up and said, "There is no ammunition shortage in Korea."

So Private First Class Sack stood up and said, "General Taylor, a lot of us heard that there's so little ammunition that they couldn't call artillery unless they saw at least fifteen Chinese on Old Baldy. Is that true?" And General Taylor said, "No, that is not true."

So following the rules of journalism, I went back to my little room in the press villa and sat down and I wrote my story for *Stars and Stripes:* "Seoul, Korea. General Maxwell Taylor said today that there is no ammunition shortage in Korea." But also I know what he said was a lie. But under the rules of journalism, there is no way I can say so.

To the class at UCLA: "Now," I said. "If Hunter Thompson

had been in Seoul, he would have written: 'Seoul, Korea. General
Maxwell Taylor said today that there is no ammunition shortage
in Korea. And the man is a motherfucking liar!' "

—JOHN SACK

9

I met Hunter in the mid-seventies after my husband's novel *Stay
Hungry* had been filmed in Alabama. We flew out to L.A. to
watch a rough cut and we stayed with the director and his wife,
Bob and Toby Rafelson. Toby was having a party after the screen-
ing and I walked into her kitchen and everybody in the kitchen
was famous. You know, like Jack Nicholson and Anjelica Huston,
and I looked around the room and the only person who didn't immediately strike me as being so famous that I couldn't possible go
up and start talking to him was this man standing over in the corner, wearing something strange around his neck. So in a very
smartass, flip way, I said, "What's that around your neck? Your
roller-skate key?" It was a little dark thing, and it had two little
ears that almost looked like Mickey Mouse. And he just glowered
at me. All this bile and hostility came up and he grew so angry! He
slammed his fist down on the kitchen counter like a karate chop,
and he glowered at me. And he said, "That is my magic mush-
room!"

And he just turned and walked out. It was a bad beginning. I
walked into the other room and he was sitting down on the couch
unloading his famous TWA bag. It was blue and white plastic, the
size of a bowling-ball bag. He spent the rest of the evening glow-
ering at me.

So when my husband [Charles Gaines, the writer] said that
Hunter was coming to stay with us because he wanted an unoffi-
cial headquarters for the New Hampshire primary with Jimmy
Carter, I immediately felt upset. I had young children in the house.
And I felt this guy would be hostile and mean and wouldn't like
me.

So Hunter arrived.

He walked in the house wearing a blond woman's wig with
enormous limpy curls. He was carrying his TWA bag. He had a

day-old beard. And he was wearing sunglasses. I said, "Why are you wearing the wig?"

He said, "Because I'm being followed. The FBI and the CIA are after me."

> —PATRICIA GAINES, friend of HST; former Miss
> Alabama; famous New England hostess;
> celebrated artist

I think Hunter did a lot to get Jimmy Carter nominated and elected. His early endorsement of Carter in *Rolling Stone* was very influential, not so much on the voters, but on the media, who weren't too sure whether Carter was some pious Southern hypocrite or someone to be taken seriously. And Hunter, as the Number One Scourge of Hypocrisy, was suddenly writing in a heartfelt way about their mutual understanding of the implications of Bob Dylan. It certified Carter to the skeptics.

> —RON ROSENBAUM, journalist; contributing editor
> to *Vanity Fair*; author of *Manhattan Passion:
> True Tales of Power, Wealth and Excess; Travels
> with Doctor Death and Other Unusual
> Investigations*, etc.

That early piece was very helpful to Carter. I would not underestimate it. What Hunter wrote certainly had an effect.

> —DAVID BRODER, *The Washington Post;* syndicated
> columnist; television commentator

He worked in the guest room and one day he went crazy. He couldn't find his files. He was all upset. He said, "My files! My files!" He searched all through the house crying, "My files! My files!" By this time the whole family adored Hunter, and I was running around too looking for his files, but I didn't know what to look for. And finally he found the Sunday *New York Times*. He had written in blue ballpoint pen all the way around the margins of the newspaper. All of his thoughts. Those were his files.

> —PATRICIA GAINES

Carter was grateful, and over the course of the early 1976 campaign, Thompson felt he had a special franchise with the candidate. But after Carter ducked out of an interview, Thompson besieged the hotel room where Hamilton Jordan—Carter's campaign manager—was still sleeping. When Jordan refused to respond to Thompson's screeching, the national affairs correspondent for *Rolling Stone* soaked the base of Jordan's door with lighter fluid and set it ablaze.

> —CURTIS WILKIE, *Boston Globe Magazine* (a
> slightly different version by Wilkie appeared in
> *Image*), February 7, 1988

Then Hunter decided he was going to go to Manchester [New Hampshire] to check into the Wayfarer Hotel. Everybody was there. All the news crews. Everybody. And he went up to the counter and he said he wanted to check in. And the woman behind the desk said, "Oh, Mr. Thompson. You have been transferred to the Cadillac Motel."

Well, Hunter just went berserk.

He started shouting and saying if the manager didn't find a room for him he was going to personally remove the manager's ear with a fork.

> —PATRICIA GAINES

Fritz Mondale [at the 1976 Democratic Convention] was okay with almost everybody. The vice-presidential roll call ended with 2,817 votes for the Minnesotan, 20 for Representative Dellums, 12 for Gary Benoit, 11 for Fritz Efaw, and 148 for persons known and unknown, including Hunter Thompson.

> —RICHARD REEVES, *Convention*, Harcourt, 1977

So he started working the Wayfarer dining room. It was huge! And all the waitresses came up and spoke to him. He had been there four years before and it was clear they had fond memories of him. I saw him from time to time sitting down at different booths and talking to people. I remember distinctly that Douglas Kiker [NBC correspondent] was at one of the booths. After a while Hunter came back and sat down to eat dinner with Charles [Gaines] and me, and Douglas Kiker came over and he was trembling with rage. We looked up at him and he said to Hunter, "You have a lot of nerve coming over to my table and asking me for information after what you wrote about me and Walter Cronkite!"

Hunter said, "What are you talking about?"

Kiker said, "You described me and Walter as puking our brains out in the parking lot at the Miami convention."

Hunter just looked at him and said, "Hey man, don't you have a sense of humor?"

—Patricia Gaines

At 3:00 A.M. . . . Clare Smith went to the Americana to try to find Hunter Thompson. . . . She knocked and someone said, "What?"

"Is Hunter there?"

"No."

"Bullshit!"

That brought the man himself to the door. Clare said she wanted his autograph. She was very scared because her hero was making growling noises and jumping from side to side in the doorway. She figured, though, that he didn't have glasses on and probably could not see her well. She pushed a white envelope into his hand, and he held it against the wall and scrawled: "H. S. Thompson, 7-14-76. NYC."

"Hunter, why aren't you writing *Fear and Loathing in 1976*?"

"Because of shit like this!" he shouted. "Now get out of here."

—Richard Reeves, *Convention*

He put all the choicest bits from his dinner onto another plate. And then he asked me to take it to the young woman that he yelled at at the reception desk. When I told the young woman who it was from, she just started hooting with laughter and she took it and ran back to the manager's office and I heard her say, "You know that maniac that threatened to remove your ear with a fork? He's just given me a plate of hors d'oeuvres!"

—Patricia Gaines

10

I was at home one evening and I got a telephone call from Hunter. He was just having a fit. He said there were spies preying on him. They were getting information and giving it to Garry Trudeau. And Trudeau was putting the information into the Uncle Duke stuff. He was just furious!

"You're a friend of Trudeau's," he said. "This is terrible! It's got to stop! They're spying on me in my own household! You talk to him!"

Hunter and Garry had never met.

So I called up Garry and I said, "You're driving Thompson nuts! You've got him going around the bend. He said you've got spies all over the place getting this information."

Garry just laughed and laughed and laughed. He said: "Well, you know who my spies are?"

I said, "No. Who are your spies?"

And Garry said, "I've gotten all of it from his own writing. That's where every bit of it comes from."

Garry is a completely aboveboard citizen. He wouldn't get a spy or anything like that. I called Hunter back. I reported the source of all Garry's information was himself. Hunter wouldn't believe it. He wouldn't believe it!

—NICHOLAS VON HOFFMAN

People think it's a joke—like I get paid for it or something. You know, me and Garry must be big buddies. Well, fuck that. I've never even seen the little bastard. All this stuff avoids coming to the point that matters, which is what I turn out. Funny, I almost never get questioned about writing.

—HUNTER THOMPSON, in an interview with P. J. O'Rourke, *Rolling Stone*, November 5 to December 10, 1987

I got a very nice letter from Trudeau once. Jann had told Garry that I would be very upset by what's-her-name, the Chinese girl, Honey, if she and Duke wanted to get married.

So Garry sent me a letter which was really sweet. He said, "I never meant to hurt or upset you. That had not been my intention." I respected that.

—SANDRA DAWN THOMPSON TARLO

I wonder who else in the history of this country has to be a comic strip character and try to work at the same time?

—HUNTER THOMPSON, appearing at California's College of Marin (after which irate members of the audience demanded their $4 admission back), quoted by *People*, November 5, 1979

But there was a strip where Hunter comes home and walks in Owl Farm and he says, "Goddamn it," to what's-his-name? To Zonker. "Where's Sandy?" And Zonker says, "Sandy's gone. Don't you remember? Sandy's gone. And she's not coming back."

—SANDRA DAWN THOMPSON TARLO

11

I was sitting on the floor and there was one more outburst, one more Hunter explosion, and I was really calm and I looked up at him and I said, "Hunter, I want a divorce." Just like that, very calmly. Well, things kicked into gear then! He flew into a rage. I ended up calling the sheriff for help in leaving. He was a friend of ours, so he didn't want to come out. So he sent a young deputy instead.

The deputy arrived on the porch. Hunter went to the door totally wired and turned on the charm box and said, "Oh, I'm really sorry you had to come all the way out here. This is just a little family quarrel. You know how things are when the wife drinks."

Well, I wanted to *kill* him. I hadn't had a drink in a year. Hunter went into the kitchen; and the deputy, a very sweet and a very young man, whispered to me, "Does he have any guns?"

"*Guns?*" I said. "Does he have any *guns?* I think he has twenty-two guns and every single one of them is loaded."

The deputy just crumbled.

THE FRIENDS OF HST

Ralph Steadman.
(© Carol Kovinick-Hernandez)

Jim Harrison.
(© David Brigham)

Margot Kidder, Tom
McGuane and baby Maggie
McGuane in Montana.
(*People* weekly / © Harley
Hettick, 1977)

Russell Chathem.

HST and V. S. Naipaul in Grenada after U.S. involvement. (© Matthew Naythons / *Time* magazine)

Below: George Plimpton.

Debi Sundahl, the fiery feminist pornographer. (Courtesy of Debi Sundahl)

Ed Bradley. (© Mary Grasso)

Gail Palmer-Slater. She never wanted to press charges. (Courtesy of Gail Palmer-Slater; photo by Michael N. Marx)

Judge Charles Buss presides over HST's court case when he is charged with sexual assault and drug possession.

HST and Ms. Sabonis-Chafee leaving the preliminary hearing. As HST gets older, his girlfriends get younger. Usually they leave him to go back to school. (© Frank Martin)

HST's supporters from the Mitchell Brothers' O'Farrell Theatre, the Carnegie Hall of Sex. (© Frank Martin)

(© Frank Martin / *Aspen Times* / Picture Group)

(© Frank Martin)

Jubilant HST, after charges are dropped, just before he begins shooting into the cheering crowd. (© Peter McClain / Picture Group)

**HST'S JAPANESE
TRANSLATORS
COME TO VISIT**

In front of the Woody Creek
Tavern. (© Kanzunobu
Kakishima and Takahiko Soejima)

Mr. Soejima and E. Jean Carroll.
(© Kanzunobu Kakishima and
Takahiko Soejima)

Mr. Soejima.
(© Kanzunobu
Kakishima and
Takahiko Soejima)

HST takes aim at a barrel of dynamite. (© Kanzunobu Kakishima and Takahiko Soejima)

HST hits barrel of dynamite. (© Kanzunobu Kakishima and Takahiko Soejima)

Sheriff's deputies arrive to check complaints that HST has shaken the foundations of three of his neighbors' houses. (© Kanzunobu Kakishima and Takahiko Soejima)

I began packing. Hunter grabbed a stack of papers that I had, the only writing I had done in all those years, and threw it into the fire. I was outraged and really really angry. But you know all that writing was totally pathetic. How Sandy was so little and how great Hunter was over and over again. It would be interesting to see it now, but not *really* interesting. He was screaming about how I would use it against him. Publish it. I'd never thought about it. He also told all our drug dealer friends that I'd turn them in.

No. No. All I wanted was a little peace. So it was a fiery end. It had had a fiery beginning. First time it was love. Last time it was fear.

—SANDRA DAWN THOMPSON TARLO

Does it *look* like [drugs have] fucked me up? I'm sitting here on a beautiful beach in Mexico; I've written three books. I've got a fine one-hundred-acre fortress in Colorado. On that evidence, I'd have to *advise* the use of drugs.

—HUNTER THOMPSON, *Playboy*, "Playboy Interview" conducted by Craig Vetter, November 1974

C H A P T E R
SIXTEEN

Like the soldier for whom the final moments are
precious, he awaits the enemy attack and
masturbates.

—KOBO ABE

1

I am sick and tired of writing about the Doctor.
I am sick and tired of writing about the Doctor.
I am sick and tired of writing about the Doctor.
I am sick and tired of writing about the Beast.
I am sick and tired of writing about the Monster.
I am sick and tired of writing about the Doctor.
I am sick and tired of writing about the Doctor.
I am sick and tired of writing about the Worm.
I am sick and tired of writing about the Doctor.
I am sick and tired of writing about the Fiend.
I am sick and tired of writing about the Doctor.
I am sick and tired of writing about the Swine.
I am sick and tired of writing about the Doctor.
I am sick and tired of writing about the Doctor.

2

Not satisfied with making me the target of the boldest scenes, yesterday the Hyena declared that I had to wear crotchless apparel

while composing this idiotic biography. The Reader will not be surprised, therefore, to find my style somewhat contracted. Frankly, I dread impaling myself on the Cesspool furniture. Indeed, I refuse to sit for more than five minutes writing——and I see my time is up.

3

The Pest comes and lifts the lid of the Cesspool at odd times to check my compliance. If I am found in arrears, I am to receive no dinner. I had planned to dazzle the Reader with the arrival scene of Takahiko Soejima, the Doctor's Japanese translator, and Kakishima Kazunobu, Mr. Soejima's editor, employing such phrases as "gaily but not foppishly dressed in a bottle-green linen suit" in reference to Mr. Soejima, and "hair like a cape buffalo" anent Mr. Kazunobu. But now——excuse me, I have to change position.

4

Numbed, panic-stricken, shaken about, blathering in their melodic language, and dazed to such a degree by the pig-squealer, the dog-barker, the gunshots, and the beating and flagellating tape, the Orientals barely summoned the strength to raise their cameras to their faces.

They then waited three hours for the Doctor (who was hiding in the Hot Tub). I would elaborate, but I'm being pressed in a manner that cannot be denied.

5

Dragged from the water by Deborah and shoved drunken, red as a lobster, and still wet into the leather chair on the porch, the Doctor greeted his guests. I am sorry.

6

Quivering like delicate cherry blossoms

7

The Orientals approached the Doctor bowing and smiling like——
well, Mr. Soejima's face wore the identical expression as the
fellating Republican. "Allow me to say, Dr. Thompson, we are
greatly thankful for your kindness in speaking to us," said Mr.
Soejima, bowing.

The Doctor was wearing sunglasses and his Australian snap
hat. He was an extraordinary color. Between an artificially ripened
tomato and a brick. His nostrils were enlarged to the size of small
McIntosh apples and he was covered with sweat like a yak. In one
hand was his cigarette, and in the other a Molson. His upper lip
quivered like the lid on a pot.

"Turn off that goddamed dog-barker!" he cried in misery.

8

"I venture to hope your injury will soon be better, Dr. Thompson," said Mr. Soejima, bowing again. (Deborah had told the Japanese the Doctor had fallen off the tractor and "crushed his
back," and this was the reason he had to spend so much time in
the Hot Tub.) What a long explanation! And I thought my lips
were sealed.

The Doctor nodded and Mr. Soejima presented him with a gift.

"Jesus! I hope the bastards don't give me a goddamed fan," the
Doctor had said earlier. He opened the box. It was a fan. At this
point Molly appeared on the porch——Oh Gads! You don't know
who Molly is, do you, Reader? I confess she was a looker. Come
now! Molly would have placed second in the Miss Indiana Pageant! If that doesn't tell you everything, nothing will. She had long
black hair and a big bottom.

She sat down next to the Doctor.

Deborah whispered that Molly was the wife of one of the Doctor's "dearest friends and dealers." My impenetrable nature, of which I have given such noble proofs throughout this biography, blinded me. And so what was my amazement to observe Molly, a married woman, sneak her arm around my handsome Fiancé and rub his

9

Turn the page! Turn the page! Reader! go to the next biographical section! Leave Laetitia in the depths of her sewer, without recourses, without honor, without hope, exposed to every peril and wearing a crotch-free trick teddy with matching finger-tip gloves with black velvet wrist bows, and return to that chronological crowd of horrors that is the Doctor's life.

I just pray you have the balls to sit through it.

CHAPTER
SEVENTEEN

It's a hell of a life.
—ERNEST HEMINGWAY

1

You silly little fart. Don't lay your karmic nightmares on me, and don't bother me with any more postcards about your vomiting problems. . . .

And what lame instinct suddenly prompts you to start commenting on my material? You've done pretty well by skimming it for the past five years, so keep your pompous whining to yourself and don't complain.

If you *must* vomit, go down to Mory's and use that special low-rent stall they keep for lightweight Yalies who steal other people's work for a living. . . .

—HUNTER THOMPSON, in a letter to Garry Trudeau after Trudeau had lamented that Thompson had sold out to Hollywood; quoted by Craig Vetter in *Playboy*, June 1980

Felton: [*The Great Shark Hunt*] is probably the worst-edited and most self-indulgent book since the *Bible*. There doesn't seem to be any order. One-fourth of the book is either stuff that's been in previous books of yours or old, hack, pregonzo stuff that reads rather flat and uninspired.

Thompson: That's the way I wanted it.

Felton: For what reason?

Thompson: I just thought it should be in a permanent record. I thought it would be pretty fun to see the development from the Air Force to the Ali piece. It seems like I've been writing the same thing, really, since I was eighteen years old. Looking back on it, I was surprised at the consistency of even the style, in terms of the attitude.

. . . I'll stand by this. It's messy, it's fucked up; it's not a bad book.

—HUNTER THOMPSON and DAVID FELTON in "Hunter Thompson Has Cashed His Check," *Rolling Stone College Papers,* Spring 1980

We hadn't started the movie yet. We got off the plane around midnight and Hunter said, "We gotta find some chicks."

I said, "Hunter, it's twelve-thirty."

He said, "You know where the chicks are in L.A., Kaye. We'll go to a bar and we'll find some women."

So we went to Joe Allen's. And there were five single guys standing around. We walked in and Hunter said, "Jesus Christ! You've taken me to a fag bar. We have to find women!"

I said, "Let's go back to the hotel."

Hunter said, "Good. We'll call some hookers, how about that?

I said, "OK."

He said, "We'll put it on the Universal tab."

I said, "We can't do that, Hunter. We can't charge it to anybody."

He said, "We'll get hookers anyway. It will be interesting."

So we went back to the Hermitage, up to the suite, and I phoned a Beverly Hills out-call service to send a couple of women over.

Soon two women knocked on the door. They were your basic kind of trampy, slattern Midwestern hookers. They were both white, in short skirts and regular hooker clothes. One was blond and one was a brunette. There was nothing elegant about these women. They looked like they could have been working a strip

bar in Akron, Ohio. Hunter looked at them both and said, "Jesus
Christ! Lovely!"

> —JOHN KAYE, friend of HST; screenwriter; author
> of *Where the Buffalo Roam,* the film "based on
> the twisted legend of Hunter S. Thompson"

I got a call from Lynn Nesbit, my agent. She said there's this person, Thom Mount, who wants to buy the magazine article about
the Brown Buffalo ["The Banshee Screams for Buffalo Meat," a
eulogy for Oscar Acosta] for $100,000 and make a movie. I
thought, "Well shit, that's wonderful."

They wanted to make a movie about whatever they perceived
to be the relationship between these two characters. It was a weird
idea. Actually it was *so* weird that it never occurred to me that it
would be made.

. . . I don't know why people are so concerned about my image.
I'm an egomaniac. *I* should be the one concerned about my image!
Why are you and Garry Trudeau so worried about this film hurt-
ing me? *I'm* not.

> —HUNTER THOMPSON, "Hunter Thompson Has
> Cashed His Check," *Rolling Stone College
> Papers,* Spring 1980

Then he said to the girls, "Look, we have some cocaine here. We
might as well start off with that." Well, the girls got into that
whole aspect. Then finally one girl said, "Well, we have to talk
about money here."

Hunter said, "What do you want?"

The girl said, "We get a hundred dollars apiece."

He said, "That's very reasonable. But we want to party. We
don't want to spend an hour with you. We want to have like a
party here."

The girl said, "It could cost four hundred or five hundred dollars."

Hunter said, "Four or five hundred dollars is no problem at all.
We want to go up top, don't you?"

The girl said, "Up top?"

> —JOHN KAYE

I remember them calling when I was still at Owl Farm and saying, "We're going to do this great movie on the sixties, and what the sixties meant, and it's going to be fantastic." And I said, "Bullshit. It's not going to be about the sixties, it's going to be about crazy Hunter Thompson. It's not going to be a serious film."

—SANDRA DAWN THOMPSON TARLO

He said, "Oh yeah, there's a Jacuzzi up on the roof. We'll take some beers and some cocaine and we'll go up."

The girl said, "That sounds great, we have to have some money first."

Hunter said, "Of course. There's no problem with that. I have no money *on* me, but ultimately, there's no problem. I'll just call downstairs and I'll have them open the vault. I have unlimited money on my Gold Card. I'll just call them up."

He called and he said, "This is Dr. Thompson in Room 605. I happen to need four or five hundred dollars." There was a silence. Then he said, *"What are you talking about?* What the fuck do you mean I can't get any money? What do you mean the safe is locked? Open the safe! I have some women and I'm negotiating the sale right now!"

—JOHN KAYE

The film company flew us out to the Beverly Hills Hotel. We had a suite. Everyone was doing cocaine and carrying on and I went to bed. It was a very expensive suite. It had a bedspread that matched the lampshade, that matched the wall tapestries, and it was very, very fancy.

Hunter came in about three o'clock in the morning and decided he wanted ice cream. I was trying to sleep. So he ordered chocolate and probably vanilla, and then he wanted me to wake up and play. I wanted to sleep. And he got angry. I wasn't supposed to sleep.

And so there was a scene. And he took the chocolate ice cream and he threw it at me. And I ducked, and it hit the lamp, and it broke the lamp, broke the shade, and the ice cream splattered all over the wall tapestry. They told me later that it cost the film company several thousand dollars for just that little number.

—SANDRA DAWN THOMPSON TARLO

I said, "Hunter, relax!"

He was kicking over furniture. The girls were stunned. He was screaming. He yelled into the phone: "This is Dr. Thompson! I'll make a warehouse out of this fucking room!"

He hung up the phone and then he said, "This is a terrible turn of events. I'll have to wait till morning to get the money. That shouldn't make a difference. You've seen what I've done here. I've gone out of my way to try to get the money. I'm good for it."

The girl said, "Listen, we can't do this without money."

He said, "What do you mean? That's absurd! This is a terrible thing to happen!"

The girl got up and said, "Look, we've been here an hour. We're going to need some money."

Hunter said, "What? We haven't done anything! What the fuck do you want? *A turn-down fee?*"

—JOHN KAYE

Where the Buffalo Roam is a raunchy comedy . . . the most surprising thing . . . is how much of Thompson's tone gets into the picture. . . . It is made, for me, by the performances of Bill Murray as Hunter Thompson and Peter Boyle as Thompson's sometime lawyer and fellow-zany, Lazlo.

—ROGER ANGELL, *The New Yorker*, May 12, 1980

Hunter's a moving target on sprockets. Billy [Bill Murray] really got Hunter down. You know, that kind of off-centerness. It was fun to do the movie. But when Hunter came to the set, at that point I would leave because I knew things would be changed in the script and I didn't want to be part of it. And he did, he did make changes. And he and Murray fucked with stuff. And that was OK. And they did some funny stuff together. But I felt my role had become diminished. Which is the way it goes. They're doing the Hunter Thompson story and if Hunter wants to go out and write something, great. And at that point I just split. When he came on the set there was a kind of general rumble of excitement.

It was a little embarrassing for him. He didn't know quite what the role was he was supposed to play. I think he wanted to withhold any kind of affirmation about it.

—JOHN KAYE

The scream. That was my horror. The scream, that I couldn't get the scream right. I was really afraid that I wouldn't be able to scream like him.... It's anger and surprise and shock and pain, like a baby's scream—just a noise, a roar ...

—BILL MURRAY, "Bill Murray's Savage Journey to the Heart of Hunter Thompson," *Rolling Stone College Papers,* Spring 1980

I felt that Hunter wanted to protect himself. But I had seen that he also wanted the movie to get made. He did a very astute job. He's probably the best person I've ever seen do something like this—passively support something while distancing himself at the same time. And I thought that was a very diplomatic position to take. He didn't want to hurt the movie. At the same time, he didn't want to endorse it.

—JOHN KAYE

The film is, at best, gonzo dreck.

—MERRILL SHINDLER, *Los Angeles Magazine,* June 1980

I gave Hunter Thompson the only *real* money he ever had.

—ART LINSON, director of *Where the Buffalo Roam,* quoted by Craig Vetter in "Destination Hollyweird," *Playboy,* June 1980

——What did you do with all that money, Hunter?

——I don't know. Bought drugs.

—HUNTER THOMPSON interview

2

Let me tell you something. Tom McGuane could consume a lot of drugs but Hunter Thompson could consume more drugs than anyone. He came over to the house in Key West and had a contest with Tom as to who could take the most drugs without dropping dead. I was very upset. I was screaming, "Hunter! Hunter! You're going to kill my husband!"

They lined up piles of white powder, brown powder, pills of various colors, I guess smack, I don't know. I think there was a little acid. I have no idea what it was. I just remember that each of them had a line in front of them, on either side of the dining room table under the big ceiling fan, the Tennessee Williams fan. And they started at one end, and they had Wild Turkey on the table, 'cause Tom had to have a drink. And they went through to the end to see who could stay up. And, of course, they both did. Neither of them dropped. It was the strangest kind of cock-length contest I'd ever seen. It was like, "Who can not die?"

—MARGOT KIDDER, friend of HST; actress and
    writer

I was a senior editor at *Playboy*. We wanted to excerpt Hunter's *Curse of Lono* manuscript in the magazine. We paid him what seemed at the time like a lot of money for it. I was a tremendous admirer of his work. He was the political writer of our generation. I came to the manuscript with a great deal of enthusiasm.

The first thing that struck me was that the initial story, a piece for *Running* magazine and the genesis of the book, was terrific. On one level it was about the Honolulu Marathon, but it was really about the whole running and fitness culture. It was brilliant. It all held together. It was Hunter in his top form.

But as I got into the book, I found the best story had already been published. The rest of the book was mostly a series of false starts and half-baked ideas. I was surprised by the degree of degeneration in Hunter's work. I was disappointed as much as surprised.

He still had interesting thoughts, but in *Lono* he couldn't sustain them and control them in the wonderful ways that he once did—and make it look effortless. That's one of the things that made him great. He made it look easy. So I pulled an excerpt. A good, substantial hunk, woven together from here and there. I tried to re-create the best of the book in miniature.

So Hunter flew in, I think from Key West. I arranged a room for him at the Drake. At *Playboy*'s expense. Everybody knows what that can mean. But we were ready to do whatever it took to crank this thing out and make sure it was done right. Now I *sort of* knew what it meant to work with Hunter—but you don't really know until you've been through it. I'd heard the stories—but I didn't know. Nobody knows except veterans. All those people who have been stuck on the pin and had their wings pulled off.

—ROB FLEDER, formerly an editor at *Esquire* and *Playboy;* now feature editor at *Sports Illustrated*

Down in Key West Hunter had a police scanner. He could listen to what the police were talking about. He could plug it in anywhere. We took him fishing one day. It was a terrible day. He had his scuba gear and he shot a ray, which we thought was in bad taste.

—JIM HARRISON, friend of HST; author of *Legends of the Fall, The Woman Lit by Fireflies, Sundog, Warlock,* etc., considered by the lit set as one of America's greatest living novelists

I was fucking every girl I could get my hands on while pretending to fish. Harrison was there, Caputo was around. We had a pool which only naked girls were allowed in. Hunter was very funny. We would make our little runs to go get our dope and stuff. I don't know if you know this, but Hunter is very funny about food. He was always looking at his food and wondering what the hell it was. He's in great shape, you know. To my knowledge he didn't choose any of the girls in the pool. In fact, I thought it rather odd. He didn't seem too interested in that. For some odd reason he was busy learning to run a boat.

I remember the year he ran the boat amuck in the harbor.

> —RUSSELL CHATHAM, friend of HST; described by
> HST as "the legendary Montana artist" and
> "profoundly eccentric"; president and editor-in-
> chief of Clark City Press.

He flew in from Key West with a big carry-on bag and a club that
he got in Hawaii while he was there doing *Lono,* which he carried
around.

That first night, his friend Bob Franks [name changed at insistence of publisher's lawyer] arrived. Franks was a semi-big-time political operator and he showed up at the Drake—an elegant old
hotel—wearing bathing trunks and a T-shirt, with a bimbo on his
arm. Hunter got on the phone and started ordering stuff—a dozen
Heinekens, a bottle of scotch, a bunch of sandwiches. Cocaine was
being consumed. He was on the telephone quite a bit that night
with Laila. [Laila Nabulsi, former talent coordinator for *Saturday
Night Live,* HST's girlfriend during the early 1980s, one of the
most beautiful women in New York City, currently flogging *Fear
and Loathing in Las Vegas* as a play, refused to speak *on* the
record.———Ed.]

That situation seemed tense. I think the personal side of his life
was upset. The conversations on the phone were quiet. They
weren't animated. They weren't delightful conversations. I don't
know if it was fighting, but it seemed kind of grim.

Other than that he was in a good mood. I gave him a copy of
the excerpt. I said, "You read it, and we'll talk about it."

> —ROB FLEDER

Hunter tried to throw a girl out of his boat. He turned the boat
so suddenly that he threw he and the girl out of the boat. The boat
continued up on this person's lawn. OK. Now. About ten days
later something similar happened to [Jimmy] Buffett. It went up
on the same yard. This is a true story. Oddly enough Hunter is extremely well-coordinated. He's very good at any kind of sport.
He's also very strong.

> —JIM HARRISON

We told him if he ever fell out of his boat, which we were certain he would, to be very careful because the boat would come back around and get him. We said he would have to dive to get out of the way of the propeller. He thought we were making it up. I think he couldn't stand it. He had to see for himself.

He told us, "I was getting out of the boat. My foot slipped, and I fell. My hand hit the throttle and the boat took off!"

He sent the goddamn boat away from the dock at top fucking speed and it circled the fucking harbor and came back at him and he had to make a run for it. It came back around, careened off the front of about three dozen boats and ripped the fucking fronts off half of them, and fired up across the dock and across the lawn and into the country club.

—RUSSELL CHATHAM

The next day we began work.

He would lie on one bed, and then I would lie on the other bed. It went on for hours and hours, on and on. And at some point that evening Franks [the political operator] and Hunter had a dispute. I think the whole thing was over the girl, but I can't remember exactly what happened. Franks was about six feet tall, maybe a hundred eighty-five pounds. Hunter wanted to kick him out of his room. And he *did* kick Franks out. There was some stuff thrown, some low-level violence. And then Hunter called hotel security.

Security came up to the room and pounded on the door and Hunter said, "Get this guy out of here." So Franks and the girl were led away. As he went out the door, Franks had this satanic little smile on his face and he said, *"I'll be there when you check out."*

Now, I'm sitting in my chair watching all this occur: Hunter coming to blows with his old friend, then having the guy hauled away. We went back to the manuscript. Hunter continued to go through the galleys of the book and say, "What about this story here? Why don't we use some of that?" And I would say, "OK, we could work that in." Then he would change the subject and say, "What about this? What about this?" And I would write *that* down.

He was just sort of jumping around. And by this time I was starting to get the point. I think what he mainly wanted to do was wear me down. It seemed like fun for a while, then it got a little bit—it got more contentious. A guy named Craig Vetter, who was an old pal of Hunter's and a good friend of mine, was there the whole time, trying to act as a sort of mediator in this whole process. But I don't think Solomon himself could have done that job in that situation.

We had at least two long night sessions. Hunter continued to say, "What about this?", pointing out new sections. I would say, "I like that piece of writing, but it doesn't have anything to do with *this* piece of writing."

Because I'll tell you what: I'd gotten the best stuff out of there already, and there were some little things, some little flights of writing that were nice in the book, but they didn't have anything to do with the story we were trying to tell in the excerpt.

It became increasingly contentious. He realized at some point that I wasn't going to roll over. It got tenser and tenser. The phone rang constantly. People would drop by to visit. Hunter would pace back and forth like a caged animal, and you know, he's a very imposing physical presence. He drank. There were drugs. He would be on the phone. I ached. My body. My back hurt. So I would lie on the floor and we would talk or I would bend myself backwards over a chair, anything to stretch my back out.

Now, Hunter is brilliant. It was *his* work, his book, and if he was going to have a good idea about how to excerpt it, then I was perfectly happy to go along with it. So we went into the third day. The drugs were the only sustaining energy in the room. The phone rang. Hunter answered. Then he hung up and said: "Do you know who that was?"

I said, "No."

He said, "It was the front desk. The credit office. They were saying that *Playboy* cut me off, that this man Rob Fleder called and said *Playboy* was no longer responsible for Mr. Thompson's bills."

I said, "That's not true!"

It was a touchy moment.

I hadn't slept in a long time. I thought he was going to pull the Hawaiian cudgel out of his bag and bash me over the head.

—Rob Fleder

Then Hunter, Tom and I ended up in some large van driving around in Key West in the middle of the night with Jimmy Buffett. I was in the back sobbing on two mattresses, crying, "They're gonna kill Tom! They're gonna kill Tom." And Tom would go, "Shut up." [Laughs.]

—MARGOT KIDDER

Our typical day in Key West? We were American Sportsmen. We tried to get out on the water by nine o'clock. Hunter didn't fish. We would meet at the bar at five o'clock. One day Hunter and I bought a whole cardboard box full of mushrooms. We ate handfuls of them like truffle ragout. We would watch shit on TV. But you know, that took a back seat once the girls got out of the pool. Then we would eat. Then we might go out to a bar, or we might stay in the house, depending on the number of girls there—we might fuck the girls. We did. Repeatedly. . . . To tell you the honest truth, there may have been women around him, but that was not an issue with Hunter at that time. In fact, that's why it surprised me when he was in San Francisco later on and got such a kick out of hanging out with the Mitchell brothers [at the O'Farrell Theater, "the Carnegie Hall of Sex"]. I saw quite a bit of Hunter there because, of course, that was right up my alley.

—RUSSELL CHATHAM

Hunter said, "You gotta help me!" He had a fax machine Jann Wenner had given him so he could send his story in on time. But he hadn't written anything. So he wanted Tom and I to get down on the floor and pull this plug in and out while he called Jann and pretended to feed the story through, right?

So Tom and I got on the floor and Hunter called Jann and said, "Jann! It's coming through!" And Jann said, "There's nothing coming through—it's gobbledygook." And Hunter said, "I'm feeding it through! I'm feeding it through!"

He was so munglingly ineffectual as a human that I adored him. I just thought anyone who was this bumbling was wonderful. He was very dictatorial in his insistence on us getting down on our hands and knees and pulling the plug in and out of the floor. I'd never seen such total anarchy within the publishing community!

—MARGOT KIDDER

I left Hunter and went down to the credit office.

It took a while, but I finally figured out what had happened. I remembered Franks had said, "I'll be there when you check out." He had watched enough of the whole scene up in the room to know that Hunter and I were going to do battle. He knew there was a real good chance that he could cause the whole thing to explode violently. This guy was a political person. He saw the seam and he went right for it.

By the third day of working on the manuscript, it clearly was not going anywhere. Hunter was still saying, "What about this? What about this?" He just sort of kept looking through the galleys, saying, "What about this?" It was pointless. We would talk for two hours and end up adding a sentence to a ten-thousand- or fifteen-thousand-word manuscript. By the end of three days I was ready to kill him. And he just about *had* killed me.

You do just wear down. You get tired. And you get sick of dealing with him. It's great to goof around and watch the evening news with him and talk about what's going on in the world and get his unique, twisted take on things. That's great, but when you're trying to get a job done, trying to accomplish something, it's tremendously frustrating.

In the end, the excerpt ran in *Playboy* almost exactly as I had pulled it. And we somehow went on working together after that. We talked and corresponded. Then more than a year later, I flew to Colorado to try to get him to finally write "The Night Manager," a story about the pornography industry and the O'Farrell Theater.

—ROB FLEDER

William Blake said, "Energy is genius." Of course, Blake was nuts too.

—JIM HARRISON

3

Oh! No!

—ROXANNE PULITZER to her lawyer when told that
Hunter Thompson had arrived to cover the
Pulitzer trial

4

The O'Farrell Theater is a huge place. Thick carpeting. Very subdued. They filmed *Behind the Green Door II* there. Throughout
the theater are posters of all the Mitchell brothers' movies. It's
very comfortable. Very clean. You could literally spend hours
there. The dancers here in San Francisco are more avant-garde. In
the Copenhagen Room the couches are cream-colored. The live
sex acts are female to female.

Lesbian sex.

By law it's not real sex. That's one way lesbian invisibility
worked well for the dancers at the O'Farrell, because they could
fuck right there and get all kinds of money. You can ask them to
do anything. Masturbate, have oral sex with each other. Finger-
fuck, or fuck each other with a dildo. Talk dirty. Sometimes you
pretend you're sucking a cock.

I worked in all the rooms. I was pretty good. I look good. I
have a great body. Good ass. Hunter usually came at night and sat
on the pool table in Jim and Artie Mitchell's office in one of his
short-sleeved golfing shirts and his sunglasses. He was drunk a lot.
He gibbered to me. A couple of the girls were attracted to him.
But half of them didn't pay him the time of day. Well, dancers on
the whole are attracted to men who dress more stylishly.

—DEBI SUNDAHL, publisher of *On Our Backs*
magazine, president of Blush Entertainment and
Fatale Videos

Hunter came out to the College of Marin in 1984. Our mother
happened to be here visiting me at the time and we went. And you
can imagine! For an hour and a half nothing happened. The stage
was empty. The house lights were up. It was a gymnasium filled

with raging, screaming students. It was like a pep rally. People were throwing things, a very raucous group. We were in the front row. Then someone came out and said, "Hunter's here, we'll be starting in fifteen minutes, if you can hold on." I could already sense that something very strange was happening in the dressing room. I had heard before that these Hunter lectures had often been very late starting. And my mother was absolutely horrified at being—at the crowd.

Well, Hunter came out and gave his little speech stoned to the gills drunk! Visibly drunk! And that's really drunk! He brought his bottle of whiskey and he got up there and fielded questions. The whole thing was terribly disorganized.

My mother and I were both so nervous we could hardly even look at or talk to each other at that point. I was nervous for her, wondering what she was thinking—they were throwing shit up on the stage. And it got worse.

Hunter made his famous statement in favor of nuclear power. And everybody booed and hissed.

Half the things he said I couldn't understand. My mother and I were turning to each other saying, "What? What was that?" She has a terrible time understanding Hunter and I don't understand him very well, either. He mumbles. We were both so nervous we really wished, I'm sure, we both wished that we'd done something else that night, because it was ugly. And they were raucous. I thought the College of Marin might have, you know, civilized people, but they were like the University of Tennessee or something.

I'm not sure who the audience was mad at or why they were making so much noise, but I have a feeling that they felt a little ripped off. Because the format was so disorganized and stupid, and people were screaming from the audience, and Hunter was screaming back—I don't remember specific comments, but it was ugly.

The crux of this whole story is that when the thing was over, and everyone was dissatisfied, and noisy and screaming and throwing things—they had asked him questions like, "What's your favorite drug?" That kind of thing, you can imagine. "I've taken 'em all and love em all"—there was a door off to the side of the auditorium and we went to head Hunter off as he left the stage.

And here he came.

He looked at me. His eyes popped out of his head. Then he looked and saw Mummy, standing right next to me. At that point he went, "Ho! Jesus Christ!" And just turned, waved his arms and ran with his head down. Just ran past her into the dressing room. And that was the end of that. He looked at her and said, "Ho! Jesus Christ!"

—Jim Thompson

The O'Farrell? There was more pussy than you could shake a stick at. Oh! Three hundred girls! Three hundred beautiful girls that would do anything. I went down there dozens of times. Hunter was deeply amused by the scene and the ambiance, as anyone would be.

—Russell Chatham

I saw Hunter at Stanford [at a college speaking engagement]. I was backstage with him and he was in such a state. Agitated. Absolutely paranoid. That was the day that I understood that this just wasn't a part of the persona. That was serious pain. I asked him about it. "Why do you do that at these colleges? You just drive people nuts."

He said, "'Cause I'm terrified."

—David Burgin, longtime friend of HST; currently editor-in-chief of Alameda Newspaper Group

Most of the men who came to the O'Farrell were in awe of the dancers and of their beauty. Of the way they moved their bodies. Of their comfort with their sexuality. Hunter used to flirt with them. It was more of a bravado type of flirt. He would be talking and engaging their attention, and then he would throw his arm around them. To me, that's flirting. I never saw him corner anyone or kiss them.

—Debi Sundahl

One of my mother's statements was, "Hunter will never hurt me again."

—Jim Thompson

Anyway I was just bringing out my magazine, *On Our Backs*. It's women's erotica. The fact that I was a feminist ran contrary to the view of feminists being antiporn. Plus, gay men have tons of erotic magazines. Lesbians had nothing. Zero. So I was the first. I made the first erotic magazine for lesbians. So I wanted to show it to Hunter. I thought he would be interested.

So I introduced myself to him very professionally. I mean this man was a writer and well known. He was a progressive person, so I felt like we had something in common. So I said, "I publish this erotic magazine for lesbian women, *On Our Backs*. It's one of a kind. I thought you would be interested in taking a look at it." I don't know what he said. It was incoherent. It was gobbledygook.

I think later I performed with my partner, Ramona, a fistfucking act on the pool table. I believe Hunter was there. It may have been for Artie's birthday. I remember there was a big cake with boobs. I may have a picture of it. I don't have any pictures with Hunter. I'm not an opportunist, you know.

—DEBI SUNDAHL

I guess I should have learned my lesson. But the prospect of publishing what had the potential to be a great piece by Hunter Thompson was sufficiently tantalizing—to *Playboy* and to me personally—to justify the effort, and the risk.

"The Night Manager" started out as a nicely focused magazine story about what we were calling "feminist pornography"—though we didn't know exactly what we meant by that at the time. Well, before long, Hunter was pretty deeply into the story. At some point he basically moved out to San Francisco and went to work at the O'Farrell. I guess he spent the better part of a year reporting this story, or living it. I talked to him fairly regularly, and he wrote some letters that made me think he was on his way to producing a great piece of writing. He had tremendous material, and with the onset of Reaganism and the conservative backlash and the first hint of AIDS, it had become more and more of a political story. It was perfect turf for Hunter to be working.

—ROB FLEDER

I had never seen him demonstrate such a completely hysterical interest in women. The first time I saw him in San Francisco he said, "Listen, there's this girl dying to meet you." We were up in Jim and Artie's office and he brought a naked girl in because he knew I would be dumbfounded. She just stood there matter-of-factly telling me how much she liked my work.

Hunter was off to one side. I kept looking at him. And he had the funniest look on his face that I had ever seen in my entire life. I don't remember her name. She was also a big fan of Harrison's. She was really a lovely girl, but she was naked, you see. You couldn't beat it with a stick as far as I was concerned.

—RUSSELL CHATHAM

One night I was walking home, I'd been out with some number that I'd picked up and it was a nightmare, so at three o'clock in the morning I found myself in front of the O'Farrell and there was Hunter working the counter. Not only that, but then he moved to the Ultra Room. And he worked there. He was the ticket-taker at the Ultra Room. He was working on a book called *The Night Manager*. That was when he was having that affair and he was involved with the Mitchell brothers. You know one Mitchell brother killed the other Mitchell brother. They were my customers for years.

—"DANNY JOHNSON," famous dealer to the stars and political activist (does not wish his true name revealed)

Somewhere along the line Hunter had made a book deal based on ["The Night Manager"]. So now he had a year's worth of material, and he owed *Playboy* a magazine piece and someone else a book. I figured that if I had any hope of getting an article out of him, I had to get up there and see if I could help get the thing rolling.

To make a long and painful story short, it didn't work.

It was summertime, and I flew to Aspen and took a room at Snowmass, one of the ski resorts. I spent four or five days there, almost none of it at the hotel. Mostly it was long, late-night sessions up at Owl Farm, talking about "The Night Manager," trying to figure out what the story was and get Hunter moving on it. There was none of the bullshit and posturing that we'd gone through in Chicago, no macho dance of death.

There were other distractions and diversions, of course. This was Hunter's home, after all, and there were firearms—he was trying to blow away some wild cats that were attacking the birds he kept in front of his house—and ringing phones and odd people dropping by at weird hours.

This time around, he wasn't hostile or fundamentally suspicious, as he had been the first time we worked. In fact, he was downright gracious, friendly, in great spirits. This time we were both pulling in the same direction, but it was still a torturous process. It was like suffering someone else's writer's block. Like feeling someone else's pain.

Maria [Maria Kahn, Thompson's very young, sweet-tempered girlfriend after Laila Nabulsi] was there, writing down whatever coherent thoughts came out of our conversations about the story. But I'm afraid there weren't many—not enough, anyway. We actually did get a bunch of stuff down on paper, but it was all false starts and blind alleys. That's the strange part, because it struck me at the time that Hunter still had an absolutely original way of looking at things. He was still a genius. And I felt somehow complicit in his failure to pull off that story. To this day, the fact that "The Night Manager" never got written is as great a disappointment as I've had as a magazine editor.

—ROB FLEDER

That was the year Hunter discovered sex.

—JIM HARRISON

Hunter Thompson Pays Some Dues

Hunter S. Thompson, the founder of gonzo journalism, was fined $800 yesterday after pleading no contest to a drunken-driving charge in San Francisco.

Municipal Court Judge Lenard Louie also ordered Thompson to pay damages and medical bills for three people who suffered minor injuries when he hit a car while driving drunk. . . .

Thompson's speech was described as repetitive, wandering and slurred by the CHP, which said he failed several coordination tests at the scene.

—*San Francisco Chronicle*, July 13, 1985

5

I met Hunter during the Democratic Convention in San Francisco. The very first night I met him, actually, I was with, who was it? It was Pat Caddell and Margot Kidder, who was covering it for *Vanity Fair*, and I think Frank Mankiewicz, and we got a call that Hunter was over at a house on Pacific Avenue and he had taken his clothes off. And he was having an argument with Linda Ellerbee. He was calling her "a dyke news hen."

Ellerbee was having a fit. She was just furious with Hunter. Oh, he was just impossible. He was so drunk. We got him into the car and we were driving him back to the hotel, and, of course, he was doing coke right out in front of everybody, you know, and there were cops everywhere and Mankiewicz was trying to get him to stop, and he finally said, "You've got to drop me off, because I'm not having anything to do with this."

—Danny Johnson

Hunter ended up with my friend Danny, and they became best friends. Danny was Hunter's confidant. Danny and Hunter would go out. Danny took care of Hunter during the Convention, and then for months afterward.

—Margot Kidder

Well, let's see. To tell you the truth it would be hard for me to say that Hunter did more than two grams a day. But I can't tell you the amount of waste that boy was capable of!

He'd put it on the dresser in his room, in his suite, and throw his notes on top of it, and it would go everywhere. And when he wanted to do acid he'd take two or three hits at a time, at least. Sometimes he'd take four or five in one night. He had no patience. Maybe it was thirty to forty minutes to work. He was Mr. Clockwatcher. And if it didn't kick in within thirty-two seconds, he'd already have taken another one, you know. "This stuff's no good, where'd you get this?"

His favorite thing at that time was Xanax. To calm down and get some sleep. And I must admit, by the way, whenever he was smoking dope, he always thought much more clearly. Coke would drive him crazy—after three weeks of spending time with him, every single day, and constantly doing the coke, after about the eighth day I turned to a friend of mine, who worked for Senator Cranston, and I said, "I don't know about you, but I can't take much more of this."

—DANNY JOHNSON

Hunter had fallen in love with a porno queen. Totally in love. Hunter spent all of the '84 Democratic Convention at these porno shows or underneath the pool table with Ronald Reagan, Jr., snorting coke. And Ronald Reagan, Jr., was so smitten with Hunter that he followed him around like a puppy dog. And Hunter would say, "Sit here, sit here." And they'd get under the pool table and Hunter'd do more coke. It was good for Ronald Reagan, Jr. Hunter then stayed on in San Francisco for months after the convention and got a job writing a column for one of the San Francisco papers.

And he was in love with the porno queen.

I remember sitting one night with Hunter, and he was in tears. He was telling me how she had broken his heart. He was just devastated by this woman.

—MARGOT KIDDER

[All efforts to locate "the porno queen" have failed—Ed.]

Hunter stayed at the San Franciscan Hotel on Market Street. I picked him up and drove him to the Convention every morning and then I spent the day with him. We were supposed to be there at eight o'clock to get his press credentials for the day. Of course, we never had that covered. Hunter would be in the shower forever, then we would go get something to eat, and then we—then drugs—and, you know, then we'd go off to the Convention. He made me a super-delegate so I could get in all the time.

He was close to [Pat] Caddell, he was close to Warren [Beatty]. They were very quiet when they talked politics. They would talk very quietly. He was friends with all the presidential families and all the presidential kids—the Ford kids, the Carter kids, the Reagans and the Kennedys. It was amazing. He was friends on both sides. I mean, he knew everybody. He had that whole collection of kids in the palm of his hand. I remember thinking at the time: "God, these kids are easily manipulated."

Ron Reagan was just like a child. He was so impressed with Hunter. He would kind of scamper after Hunter. He was there covering it for *Playboy*, I think it was. Ronnie was only around a couple of times. Ronnie was a very dull boy. Hunter didn't spend very much time with him and made fun of the fact that Ronnie was there and here his father was President.

And these people would compulsively talk to him, which I could never understand. Yes, he is the greatest American political journalist, there's no doubt about that. But he was crazy.

—DANNY JOHNSON

The myth has taken over. I'm really in the way as a person.

—HUNTER THOMPSON, in the documentary film *Fear and Loathing: On the Road to Hollywood*, directed by Nigel Finch, the BBC, 1980

6

There's also a theory out there that his brain is fried and his stuff is no good anymore. I don't buy it for a second. I think he's just as lucid and clear as he ever was. Maybe we're a little tired of him, like we got a little tired of Hemingway. But he's just as good as ever. In '85, when I hired him at *The San Francisco Examiner,* I edited his stuff, whatever he wrote, and I didn't have any problems with it. Well—he got off the wall once or twice, but usually he was fighting with Maria.

That is probably the most intense and wild time I've ever had with him. That whole period. I became editor in June of '85. I was fired in January of '86. And frankly, the whole thing with Hunter probably cost me pretty dearly. But not that I would want to blame it on him. I got so distracted with the problems that Hunter had that it really cost me in other areas.

Here I was, The Editor, and I was in the office at four o'clock in the morning, trying to get Hunter's column in, and I should have been home sleeping so I could get back in and run the paper. Hunter kind of treated it like it was another *Rolling Stone.* Here was a serious newspaper with problems. It really cost me.

But I loved it. You know? And that's why I can't blame him. I loved it. I loved editing his stuff. It was the first time I ever had gotten to edit it. And it was probably the greatest—well, technically he's not the greatest writer, but the best I've ever been around.

His column ran on Mondays. So his deadline was Friday. So, I'd have to spend Friday, Saturday, Sunday and well into Sunday night—three days of my time! just to—looking back, I wouldn't trade it for anything.

—DAVID BURGIN

Hunter had a real tender side. I had a good friend who was dying of AIDS, who was very sick. And Hunter gave Margot a copy of *Curse of Lono* to give to him. He said, "Here, this is for your friend. I hope he feels better." I mean, it was that kind of thing. And then from the other room, "Bowl of Fruuuuit!" That's what he would always call me. "Bowl of Fruuuit." He would always call me Bowl of Fruit right to my face. I finally said, "Hunter, give me a break with that." And he said, "Well, is it better to call you fag?" And I said, "Well, actually, no, I wouldn't appreciate that either."

—DANNY JOHNSON

Will Hearst was one of our oldest clients. When he took over *The San Francisco Examiner* he wanted us to make the commercials. So we said, "Let's show what Will's doing to make the paper better." Hunter was going to be one of the new columnists, and we wanted to show that. Now Hunter, as you know, is the Gonzo Journalist, so we filmed him at the Presidio Army Shooting Gallery.

WHAT A MISTAKE!

Hunter wanted live ammunition. He wanted a submachine gun. We didn't want to give him a submachine gun. He wanted a .357 Magnum. And that's what he got.

We had a gun specialist from Hollywood bring the guns in with blanks. Hunter didn't like that. We quickly found out that Hunter didn't want to be told what to do.

We had a script for him. We said, "This is what we have to communicate." He didn't want to hear about it. First of all, he wasn't even on the set. So Will Hearst had to be called. We said, "Will, go to the hotel and pick up Hunter." We were frustrated that the money ticker was going. So Will went and got him. And that wasn't easy. I think there was a girl in the room. I think there were other things going on that got even stranger.

We also had a director who couldn't control him. The director threw up his hands. He couldn't get anything out of Hunter. Hunter wasn't going to listen to him. Then my partner tried. Then I tried. It was painful.

What it was, was after spending a lot of time going back and forth from the motor home, Hunter wanted live ammunition and he didn't want any of these chickenshit fake guns. He said, "What is this chickenshit stuff? This is a *fake* gun. I know how to shoot a gun. I want a gun!"

There were fifty people around the set and we were not going to give Hunter Thompson live ammunition. He got fairly hostile because of that. He said, "You guys are a bunch of hacks."

Will was the only guy who could try and calm him down.

Hunter came up with his own lines. The commercial started with the firing range. It said, "Will Hearst is going to find the best people." And then the camera came up on Hunter Thompson shooting a gun. And then Will interrupted and said, "Hi, I'm Will Hearst. I would like you to work for the paper." Then Hunter ad-libbed. Something like, "We'll chase them like rats across the tundra." There was a lot of babbling stuff we couldn't use. I mean, we just happened to pull that line out. In truth, the commercial could have been great. It was just OK, because of Hunter.

In the end, we had to shut down the set because the cameraman—a famous cameraman, he shot *Who Framed Roger Rabbit, Back to the Future*—was not going to shoot any longer because Hunter was waving the gun around. Inches from the camera. It was frightening.

You know, after watching his behavior, I realized that all Hunter's writing is true. That was the thing I didn't believe. I was reading what I thought was all fantasy. It's reality.

—RICH SILVERSTEIN, partner in Goodby, Berlin &
Silverstein, a San Francisco advertising agency

He just didn't understand women. He didn't comprehend them. He didn't try. Oh, he loved to have women around twenty-four hours a day. And then he would become tired of them and then he blamed them for being around.

He said they were draining him. One of his great things was that they were draining him. Life—everything was kind of a drain on him.

—DANNY JOHNSON

I fell in love with Hunter actually. I literally fell in love with him. Love at first sight. It was a very sensitive connection. I could read his mind and he could read my mind. It was the highest level of mental communication with the opposite sex I've ever had in my life.

We met in a house of a friend of mine's. We started talking immediately. We lay down in another room, in a bedroom together. I don't remember a single sentence that passed between our lips. I only remember the feeling when I was in the bed with him in the dark. Being pressed up against his body, the full length of his body, having a communication of souls. I remember the feeling of—that I couldn't believe that anybody could be so incredible. Oh! I'm ready to cry just talking about it. I'm ready to cry right now. I'm so ready to cry right now. I was so humiliated. So humiliated! You can print this. *You can use my name.* You can say I was never so humiliated in my life, you know, or so disappointed. Because I felt so heavenly with him, talking to him, the instant intellectual and spiritual communion I experienced with him was so divine and then the letdown——

I didn't care that he couldn't get it up. I didn't care that he couldn't get it up, and that was all the point. I didn't care.

—FAMOUS BLOND MOVIE STAR, name withheld for her own good

Remind me to tell you about the negotiations for his pay at the *Examiner.* I think it might have been one of the few times somebody besides Jann Wenner bluffed him out. We were at Tosca's, right there in North Beach, in the back room with the pool table. That was where the negotiations were. Hunter wanted some outrageous sum and satellite equipment installed in Woody Creek.

So I just told him: "Twelve hundred dollars a column." And *that* was an incredible amount. And I walked out. And I was walking up Columbus Street and here came Hunter chasing after me. He had a pool cue in his hand. And I thought for a second, "Oh, God, he's going to kill me." He said, "OK, OK. You got a deal. You got a deal. Come on back in and play some pool."

I knew it was a time when he needed the money. It was a good deal.

—DAVID BURGIN

I don't remember if he had started doing the column, but Hunter called me howling and moaning into the phone one night about two red-haired Malaysian strumpets who were covering him——as he spoke!——from head to foot in Gillette Foamy and were about to shave every hair off his body up to and including his eyebrows. He wanted me to come over immediately and supervise.

He was staying at the Mayflower on Central Park West under the name of Mr. Walker. He greeted me wearing a shade of lipstick I found so attractive I purchased a tube myself at the first cheap five-and-dime I ran across. It soon transpired the reason he called was not to supervise the trollops who had already departed, leaving water all over the floor, but because Bob Wallace, the editor of *Rolling Stone,* was due the next morning to pick up Hunter's Vietnam piece, which they were running, in a fit of Hunteralia, ten years after the evacuation.

We ordered in, watched a game on TV, washed out his laundry, rode up and down in the elevator, ran back and forth in the hall-way, I think Hunter did actually shave a couple of times, we ate six or seven meals, no we didn't make love, and Hunter, the great-est stylist in the English language since Jane Austen, turned in the piece the next day——*on time*. I'll never forget the look on Wal-lace's face.

—E. JEAN CARROLL

7

One day I was going to play golf with Hunter and Buffett in Col-orado. They were taking along guns to shoot gophers with while they were playing. I decided I didn't want to be isolated out on a golf course with Hunter and a nine-millimeter Walther.

—JIM HARRISON

Golfing with his friend Ed Bradley of *60 Minutes,* [Thompson] was charged with firing a shotgun on the Aspen municipal course. My sources say he fired two "warning shots" near a man on a lawn-mower tractor. . . . Bradley testified he heard a mysterious shot, but saw nothing. Thompson was fined $100.

—CURTIS WILKIE, friend of HST; reminiscing in
Image, May 29, 1988

I met the woman who fell in love with Hunter when he gave a lec-ture at the University of Arizona. This was when he was beginning to write columns for *The San Francisco Examiner.* Maria. That's right. Very sweet. Very young. Very cute. Her father was a red-necked golf champion of the state. So when I went out there to Owl Farm, Hunter was obsessed with golf. Terry McDonell [editor of *Esquire,* former managing editor of *Rolling Stone,* founding ed-itor of *Outside, Rocky Mountain,* and *Smart*] and I went out there to try and interview him for *The Paris Review.*

On the art of writing!

We got nowhere. All he wanted to do was play golf. So we went out and we played golf. At about eight o'clock in the evening the sun went down and we played night golf. Again typical of Hunter, he played the worst golf I had ever seen. But he hit his father-in-law in the leg with a golf shot.

He was absolutely obsessed with this thing and we went out and played in the darkness. We had some booze with us, I think it was Wild Turkey. So it was hysterical. You would hear Hunter take a swipe at the ball and miss it. You could see this ghostly golf course. You could see it in the moonlight. The thing about Hunter is that these lunatic things don't seem to amuse him.

We stayed two days. We didn't sleep. A lot of the time was spent trying to get Hunter to do his *Examiner* column.

I remember Maria was very young, very desirable, very sexy, and very devoted to Hunter. Adoring. Protective. I thought she was wonderful. She had a notebook and wrote down Hunter's conversation.

I fell in love with her!

You want that sort of fawning. Someone as pretty as that and so in love with you! And very worried about Hunter getting his column in.

It became frantic. It became the sort of deadline you would expect to see at newspapers. There were phone calls to Hearst or whoever it was, and his editor. He hadn't started. And we didn't know what to do.

Then we thought we ought to go out and play some golf to get his mind relaxed. It was all sort of a frantic preamble to sitting down and writing this thing. It was like an Irish setter who was trying to find a place to sit on the ground and rolls around and around. I never saw him settle down to it.

At one point Terry and I tried to write it for him. Because it was terribly important! He had to get this thing in or he wasn't going to have the contract. Then we dissolved, as I recall, into this golf game. Then the next day, cold sober or whatever his condition was, he sat down and wrote a very funny column.

—GEORGE PLIMPTON, friend of HST; editor of *The Paris Review*, and author of *Paper Lion, Shadow Box*, etc., co-author of *Edie*

Vegas was like four or five drafts. Probably the further back you go in time, the more rewrites we get in each piece. The newer stuff, almost without exception, is essentially journalism, as it was written on the day, sent in for a deadline, not edited, either then or now, and published.

> —HUNTER THOMPSON, quoted by David Felton in
> "Hunter Thompson Has Cashed His Check,"
> *Rolling Stone College Papers,* Spring 1980

The content of *Generation of Swine* was culled from the Pulitzer Prize–nominated columns Thompson wrote for the *San Francisco Examiner* between 1986 and 1988. The entries run about three or four pages each, and their brevity is their main drawback.

> —CURT HOLMAN, "Thompson Still Gonzo
> Patriarch, but Short Columns Dull His Razor," a
> review of *Generation of Swine*, *Nashville Banner*,
> August 27, 1988

The result isn't just classic Thompson. It's Thompson at his fuming, bug-eyed best (and occasionally worst), seized by a new intensity of fear and loathing and staking everything on his brash style.

> —RAPHAEL KADUSHIN, "Thompson's Cheap Shots
> Force Us to See the Truth," a review of
> *Generation of Swine*, *Capital Times* (Madison,
> Wisconsin), July 30, 1988

I *need* information, I *want* money and expenses from the syndication deal, I *must* kill pigs—and if I'm going to be a goddamn syndicated columnist on a level that we can put up against *anybody* else in the nation, *I want to be treated like a wizard and a main player and the best political columnist in America or anywhere else.*

> —HUNTER THOMPSON, fax to Will Hearst,
> September 11, 1987, quoted in *Songs of the
> Doomed,* Summit Books, 1990

8

Hunter likes his stuff read aloud. Once he asked me to read his poem "Collect Call from a Mad Dog" that was in *The Great Shark Hunt.*

So I began to read. He stopped me on the second line. I reread it. He glared at me. I became nervous and my pronunciation, of course, sounded like my head was stuck in a bowl of ice cubes. He began to insult me quite rudely. I rushed on to the second stanza. He lost his temper, winced, rolled angrily in his chair, ridiculed me, and said if I couldn't get his meaning, he was *afraid* of what other stupidities I was capable of.

I went on reading, messing up, of course, more and more horribly, stumbling, getting flustered, wondering when the end of this stupid poem was coming.

"Jesus!" he kept shouting. "You're so dumb!"

I read on. "What? *What?*" he screamed. I repeated the line twice. "There's no punctuation there!" he shouted. "Read it again! Jesus!"

Finally, I finished. "I'm sorry," I said. "I made it sound awful. It's a wonderful poem." I was lying. Danielle Steel will write like Emily Dickinson before Hunter turns out a good line of verse.

"Well, I don't know how to punctuate a poem," said Hunter, all calmed down by this time. He said, "I'm still learning to punctuate, even my prose."

So I suggested that his secretary, Deborah, read it out loud, because she was a good reader. Hunter liked that idea. And so Deborah started reading. He stopped her cold on the second line. " '*And* Dawn'?" he shouted. " '*And* Dawn,' " repeated Deb. " '*And.*' " She showed him. " '*And.*' "

"Jesus!" screamed Hunter. "What a typo! It's '*at*'! '*At*'! Jesus! The meaning is fucked!"

Well the whole "and/at" thing rattled Deborah so much that even she stumbled two or three times and you could see Hunter was ready to burst into a rage any minute. So she stopped reading and put the book down. You couldn't have *paid* her to read another syllable.

"Here, *you* read the motherfucker," I said, and gave him the book. Well, he began wonderfully. He has that low, deep voice, perfectly controlled, lyrical! musical! He practically sang!

Well, around the third stanza, he started flubbing. Then he stumbled completely. Then he had to reread a whole line to himself again out loud and flubbed again. Of course he ended up slamming the book closed and throwing it. And he said: "This is *stupid!* No wonder poets don't make any money. This is *shit!*"

—E. Jean Carroll

9

Going to visit Hunter at various hotels in San Francisco over the past few years, and you knock on the door, and you almost hope that no one's home, because you don't know what to expect when that door opens.

I can remember specifically a time that I visited my brother out at the Seal Rock Inn. Pouring rain, the middle of January or November, there was a football game on. Hunter called me. He said, "Why don't you come on out? We'll watch the football game."

I was very happy. Hunter wanted to watch a football game with me!

I got on my motor scooter and drove all the way out to Thirty-eighth and Geary in the rain, took me about a half an hour to get there and when I got there Hunter wouldn't let me in. He opened the door in his Jockey shorts.

He peeked around the edge of the door with the chain still bolted and said, "Uhhhh, really sorry, uhhh, Maria"—I believe it was Maria—"Maria has got herself into quite a fix. And we are in a situation right now and we just can't let you in."

"You mean to tell me, Hunter, that you had me come all the way out here in the rain and you're not going to let me in?"

"Well, Maria's got this—she's in quite a state." Hunter was the one who was in quite a state. Maria was probably trying to straighten things out. And I got back on my motor scooter and cried all the way home.

—Jim Thompson

When I moved into the Creek, my first encounter with Hunter was down at the Woody Creek Tavern. He mumbled some obscenities about me destroying the valley. So I told him, "Now, since I own the property, I have every intention of doing exactly what I want to do with that ranch and I don't give a fuck what you think." And I walked out of the tavern.

Then a few days later I ran into Hunter at the post office and he said I had no right to pour any concrete and that I should leave the valley like it was. And I told Hunter that he probably would do well to keep his nose in his own business and to straighten out his personal life.

After that someone painted a sign on my property which said, "Fat Floyd's Trout Ranch." I went to Hunter's house and said, "Hunter, this certainly looks like your handwriting and I'm going to stick it right up your ass, so you better be prepared." There was a girl living with him. She was quite attractive. I took the sign and threw it down on his front porch.

After that he and I said hello down at the tavern a few times. Then there was the fateful night when he came up here and shot up my ranch.

—FLOYD WATKINS, wealthy neighbor of HST on Woody Creek; sold Transworld Systems (a computer software, hardware and service company) and retired at the age of 42

The first time I ever met Jim's brother was at the Miyako Hotel. Hunter came to the door, and he was in his Jockeys. The place was trashed. The armoire was moved into the middle of the room, there was a typewriter, typewriter paper everywhere, the basketball game was on, the radio was on, there was about three days' worth of room service spread out, half-eaten, like melted sundaes covered with Saran Wrap, coffee, beer cans, whiskey, it was all over the place, and Polaroids of him and Maria, like him licking Maria's toes.

She was very nice. Hunter was writing his tattoo article. He had a tape recording of Maria getting the tattoo. When he played it, all we heard was the buzz from the tattoo gun. And that was his proof that she had gotten the tattoo. She was sitting in her bathrobe on the floor, very young and pretty.

JIM: Shall I talk about the pot?

JEFF: OK. He filled up a pipe bowl with pot and he lit it and he smoked it and he just like smoked it, smoked it, smoked it, and then gave it to Jim and proceeded to cough for about three minutes solid. Banging his head on the wall and kicking the wall, and going around coughing and hacking, gave it to Jim, and Jim lit it up and of course there was no pot left in it, you know, and Hunter didn't even ask, and Jim said, "This is how he always is."

Maria was sitting there and then they disappeared together in the bathroom.

JIM: Twenty minutes.

JEFF: In the bathroom.

JIM: The tub was full of water when we got there.

JEFF: They screwed, who knows?

JIM: Do you remember all the noise?

JEFF: No, I don't.

JIM: Going, "*AAWOOOO!* Goddamn it! God! Shit!" He spilled his cocaine all over the floor, I think that's what happened. 'Cause he was in there moaning and groaning and bitching and cussing.

> —JIM THOMPSON and JEFFREY PORTER; Porter is a
> performimg arts teacher, a volunteer worker with
> the disadvantaged, and bon vivant

I had just gotten through pouring about sixty yards of concrete in the driveway when I got a telephone call from an anonymous individual that there was gonna be trouble that night, and that I should be well prepared. So I called Bob Braudis [Pitkin County sheriff]. And Bob said, "I have only two deputies available and I can't spare them for some wild goose chase." So I said, "OK, Bob, I'll handle it myself." And he said, "Floyd, don't do anything crazy." And I said, "Look, somebody's threatened my ranch. And my son, Lance, and I will be properly prepared."

Braudis knew exactly what that meant. We had two A-R 14s with hundred-shot clips with laser sights. And we had a Jeep with a three-sixty souped-up engine in it.

We took turns every four hours guarding. We had a million-candlepower light. It was hooked up to a twenty-four-volt battery. I figured the trouble would come somewhere around the entry gate. So I closed it electronically and then I took a fence down where I could slip through with the Jeep.

Then at about four in the morning, I had just gotten out of the Jeep and was stretching and saying to myself, well, probably nothing was going to happen, when I heard forty shots. It sounded like a three-o-eight or a thirty-ought-six. Then about five rounds from a shotgun. I could hear the noise was coming from the entry gate.

I started the Jeep, pulled around and turned on that million-power light. And there was Hunter Thompson with his girlfriend standing there with a rifle next to his Jeep.

He saw me and jumped in his Jeep and took off. And I chased him at the rate of sixty miles an hour down the road. He pulled in George Stranahan's ranch. His girlfriend jumped out of the car, ran up to the door and started beating on the door and screaming. I kept the million-candlepower light on Hunter and told him to get out of his car. And if he had anything in his hands, it'd be the last time it ever happened.

He had a white tennis jacket on and shorts and he had his cigarette in the holder. He got out of his car. I told him to take his hands out of his pockets. I can't tell you what was in my hand because of lawsuits. But let me say I was well prepared.

—FLOYD WATKINS

I was going to tell you—I wanted to touch upon, as you may or may not have heard, in April of 1989 I was diagnosed with AIDS.

I have absolutely no regrets. This is a bad break for me, as it has been for thousands of others. But I don't have a lock on personal tragedy. No one is immune from occasional trouble and deep sadness. I've lived a joyous, charmed life. I've never been seriously ill. I accept my fate. Do I have a choice?

—JIM THOMPSON

And I said, "What do you think you're doing?" He had a twelve-gauge shot gun and a pistol in the front seat. I'm guessing it was a .454 pistol or a .44 Magnum. And a .3006 or a .308 in the back. Automatic.

And he said, "I'm the only friend you have in this valley. I was giving you a friendly warning."

So I told him the next time he comes to my ranch with a gun it better be a small one because I was going to stick it right up his ass.

And Hunter said, "Here, have a drink."
I have to admit, it was funny.

—FLOYD WATKINS

The last time I saw Hunter was in September of 1990. I felt so sure of his lack of concern for me. He tried to fake it, but his actions did not ring true. He just seemed so bored when I was there. I didn't know what I could do to cheer him up.

He fell asleep. And then after the girls came over he perked up. That was right after dinner they knocked on the door.

He was at the Pan Pacific Hotel. The room was a mess. Suitcases, bottles, half-eaten desserts, and fruit on every table, TV on, turned way up, all the lights on, all sorts of nude pictures out on the table. He had just finished with some woman that he'd been taking naked pictures of with his Polaroid. She was buttoning up when I walked in through the door, and I said, "Well, don't let me interrupt anything."

She said, "No, I have to go anyway," and out she went; but as soon as she left, Hunter kind of switched gears. He didn't really know what to say. He was ill at ease. He appeared to be kind of pained, and didn't feel well. He had a bad leg or a bad back or a nerve or something. And he began to sink lower and lower and finally, he said to me—this is an interesting quote—he said, "I'm in much worse shape than you."

I said, "OK, you're in much worse shape than I am."

And then the girls arrived and he forgot all about it.

—JIM THOMPSON

The neighbors, of course, had called the sheriff. Braudis told me, "Look. Don't press charges because Hunter's already on probation. For shooting that shotgun on the golf course with Ed Bradley." So when the police asked Hunter what he was shooting at, he said . . .

—FLOYD WATKINS

—— I was out in front of Watkins' and I was charged by this [pointing to it, stuffed, on top of the piano] gigantic porcupine. It came right at me. Running at about twenty miles an hour. It lunged at me. I had to blast it.

—— You lying bastard.

—— I've never seen anything so vicious.

—HUNTER THOMPSON interview

CHAPTER
EIGHTEEN

A female dwarf lifted up her skirts and exhibited thighs all marbled over with bites and bruises, inflicted on her, so she told us, by her lover. In one sense, it was very refreshing.

—SIMONE DE BEAUVOIR

1

It is a well-known fact that the Doctor has told the truth on only *six* occasions in his entire life——five of which have been documented in this illustrious work——so it will not surprise the Reader that the Great Prevaricator raised his eyes to the ceiling and swore a solemn oath that the big-bottomed trollop, Molly, was "just a friend."

"You bounder! You savage!" I screamed.

"Now, now, Miss Tishy, dear," said the Doctor.

"Where's *her* hot tub video?" I cried, kicking him in the shins. "Where's *her* plate of Dove Bars and fettuccine Alfredo?"

The Doctor was extremely delighted and chuckled in his melodious voice. "Now, monkey-pie."

"You sneak!" I yelled, throwing his bowl of remote controls across the room. "Walking phallus!"

"She's just an old, old friend," repeated the Doctor, putting his big brutish arms around me. I tried to push them away. I might as well have been swinging on a tree bough.

"There's nothing! I swear," said the . . .

ED BRADLEY, THE *60 MINUTES* CORRESPONDENT, HAS JUST BEEN HERE AT THE CESSPOOL. It was at 4:35 p.m. He pulled up the lid. I thought it was that pernicious vermin, the Doctor. I stared upward with my hand on my hip. "Miss Snap?" asked Mr. Bradley. For a moment I was struck dumb. I staggered backward, clutching a Fax Machine Operator's Manual to my crotchless rear-ruffled panties, and stumbled over a box of the Doctor's photographs. "HE'S HOLDING ME PRISONER!" I screamed. "That's what he tells me," said Mr. Bradley. Then he turned and said over his shoulder, "She's as cute as a button, Hunter." Then they put the lid back down and left——

2

I can't take much more of this.

By the way, if you were wondering what happened to the Japanese, Reader, they departed rather quickly after the Doctor blew up a barrel of dynamite and two Sheriff's Deputies arrived and charged the Doctor with destroying the foundations of three of his neighbor's houses. I was sick and tired of writing about those Japanese anyway. [Now here. I've lost a paragraph——I fancy I sat on it in my crotchless apparel and perhaps *engulfed* it unawares after Mr. Bradley's shocking appearance.] So where was I? I am trembling excessively. So what was I talking about? I declare! I can't remember——Oh, I covered my face with my lace hanky, and started crying, nay almost roaring, in the kitchen.

"Now, now, Miss Tishy," said the Doctor, "Next Tuesday, we're off to Meeker!"

"Meeker!" I cried. "You Priapus!"

"And then you're going to write my biography."

"Ha Ha Ha!"

"I have an offer, my dear: $950,000."

Now, Reader, I must say, I took a pause. I pulled the hanky from my face and peeped at the Doctor. He was holding out a glass of Chartreuse. "To Meeker!" he said.

"I want proof, you coxcomb!" I said, and threw the glass against the refrigerator.

"There's a fax . . . someplace," said the Doctor, rifling through the wine box on top of the stove. "It was just here," he said, removing a handful of faxes and dropping them on the floor. "Goddamn it!" He flung out an entire stack. "I CAN NEVER FIND

ANYTHING IN THIS GODDAMN HOUSE!" He turned the box upside down and shook it. "Oh, here it is." He handed me a sheet of paper.

I looked at the letterhead. It was from a hussy named Lynn Nesbit.

"You Casanova!" I yelled.

"Lynn's my agent, you little dunce," he said, handing me another glass of Chartreuse.

I began to read. So eager was my first perusal, I noticed nothing but the figure of $950,000 and the words, "The Hunter Thompson Biography." I was so much surprised that for some time I was unable to compose myself. I could only get off the stool and walk up and down the kitchen repeating, "$950,000! $950,000!" But on the second reading, I awoke to far different feelings. Lynn, whoever she was, said the $950,000 was only a "floor," and she thought she could get even *more*.

I won't attempt to describe my sensations at that moment, Reader. I scarce drew breath. My heart flew around my rib cage. The blood rushed to my cheeks, my legs gave way, and the Doctor caught me as I fell almost lifeless. In short, I was not proof against Love's solicitations. "To Meeker," I said, with tears of joy in my eyes, and lifted my glass to my bald Fiancé.

After I had downed the whole thing, the Doctor softly touched my lips and stroked my hair.

"Of course, I get eighty-eight percent for my trouble," he whispered.

Reader, that is the last thing I clearly remember. I vaguely recall slapping his face, making a run for the back door, being tackled from behind, and feeling the sensation of flying down a tunnel, hideous, with an unbearably loud noise and the smell of gas. I awoke, I do not know how many hours or days later, here in the Cesspool dressed as a ballet girl with birch marks all over my buttocks. At first I thought I was in the Fort Wayne Holiday Inn where my Aunt Hanthorne from Lima, Ohio, used to stay. There was a cot, a table, a chair, a space heater, a hose with running water, a chemical toilet——the Beast has pocketed and has, indeed, already *spent* the first half of the advance, so let us move, quickly! quickly! Reader, from the shining world of my sewer, to the penultimate biographical section and the amazing arrest and trial of Dr. Hunter S. Thompson.

C H A P T E R
NINETEEN

Supposing truth is a woman—what then?
—FRIEDRICH NIETZSCHE

1

Hunter Thompson Denies Assault

Gonzo Journalist Says He Rejected Woman's Sexual Advances

—HEADLINE, *The San Francisco Chronicle*, March 2, 1990

Well, I'm going to tell you exactly what went down.

When I got to Hunter's house, I was enjoying the evening. Hunter was so nice and he was so charming. He gave me a big cellophane thing full of play cockroaches, and he said, "Take these back to Michigan! You'll have a lot of fun with them!" And then he showed me a fake brick that you could throw against the TV and it makes a sound like it breaks the screen. It was like being with a kid. It was a really great time.

And innocently enough, the only reason I wanted to meet him was that my husband and I had bought property near Aspen, and we were going to build there, right? And I thought, I'm going into writing now, and I don't know any writers.

I had some questions to ask him about why *Fear and Loathing* was never made into a movie. I wanted to talk to him seriously about that, and then ask him some questions about publishing.

I had read all his books. So, I went to his house like that. It was fun. I was having a really, really great time.

> —GAIL PALMER-SLATER, former highly successful producer of X-rated films *(Erotic Adventures of Candy, Hot Summer in the City,* etc., etc.), former cheerleader, former National Honor Society, former *Playboy* "Girl of the Big Ten"; married to a St. Clair, Michigan, ophthalmologist; presently beginning a writing career

The broad was sloppy drunk. She might have been a *little* drunk when she got here, but I mean drooling, reeling and bumping into things. And then *she* came on to *me,* backed me into this corner right here. I was saying, "No, damn it. Get away," but she kept on lurching at me, and I finally stiff-armed her—Poom! Like this, both arms at her shoulders. *Could* I have hit her in the tit? I suppose so. But *if* I did, neither one of us noticed it at the time. All I wanted was for her to get the fuck away from me.

> —HUNTER THOMPSON, quoted by Geoffrey Stokes with Kevin P. Simonson in "Gonzo's Last Stand," *The Village Voice,* May 15, 1990

I'm five nine and a half. I weigh a hundred and fifty-five pounds. I can drink a lot of drinks. I could drink a lot of guys under the table. I had two drinks from Hunter and that's it. I skied all day. The police, or Hunter's private detectives, called my ski instructor to see if I drank during the day, and he said that I didn't. I didn't have a drink before I went over. Then Hunter made me two drinks of some concoction with cranberry juice. Well, I didn't even finish the last one with the cranberry juice, which was in a tall glass, because that's one of the things that got spilled.

—GAIL PALMER-SLATER

—— What did she do with you, Hunter?

—— She tried to have sex with me.

—— And then what?

—— (silence)

—— Did you go along with it?

—— Fuck no!

—— Was she good-looking?

—— (silence)

—— Semi?

—— (silence)

—— Fairly?

—— Had been.

—— Had been? She was an elderly woman?

—— Well? A porno queen. A porno queen.

—HUNTER THOMPSON interview

What happened was the whole evening was wonderful. He asked me if I wanted a tour of his house. He took me to the Jacuzzi room. He closed the door slightly so there was only about a three-inch gap there.

And he sat near the tub, and I sat on—there was a step there. And you know, he got real kind of nice and tender. And he told me that the girl out there [Catherine Sabonis-Chafee, sister of Terry Sabonis-Chafee, HST's girlfriend, who was away at *school*] wasn't his girlfriend but that she was his girlfriend's sister. And he said, "So this puts me in an odd predicament." And I said, "Well, what predicament?"

And he said, "Oh, well, you know, and . . ." and he was mumbling and I said, "Hunter, are you trying to say that you would like to do something, but your girlfriend's sister's here?" And I said, "Listen. I didn't come over here for that. I'm just so happy to meet you. I'm thrilled to meet you. I'm having a great time!"

I liked him, but if I was going to pick somebody to have sex with, it wouldn't be Hunter Thompson. But I think he closed the door and thought I was going to give him a blow job. And that's why he closed the door. So I opened it a little more. I didn't want his girlfriend's sister to think I was there to seduce him. Here her sister loves him! She looked nineteen or twenty at the most.

—GAIL PALMER-SLATER

—— I was *never* attracted to her.

—— You were attracted to her, Hunter. You had fantasies before she came over.

—— No.

—— Yes. You did, Hunter. It flashed through your mind. You pictured it.

—— No.

—— Yes. She had a cute body in a perky sort of way.

—— Well, I'd seen the movie.

—— So it flashed through your mind, didn't it, Hunter?

—— Well, maybe it did. I did want to go in the water, but not with her.

—HUNTER THOMPSON interview

So I said I was just so happy to meet him and I was having a great time, and, in fact, the time went so fast, it was getting about midnight, I said, "Do you mind if I call my husband to tell him I'm OK and that I'm going to stay a little longer and then leave?"

And he said, "OK," and went back to the kitchen. So I thought it was odd that Semmes [Semmes Luckett, close friend of HST; he was at Owl Farm with Tim Charles, another Thompson friend] came in and listened to my conversation. He came in and stood in the office. I told my husband, "Honey, I'm having a great time, I can't wait to tell you. I'm going to stay here about an hour more and then I'll take a cab home." He said, "OK, fine."

When I came out of the room, Hunter said, "You called the cops, didn't you." I said, "I'm *sure!*" I didn't know if he was putting me on or not.

So I went back to the kitchen and I thought everything was normal, but then Tim left, and then Semmes left, and Semmes was so drunk I thought they shouldn't let him drive. But they let him go and said he was like that all the time. I said, "Well, can I use your rest room, and then I'll call for a cab."

—GAIL PALMER-SLATER

—— And she was calling her husband, and all kind of things were happening, and she wanted to have a private place to call her husband. And I thought, Oh God, that's the last fucking thing I need! And I let her go in the office by herself. So I left her in there by herself for two or three minutes. And I came back in and she was just kinda standing there, very—

—— Clothed, Hunter?

—— Oh yeah. Yeah. Calling her husband to tell him not to worry. Meanwhile Semmes is getting stupider and drunker and the line is busy.

—HUNTER THOMPSON interview

And so I went to use the rest room. And Cat [Catherine Sabonis-Chafee] followed me in. And I was going to the bathroom and she was talking to me and she said, "You know what? Hunter would really appreciate it if you would get in the hot tub with him."

I said, "Oh!" She went, "He's had a hard time, because publishers are on his ass and he has to get things done and he's been working nonstop for a coupla days and he just got something finished," she said, "and this would be a really nice thing for you to do together."

—GAIL PALMER-SLATER

Thompson says she got drunk and approached him, and he pushed her away. He adds that he would not have asked her to join him in the bath because there would have been too much "water displacement."

—SAM KILEY, Times Newspapers Limited, *The Sunday Times,* June 3, 1990

So I was coming out of the bathroom with Cat and Hunter was monkeying at the sink and Cat said, "She won't go in." Like that. And she walked over to him, and I said, "Well, I'll just call my cab now, I'm sure you guys want me to leave." And she was saying something in my defense about not going in the hot tub and Hunter said, "You fucking dyke."

And she said, "Hunter!" And he threw a drink at me. And then she said, "Hunter!" And she went to stop him—he was starting to flail things. She said, "Hunter, you're out of control. Just calm down." He said, "You're goddamn right I'm out of control." And then he took his arm and whooooshed against all the things that were on the counter to make them fall to the ground. And she went to pick them up—and he pulled her by her hair, pulled her hair down to the floor, and said, "Yeah, get down and fucking clean it up!"

See, I thought he was hurting her. So then I went to stop him. I put my arms in between the both of them. And I said, "Wait, come on, Hunter, I'm sorry. It's my fault. OK! I'll go in the hot tub! Stop it!" And there was a cutting board pulled out from under the counter and he just threw me against it. And that's when he pushed me or grabbed me by my breast, and just pushed me like that. It was all very fast, in a second. He was swearing and cussing. And that was that.

—GAIL PALMER-SLATER

—— Well, she said, "Oh please, don't let it end like this!" She kept putting her finger on the damn phone. I was dialing the taxi.

—— What a gentleman!

—— And then she said, "I've only been married a year! He's never seen me like this!" And I said, "Boy, you must really have a strange marriage." And she said, "He knows nothing about my

past." I said, "Oh, boy. You're about to have a real motherfucker
tonight."

—HUNTER THOMPSON interview

It was a little altercation that took place between people who were
up late. I found out later he had been up for several days. That's
not good. You get crazy. It was actually Cat that he was mean to.
I just felt bad that he was mean to her because of me. So I just
kind of stepped in there, and then you know, he just hauled off on
me. The only bruise I got was from the cutting board and it went
right across my back.

—GAIL PALMER-SLATER

—— This sort of stuff doesn't happen to Tom Wolfe, Hunter.

—— Maybe it does, and it just doesn't make the papers.

—HUNTER THOMPSON interview

Do you know what Cat told me when we were alone? She told me
that he had gotten physical with his last secretary. Had you heard
that? She said that the secretary had quit because he was verbally
and physically abusive to her.

I really felt bad for Cat. She was telling me all kinds of stories
and I was starting to feel sorry for her. She said, "And he's so
mean to my sister, he fucks other girls, and my sister doesn't
know." Actually, I had a good conversation with her.

When people ask me what was it really like, I just say, "Like
one of his books." Because that's how it turned out.

—GAIL PALMER-SLATER

—— So then what happened, Hunter?

—— She wanted to talk. "Don't let it end like this. You're my
hero." I swear to God.

—— You probably were her hero.

—— That's not my problem. She was in my way.

—HUNTER THOMPSON interview

He ranted and raved, he said, "Get out of my goddamn house or I'm going to blow your fucking head off. I'm not kidding. Where's my fucking gun?" And he did have a gun there because I saw it under all the papers. And then he started going through the papers, and I thought, "I'm not sticking around."

So I ran out. And started to walk. And then Cat came out after me. She said, "Please. Don't. Please stay overnight. I don't want you to go home like this." 'Cause I was a mess. She said, "Listen. He's really sorry. He's over it now. He throws a tantrum every once in a while. I saw him on the way out. He's calm and sitting down in the bathroom. He's just fine. Please, just stay here. Your husband's going to be upset."

Then when she saw I wouldn't stay, she said, "Well, come on. Just come back in the house and let's get cleaned up before you go home." I said, "I'm *not* going back in that house." Because at that time, I really did think he might throw some bullets at me, after all the things you read about him.

—GAIL PALMER-SLATER

I'm by myself. The last dope fiend. It's hard to find the right people to party with.

—HUNTER THOMPSON, *The Los Angeles Times,*
1987

2

So what happened was, I got back to our hotel. I was wearing a white sweater. A big white bulky sweater and it was full of cranberry juice, right? And all my mascara and all my makeup—I'd been crying.

My husband was very upset, right?

He's an upstanding citizen. He was going to call the police. I said, "Don't call the police, you're *not* calling the police." And he said, "What's wrong with you? Look what happened! You're not going to stick up for yourself, Gail, that's what I hate about you! You're a doormat! People wipe their feet on you!"

He called me a doormat. So now, not only did I have Hunter

hassle me, I came home and now I was in a fight with my husband, because I wouldn't do what he was telling me I should do!

—GAIL PALMER-SLATER

D.A. Snags Thompson In Sex Case

Hunter S. Thompson, in an episode reminiscent of some of his books, has been charged with sexually assaulting a woman writer who came to his house ostensibly to interview him last week....

Thompson told the *Times Daily* he's innocent and believes the alleged victim ... is a businesswoman who wants publicity for her new venture, which is selling sexual aids and lingerie.

... Thompson offered his own headline for the case:

LIFESTYLE POLICE RAID HOME OF "CRAZED" GONZO JOURNALIST; ELEVEN-HOUR SEARCH BY SIX TRAINED INVESTIGATORS YIELDS NOTHING BUT CRUMBS.

—DAVID MATTHEWS-PRICE, *Aspen Times Daily,* February 28, 1990

I told my husband, "Don't call the police. *You're* the one who will suffer. We live in a small town. [St. Clair, Michigan] You're a respected doctor. They'll be all over the fact that your wife produced X-rated movies." He was *not* listening to me. So, I said, "Don't just take my opinion about what the papers can do, let's talk to [a friend in California]." Well, it backfired. Our friend thought I should tell the police. And when we hung up, *he* called them.

The investigators came the next day. Knocking on my door in the hotel room.

—GAIL PALMER-SLATER

Kelly: Which hand did he do that with?
Palmer-Slater: With the right, I think.
Kelly: The right hand, is that right?
Palmer-Slater: Yes.
Kelly: And which of your breasts did he . . .?
Palmer-Slater: This one.
Kelly: His right hand on your left breast?
Palmer-Slater: Uh-huh.
Kelly: . . . He grabbed it, twisted it, and pushed you away?

> —INVESTIGATIVE REPORT, District Attorney's office,
> interview with Gail Marie Palmer-Slater, Room
> #456, Wildwood Inn, Snowmass Village,
> Colorado; conducted by Michael J. Kelly

And that was how it got this momentum, and just took off.

> —GAIL PALMER-SLATER

Palmer-Slater: I don't want to press charges.

> —INVESTIGATIVE REPORT, District Attorney's office,
> interview with Gail Marie Palmer-Slater

3

Gonzo Time; Hunter Thompson, Facing Drug, Sexual Assault Charges, Claims He's The Victim Of Witch Hunt

. . . A team of investigators from the office of Milton Blakey, the district attorney in Colorado's 9th Judicial

District, pulled up, armed with a search warrant, looking for evidence of the assault and of illicit drugs.

The team finished its work at 1:15 the next morning, nearly eleven hours later.

> —DAN MORAIN, *Los Angeles Times*, April 23, 1990

That was so stupid to search Hunter's house! And also do you know that he was warned they were coming?

> —GAIL PALMER-SLATER

*A baggie containing a small quantity of a green leafy substance

*A zip-lock bag with a small amount of possible hashish

*A brown bottle with hot pink pills

*A baggie containing unknown pills

*A bronze hookah

*A glass jar with dried mushrooms

*Two bic pen shells with a white powdery substance in them

*A plastic round green canister with a white powdery substance in it

*A video tape labeled "child porn"

*Explosive materials

*A triple beam scale

*A tool box with blasting caps

*A twelve gauge shotgun

*A .22 caliber machine gun

*Various vials and containers with suspected drug residue

> —MUNICIPAL COURT FILE as reported by Eve O'Brien, *The Aspen Daily News*, March 2, 1990

The most outrageous search in American letters.

> —WARREN HINKLE, *The Los Angeles Times*

Putting a collar on Hunter was a great idea. How they did it was
wrong. When a guy can come and search you for eleven hours,
based on a third-class misdemeanor assault charge, that's wrong.

—FLOYD WATKINS, *The Los Angeles Times,*
April 23, 1990

New Fear And Loathing: Gonzo Writer On Trial

. . . Mr. Thompson said the drugs found by the
authorities were probably several years old. "I've been
living in this house for 24 years, and every freak in the
world has come through—well, not every freak."

—DIRK JOHNSON, *The New York
Times,* May 22, 1990

4

Four times they asked me, what do you want to do about this? I
said, I don't want to do anything. I just want to forget it. At the
end [Kelly] said, "Well, are you aware that we can go ahead and
prosecute without your permission?" And I wasn't aware of that.
Had I been really aware of that I wouldn't have let them come
over in the first place.

—GAIL PALMER-SLATER

Thompson Hit With 5 Felonies

"This is a low-rent, back-alley cheap shot," Thompson
muttered about the charges. He observed that many

defendants get religion when they want mercy from the court. "When you see me coming out for Jesus you'll know they really have something on me."

—DAVID MATTHEWS-PRICE, *Aspen Times Daily*, April 10, 1990

Kelly: . . . Would you just go into the bathroom and take a look at both your breasts. . . .
Palmer-Slater: The nipple's kind of sore. No. I don't see a bruise.
Kelly: OK, there are no bruises on your side . . . ?
Palmer-Slater: My nipple's kind of sore in one spot.
Kelly: Is that maybe from his twisting it?

—INVESTIGATIVE REPORT, District Attorney's office, interview with Gail Marie Palmer-Slater

What's at stake here is the Fourth Amendment. Things have apparently gone a lot farther in this country than I had realized.

—HUNTER THOMPSON, quoted in *The New York Times*, May 22, 1990

Kelly: And I believe you said there were guns all over the house?
Palmer-Slater: Yeah. Everywhere.
Kelly: It's hard for me to picture that, to get a mind's eye view of that. Is that three or four guns? Eight or ten guns? Twenty, thirty guns? How, what was your impression?
Palmer-Slater: Maybe I saw personally about ten.
Kelly: About ten. Guns are different things to different people. Are they like what some people would call a rifle, gun, shotgun?
Palmer-Slater: He had rifles on the wall, he had like a machine gun mounted in his living area which is right next to the kitchen . . . there were just guns laying everywhere. There was a gun in the kitchen, there was another gun, his house is really . . .

—INVESTIGATIVE REPORT, District Attorney's office, interview with Gail Marie Palmer-Slater

THE FOURTH AMENDMENT

The right of the people to be secure in their persons, houses, papers, and effects, against unreasonable searches and seizures, shall
not be violated, and no warrants shall issue, but upon probable
cause, supported by oath or affirmation, and particularly describ-
ing the place to be searched, and the persons or things to be
seized.

—UNITED STATES CONSTITUTION

Entertainment Tonight came to interview Hunter about his court
case and his Fourth Amendment Foundation. He placed himself in
front of the camera in such a way so that while they were shooting, behind him, through the window, could be seen——to the
film crew's utter astonishment——a beautiful blond young lady
disrobing. By the end of the interview she was buck-naked and
making underwater swimming motions like a fish. Needless to say,
it did not make the air.

—E. JEAN CARROLL

I told the police. I don't think there was a crime here. If I prose-
cuted every time someone said something sexual to me or made a
sexual advance to me I would have spent all my time, you know,
prosecuting.

—GAIL PALMER-SLATER

But be sure to make out any cheque to the Hunter S. Thompson
Legal Defense Fund, and not to him personally. Otherwise he
might spend it on drugs.

—RALPH STEADMAN, quoted by Francis Wheen, *The
Independent*, April 15, 1990

Dr. Slater [Gail Palmer-Slater's husband]: I think that somebody
has to make a stand . . . he's a dangerous person. I hate to see you
go through that but I think this man is not healthy.

—INVESTIGATIVE REPORT, District Attorney's office,
Interview with Gail Marie Palmer-Slater

Going to trial was the best fun I ever had in my life.

—HUNTER THOMPSON interview

5

Gonzo Writer On Trial

... The State of Colorado v. Hunter S. Thompson ...
Mr. Thompson, 52 years old, is to appear in court
Tuesday for a pretrial hearing on charges of
misdemeanor sexual assault and felony charges of
possession of illegal drugs and dynamite.

—DIRK JOHNSON, *The New York
Times,* May 22, 1990

I was surprised by the likeness to Duke in *Doonesbury.* He was
more subdued in court than I had expected. And I appreciated his
politeness. I think he was dressed real nicely. I recollect either a
suit with a tie or sport coat with a tie. He had two attorneys,
Gerry Goldstein and Hal Haddon.

There was an aura about him. There were a lot of beautiful
people that came into the courtroom, unlike Mesa County [Judge
Buss's district], where people look pretty ordinary like myself. A
lot of the Mitchell brothers and their dancers stayed outside. It
was fun to look out the second story—this is an old courthouse
built around 1890—and watch the picketing going on by the
dancers outside. They were wearing miniskirts and halter tops. I
think they had driven a red convertible in from San Francisco.
They were sitting in it and picketing. I forget what the sign said.
"Free Hunter," or something like that.

I couldn't tell who were the spectators and who were friends.
They all just sort of looked like the beautiful people of Aspen.

—DISTRICT COURT JUDGE CHARLES BUSS, presiding
judge

Hunter's Friends, Fans, Show Their Support

... A caravan of two Winnebagos and a red convertible with a buffalo head protruding from the back seat arrived at [the Woody Creek Tavern].

Out of the vehicles poured 12 to 14 people ... who had road-tripped from San Francisco to Aspen to show their support for Thompson....

The cast of characters ... included Jim and Artie Mitchell, owners of a chain of pornography theaters and producers of XXX-rated films, Roxi and Gigi, two young porno stars....

—EVE O'BRIEN, *Aspen Daily News,* May 22, 1990

It was a circus! He had all those people there. [Laughing] I got on the witness stand and Hunter's about three feet away. And it was hilarious. And I tried really hard to keep my attention and my focus. But I wasn't into it, to begin with, right? They said, "Tell us what his thing looked like." That thing he puts on his cigarette. And Hunter stood up and took it out of his pocket and said, "Did it look like this, hon?"

And then he took out a folded piece of paper that had pills in it, and a couple of the pills fell down on the floor. And he got off his chair and crawled around underneath his table and crawled out almost to the middle of the courtroom, retrieving the pills, and said, "Oh, God, finally!" Then he turned around, crawled back under the table, back into his chair and then took his pill. And this was going on during my testimony!

—GAIL PALMER-SLATER

—— What did the judge say, Hunter?

—— He might even have said Dr. Thompson. But I think he said Mister. "You've been a perfect gentleman." McGrory was complaining when Gail Palmer-Slater couldn't remember what kind of hideous instrument I was using to horn cocaine into my body, I thought, well wait a minute. And I pulled it out of my pocket, and I hit it on the table. And stood it up like that and giggled. And McGrory objected. I was harassing the witness. I had things on the table in front of me. I was not part of the proceeding. She was—I don't say this, it was in the paper—she was flirting with me.

—HUNTER THOMPSON interview

Drugs Not Thompson's Attorney Hints

EXPLOSIVES NOT HIS EITHER, HEARING TOLD

Hunter S. Thompson's attorney offered some intriguing theories about the origins of some of the drugs allegedly confiscated during a raid at the writer's Woody Creek home Feb 26. . . . Haddon implied the 36 hits [of LSD] were Sandy Thompson's.

—EVE O'BRIEN, special to *The Denver Post*, May 25, 1990

Having made a fortune portraying himself as a champion consumer of controlled substances, Thompson naturally took the position that the drugs found in his house must have been left there by someone else.

—LOUIS MENAND, *The New Republic*, January 7, 1991

He was funny. We were in the kitchen that night of the altercation, and he was moving some papers around by the typewriter and I said, "How can you work in this mess?" And he said, "Look what's under this paper," and there was a big pile of coke. And he put his head down to the thing, right in the pile, and he went, wheeeeeeee! and he came up, right? And he came up and his whole face was white.

He was hilarious. He said, "Look, coke. Everywhere I look in this house, there's coke." And he looked at me and he said, "That's what I like about this house." I could have died. He was like a comedian. You gotta understand it was so hilarious because his face and his mouth were white all over.

—GAIL PALMER-SLATER

It came out in her testimony that she admired him. [Thompson] had a bit of an aura about him. I suppose whenever there's a famous person in a small town it's going to be the case. He warmed up during the hearing. He became a little livelier. He had some kind of eye-communications with this witness, I forget her name, Gail Palmer-Slater.

The D. A. asked me to bawl him out and admonish him.

I forget what I said. I think I mentioned he was acting like a gentleman.

—JUDGE CHARLES BUSS

I like her. Unfortunately, she got herself into a bad situation, and I was going to prison for sixteen years. . . . At a cost of a quarter million dollars.

—HUNTER THOMPSON interview

She was an attractive woman. I liked her light attitude towards life. She wasn't trying to look conservative. She acted on the witness stand as though she was independent of the district attorney and showed a lot of spunk and was in control of herself. She wasn't going to let the lawyers get the best of her.

—JUDGE CHARLES BUSS

I don't like women who cry wolf. Because rape and sexual assault are a real thing. And it happens to people. I take responsibility for what happened to me because I invited myself over. I was *not* selling underwear and sex toys—I don't know why he said that—but I went over to Hunter's house. I mean, I've got a full-capacity brain, and I'm fine, you know? He didn't shoot me. If he'd have shot me I'd be much more pissed off.

—GAIL PALMER-SLATER

There were two hearings. This was the preliminary hearing. [It] may have taken three hours. A preliminary hearing is where the state through the D. A.'s office presents a sketch of the evidence. They try to show there's enough evidence to justify going to trial, so they don't have to put on a whole case. . . . Then the next hearing, when they made the motion to dismiss, that probably took half an hour.

—JUDGE CHARLES BUSS

D.A.'s Surprise—All Charges Against Hunter S. Thompson Dropped

"... The people would be unable to sustain their burden of proof, beyond a reasonable doubt"

—Aspen Daily News, May 31, 1990

Except for the hardship on people like Hunter Thompson who would have to go through a trial, for his sake I was glad it didn't; but for my sake, it would have been nice to have a trial.

I missed the juicy issues. The juicy issues were coming and we didn't get there because of the dismissal. The issues of the search and seizure and all of the defenses he might have had.

When we got out of the second hearing, when the case was dismissed, the chambers I was using were right next to a second-story front window, and [Thompson] was out there on the steps. He was obviously glad it was over with, but also fairly shaken. Obviously, he took it very seriously. Everybody hugged him.

—JUDGE CHARLES BUSS

Delirious Doc Looks For An Explosive Encore

... "We beat them like stupid rats. We beat 'em like dogs. They had a bad case." ... Thompson, beaming as he sped out of Aspen, stopped first to load his car with beer and then decided a more dramatic celebration was in order. Pulling a pistol from his shoulder holster, he fired a volley of blanks at anyone who approached him until he was surprisingly silenced by an elderly woman who ordered him not to shoot at her.

—SAM KILEY, Times Newspapers
Limited, *The Sunday Times*, June
3, 1990

I'm the only man in America now with nothing to hide. I think I'll run for President.

—HUNTER THOMPSON interview

C H A P T E R
TWENTY

VLADIMIR: Ceremonious ape!
ESTRAGON: Punctilious pig!
VLADIMIR: Moron!
ESTRAGON: That's the idea, let's abuse each other.
VLADIMIR: Moron!
ESTRAGON: Vermin!
VLADIMIR: Abortion!
ESTRAGON: Morpion!
VLADIMIR: Sewer-rat!
ESTRAGON: Curate!
VLADIMIR: Cretin!
ESTRAGON: *(with finality)* Crritic!
VLADIMIR: Oh!
(He wilts, vanquished, and turns away.)
—SAMUEL BECKETT

1

And so, Gentle Reader, this biography is over. If you by now do not know enough about Hunter S. Thompson, it is not my fault. I have vented my spleen against him and shewn my hatred as much as I am capable. One or two items of semi-interest, however, I must report before I finish.

First, I received the materials for the biographical sections over my fax machine here in the cesspool. Naturally, I cannot call *out* on this fax machine, but during the past six and a half months I have been the unhappy recipient of several thousand pages of yammering about the Doctor. You may imagine my boredom! Particularly in the beginning when the communications were stultifyingly complimentary. Indeed, I flushed the faxes of Warren Beatty and Jack Nicholson down my chemical toilet. Then, it is

my opinion, the fax number was compromised. Certain individuals got wind of it, without the Doctor's knowledge, without the
Doctor's blessing——Ralph "Sonny" Barger is a good example
——and the outcome is the somewhat fuller portrait you hold
now in your hands. Also at my disposal were various materials
sent along by a Miss C.C., a Bibliographer, who hails, if I'm not
mistaken, from Indiana.

Second, the Doctor has begun a new book called BETTER
THAN SEX about the 1992 presidential campaign and is in pecuniary distress again. Indeed, he actually *lowered* himself into the
cesspool two days ago (by means of the automatic winch on his
Jeep) and said he had just seen a *Geraldo,* and people were getting
a good deal of money for white babies.

"Hell, Miss Tishy," he said excitedly. "We could sell them *our*
child."

"Fie! Fie!" I screamed, backing away from him.

I was wearing the mandatory crotchless black nylon stretchlace halter suspender catsuit with strategically placed cutouts,
front and back. And a pair of red plastic six-inch platform heels
with ankle straps, to protect my feet from the damp floor of my
asylum.

"We could make a lot of money!" said the Doctor. He carried
a half-gallon jug of Chivas in one hand and a bouquet of dragon
lilies in the other.

"Don't come a step closer!" I cried.

"Goddamn it!" said the Doctor. "A child of ours could fetch a
million fucking dollars!"

Two Dove Bars peeped out of the breast pockets of his plaid
shirt——his life is one long Dionysian ritual.

"I beseech you!" I cried.

"A guaranteed *brilliant* baby! Certifiably sired by a white
Southern gentleman, male model and Doctor of Journalism!"

At the word "sired," I became almost senseless with terror. I
would have certainly fainted had not the lid of the cesspool thirty
feet above me been open. As it was, I sank down on the wet floor.

"Hell!" said the Doctor, stooping over me and trying to lift my
head. "We could have a baby every year for six years! You
wouldn't mind being pregnant all the time, would you, Miss
Tishy?"

I half rose and embraced his knees while still on my own.

"Forbear! Forbear!" I cried.

"Jesus! One every year, for nine years!" yelled the Doctor, forcing me back on the floor and throwing himself on top of my stricken frame. "This is better than selling books!"

Now, whatever my trials have been——and I admit to the Doctor's gamahuching me till I was nearly dead with climaxing——I still considered myself, more or less, in the category of an honest girl. I wept, and wept unheeded.

Fire gleamed in the Doctor's eye. He ripped my catsuit down the front, licked my nascent bubbies, thrust my thighs apart, threw my ankles over his shoulders, lodged his doodle at my door, and thrust. Reader! His rammer was rigid enough to have gone through a bank door! But my threshold was too narrow for the Gonzo Ravisher's Titanic faculty. He swore. He screamed. His strugglings were God-like. I believe three or four cups would hardly have held his fiery discharge, which looked like nothing so much as a bucket of cream of wheat.

Yesterday, he returned and repeated the operation.

But enough. There are those who question the Doctor's health. It has been well known for centuries that peacock feathers cooked in clarified butter are efficacious against disease, and the bile of the peacock, when used in the preparation of *Mritasanji-vanayoga,* removes ALL poisons from the system. So, adieu, Reader! This recital of the crimes and follies of Hunter S. Thompson is nearly done. You who have wept for the unheard-of sufferings of poor Tishy, adieu!

C H A P T E R
TWENTY-ONE

The rest was dissipation.
—F. SCOTT FITZGERALD

1

—— Don't mention the drugs.

—— *Right,* Hunter. [Laughing]

—— You can't mention the drugs.

—— I'm going to write an entire book about you and never mention *the drugs?*

—— They'll read it and come and arrest me.

—— Good. [Laughing]

—— I'm serious!

—— Ha ha ha ha ha ha ha!

—— No drugs. [Scowling]

—HUNTER THOMPSON interview

I went to lunch with him recently at Jean Pierre's Restaurant, and I wouldn't want to be quoted on this, but when the waiter asked if we wanted a drink, I think Hunter said, "Two margaritas, a glass of wine and a bottle of beer." And there were three of us. So the waiter said, "You ordered four drinks, there's only three people here." And Hunter said, "Bring me the goddamned drinks! I don't know what these bastards want."

—SENATOR GEORGE MCGOVERN

It's not just that he's going to die. In fact, probably the worst thing is just that he will continue to live. The more you try to second-guess Hunter and analyze him, the more you look like a fool. He challenges death with a con man's instinct. He knows when to pull back.

—DAVID FELTON

These drugs are gonna get me. All of this shit's gonna get me, even these peacocks, and these eighty speakers, and these fires and these excesses . . . and this weed—boy, that's good weed. It's gonna get me some day, but we don't know when, do we?

—HUNTER THOMPSON, quoted by David Felton in
"Hunter Thompson Has Cashed His Check,"
Rolling Stone College Papers, Spring 1980

Humans are very resilient. People have been able to get away with what seems like massive, astonishingly dangerous use of drugs.

—JOHN P. MORGAN, M.D., Professor of
Pharmacology, City University of New York
Medical School; one of the world's most
respected experts in the pharmacology of
marijuana, heroine, cocaine and alcohol

He told me once he was having death fantasies. He always talks about going eighty miles an hour with his feet up driving off into the desert. That's interesting. To drive in a desert where if you go off the road, you can't get hurt. That's really what he's telling you. You go off the road, you can't get hurt. His favorite place is the flat. It's interesting. Hemingway's was the mountains. Hunter should be living in a flat area. He should be living in an adobe.

—GEORGE PLIMPTON

Remember acid is the most potent drug known to mankind. Acid is very, very effective. But people rapidly build a tolerance to it. Very few people actually hallucinate on acid. Very, very few. What happens is acid makes people feel good. It makes them euphoric. Sometimes it enables them to make funny connections and to feel very smart and very bright. People grow tolerant to acid very quickly.

Of all the drugs Hunter takes, acid is probably the least harmful. My guess is, Hunter's getting very little from it. When people start taking acid on a daily basis, they start getting lesser and lesser effects. So if he's taking small doses repeatedly, my guess is the acid is contributing very little.

—Dr. John P. Morgan

I run the Death Game. Hunter Thompson has been listed every year since 1971. The man has been flirting with the Grim Reaper for twenty-one years.

In the Death Game we have career statistics, complete stats. Instead of Rotisserie Baseball, it's Rotisserie Obituary. It's fun. Every year on January first, each player draws up a list of sixty people he thinks will die during the year. A player only scores if the deceased is written about on *The New York Times* obit page. Our address is Post Office Box 433, Syracuse, New York 13201.

The Death Game is like life insurance. Insurance actuaries will work out what you're doing to yourself and how it affects how long you're going to live. And you sort of bet against yourself. You buy insurance. And they say you're going to last so many years. In the Death Game we apply the same principles. If somebody is in a high-risk occupation, like race-car driving, and he drinks and he smokes, he's a higher level of assigned risk. And naturally he'll appear on more players' lists.

So Hunter S. Thompson's a perennial. There *are* people who think he's immortal. I mean, you've got people on one hand who think this guy is going to go any minute and there are other people who think, my God, he's lived this long, he's going to live forever.

But let's look at the risk factors in Hunter S. Thompson's life. Drinking. Drugs. Driving. And weapons. Any combination of those—see, he's off the chart. So he's either immortal, or he's going to die immediately. I mean, you know, we can't really find a middle ground.

> —EVAN NESCENT (does not wish his true name
> revealed; "We've always avoided the press. We
> don't want anybody famous to think that we're
> waiting for them to die.")

Hunter's very resilient. You see, cocaine, although it can make him crazy, and can raise his heartbeat and blood pressure, it's not terribly toxic and doesn't break down the cells of the body. Neither does acid. By and large, people get away with the use of cocaine for a long time without hurting the cells of the body. For years. Forever.

The nicotine affects the heart. It bumps the heart. The real danger of nicotine is that you fill your lungs with debris and there's a very high risk of pulmonary carcinoma. Of course, the most toxic substance Hunter takes is alcohol.

—DR. JOHN P. MORGAN

We all recognize he could fall down the stairs and break his neck. Or run one of his Chevrolets into a tree. Otherwise I think he'll be around a long time. Has he had any liver damage that you know of? The liver's such a recuperative, huge, marvelous, excessive organ. You only need about ten percent of it.

—SENATOR GEORGE McGOVERN

—— You're so sorrowful, Hunter.

—— Yeah.

—— So sad.

—— [He shakes his head.]

—— I am.

—— Anyone can see you are suffering greatly, Hunter.

—— Yeah.

—— You seem to be at your wits' end.

—— Yeah.

—— You're missing something or someone?

—— Yeah, that's about right.

—— Longing is written all over you.

—— Yeah.

—— Is it a woman?

—— I don't know.

—— For what or who, then?

—— I've always longed for the thing I cannot name.

—— Oh yes! The famous thing you cannot name!

—— That's it. I'm *always* looking.

—— Well, your *name* is Hunter.

——I've never found it. I don't know what it is. I don't know what to call it. But I long for it. And I always want it.

—HUNTER THOMPSON interview

Everybody is upset, of course. Jesus! You don't want the guy to check out. He's already on borrowed time, for Jesus sake. Bob Braudis and I talked about it a couple of years ago, about doing what they call an "intervention," or whatever you call that thing. Bob didn't want to have anything to do with it.

I discussed it with Hunter. I was doing a lot of stuff myself. I suggested that both of us go off to some detox somewhere and try to do it. I don't mean come out of there and be a bunch of AA guys, but at least give it a rest, and see what it all looks like from that view. And his interest level was higher than I thought. But it never came about. In the meantime, I gave up drinking on my own.

He threatened all his friends. "Any of you fuckers try and interfere with me or try to stop something, and you're not my friends anymore."

—MICHAEL SOLHEIM

2

He doesn't work hard enough. Terry McDonell gave him the chance to write a column for *Esquire*. "The End Page." Which is one of the greatest privileges you can have. He blew it. Why? A writer who is a true writer and in control of his craft is going to be able to do that. That's Hunter's great fault.

—GEORGE PLIMPTON

In my view, Hunter has become over the years what he would have considered the enemy when he was starting out. My impression is he's become a rich, gravy-sucking pig who doesn't care about his craft anymore.

I feel that he has been somewhat victimized by Jann and by his own celebrity. People nowadays accept *People* magazine as being some kind of word from on high. And it just ain't so. That shallow and superficial view of Hunter is symptomatic of why the country is in such a fucked-up mess as it is.

—GROVER LEWIS

Who else would have given Hunter the encouragement? The space? The complete freedom? Who else would have let him go on and on for ten thousand, fourteen thousand words? Not Harold Hayes [at *Esquire*]. *Playboy* was rejecting his stuff. Only Jann Wenner. Without Jann, Hunter would not have become Hunter.

—PORTER BIBB

Hunter wanted to be a serious writer. This cartoon embodiment was tailored for him and I think Hunter was Jann's patsy. It made him wealthy and made him very famous, but I think it hurt him. I think it ruined him as an artist, frankly.

—GROVER LEWIS

Hunter has been the most fascinating journalist of our period, starting with the motorcycle book. In terms of personal journalism, Hunter gave the lead. Personal journalism depends on the writer having an actual personality. In fact, it's quite rare. I always thought of Hunter as basically an artist, rather than a journalist. He created a new form. He had enormous influence.

—JIM HARRISON

I haven't found a drug yet that can get you anywhere near as high as sitting at a desk writing.

—HUNTER THOMPSON, quoted by William McKeen in *Hunter S. Thompson,* University of Florida, G. K. Hall & Co, 1990

I don't like to write. I don't care what the fuck happens after I write. Once I've gotten the story in my mind, the rest is pain.

—HUNTER THOMPSON, quoted by David Felton in "Hunter Thompson Has Cashed His Check"

One night at three-thirty in the morning I was trying to call a cab. Hunter kept putting his finger on the button and wouldn't let me dial. Finally I reached an Aspen cab company. A nice lady answered. "Send a taxi!" I cried. "OK, honey," said the lady, "where are you?" *"Where am I?"* I exclaimed, greatly confused. "Judas! I don't know what the name of the road is. I don't know exactly *where* I am. Just a minute. Where am I?"

"Are you at Hunter's?" said the lady.

—E. JEAN CARROLL

It hasn't helped a lot to be a savage comic-book character for the last fifteen years—a drunken screwball who should have been castrated a long time ago. The smart people in the media knew it was a weird exaggeration. The dumb ones took it seriously and warned their children to stay away from me at all costs. The *really* smart ones understood it was only a censored, kind of toned-down children's book version of the real thing.

—HUNTER THOMPSON, quoted by William McKeen
in *Hunter S. Thompson*

Awwww, it's tough. It's tough. Oh, my God, that's tough. Jesus, am I bleeding. Hunter has made himself a public personality. He has made himself, purposefully. He has been a public personality since the moment I met him. So it should not be any curiosity for him and his mentality that people come over and say, "You're Hunter Thompson." I know, I know, but he bitches and moans about everything, doesn't he? Hunter's been in torment from the beginning.

—GENE MCGARR

3

[Holding out a Nepalese prayer jar.] That's where I keep my prayers and my dreams. [He removes the lid.]

I have to keep the top on or my dreams and my prayers will escape.

[A long pause as he keeps the lid off.]

I am waiting for it to fill back up.

[Getting impatient, putting the lid back on.]

Well, for right now, prayers and dreams don't respect the simple laws of physics. They go right through.

—HUNTER THOMPSON interview

I suppose if you're as brilliant as Hunter is, you see lots of missed opportunities. Various lives that might have been. He might think that with a little more discipline he might have been Secretary of State or President of the United States. Or senator from—I don't know. Or another Thoreau. He might become that anyway. You know you don't have to write *ten* books.

—SENATOR GEORGE MCGOVERN

Hunter has a peculiar uniqueness. When he gets on what I think of as a stroke—when he's inside what the Spanish call his *querencia*, it just means when you find your strongest place—he's just extraordinary and writes with a fullness of energy that you rarely find. He can make everything connect whether it does or not.

He's said things that no one forgets. His first piece about Watergate. There's a quality of moral outrage there that he shared with Mailer. Hunter says, "When I heard the news I wanted to go down to the White House and throw a sack of dead rats over the fence." Now, that's class. The only proper response.

—JIM HARRISON

4

You think Hunter's had an effect on the younger generations? Really? When's the last civil disobedience you've seen? Do you know a lot of free spirits fooling around? Only aggressive lesbians are free. They're the only ones. They're the last free group of society. And they're so busy proselytizing that they haven't got time to be free.

—RICHARD GOODWIN, longtime friend of HST;
Special Counsel to John F. Kennedy; Robert
Kennedy campaign director; former political
editor of *Rolling Stone*; author of *Triumph or
Tragedy: Reflection on Vietnam, Remembering
America: A Voice from the Sixties*, etc.

A few months ago, he was staying over at the Ritz-Carlton, and he was in a real swanky suite up there. He had just tons of things around like stone crabs and lobsters, and thousands of margaritas. But he wanted to take Eleanor and me to dinner, so he invited us to come by his room first. And a young woman met us at the door. She said Hunter was taking a shower. And you know, I just assumed she was either his assistant or some friend or something. So we were seated and I asked her a couple of questions and she said, "Well, I just met Hunter a coupla hours ago—I don't know that much about him."

He came out of the shower, he wasn't even dry yet, but he had a big white towel on, and he gave Eleanor a big hug and got bathwater from his shower all over her dress. Then he shook off like a big bear. And he kind of scrutinized this young woman who was trying to serve us a drink. Like he wasn't sure who she was. What did she look like? She was a Republican speechwriter.

—SENATOR GEORGE MCGOVERN

Let's skip the sex. Let's talk straight literature. Hunter Thompson is a unique character of our times. He is a reality, which is one thing. And he is a symbol, which is another, totally different thing. And thirdly, he's both ultimately sane and crazy. He is also drunk and sober.

—DICK GOODWIN

Do you think he's enjoying it? Well then, you tell me what the screams are about. Everybody's heard Hunter's screams. Those screams are like an animal in the middle of the night in the middle of the veld. Those screams are screams of *happiness* and *joy*.

—DAVID FELTON

When he hits land it will be six feet under. He's immortal. Obviously. Otherwise he would have died long ago. At our wedding the doctor told him he would be dead in five years. That was twenty years ago. The doctor was one of the best doctors in Massachusetts.

—DICK GOODWIN

5

I'm thriving, living in California, very happily separated from my second husband. Juan graduated magna cum laude. He's a wonderful, wise person, and has a terrific girlfriend. I've asked Hunter a couple of times, "Well, did it turn out like you thought?" And he said, "No, but—" And he looked up at me with that charming smile and he said, "But it's been glamorous."

—SANDRA DAWN THOMPSON TARLO

Hunter represents freedom.

He has confidence, plus size, plus a certain undeniable fearlessness. We all have a kind of Peter Pan ideal in our lives when we're about twelve. We're going to do this, we're going to do that, and it gets beaten out of us. It gets beaten out of us sometime between puberty and our first job. People often regret the things they didn't do. Hunter is the alter ego who got to do *everything.*

—TIM CAHILL, friend of HST; contributing Editor at *Esquire* and *Rolling Stone*; author of *The Jaguars Ripped My Flesh, A Wolverine Is Eating My Leg,* etc.

Hunter called me last night and we talked about old times, his new girlfriend, Nicole, *everything*—it made me happy, very happy.

—JIM THOMPSON

Hunter Thompson has a cookie drawer where he keeps every kind of wonderful cookie you can think of, chocolate-chip walnut, peanut butter and macadamia, fancy ladyfingers, hazelnut lace, fat meringues, butternut sandies, coconut raisin macaroons——bags and bags and bags of them. And as they grow stale, he feeds them to the peacocks and replaces them with fresh cookies. I remember, as he was kicking me off the ranch——and dashing our beautiful future together——my one regret was that cookie drawer.

—E. JEAN CARROLL

I was in love with Hunter. I'll always be in love with Hunter. I was in love with him the day he threw my hat into the mud. I feel like when Hunter dies it's going to be—"Gosh, it's really the end." I can't put into words what I'm trying to say. It's kind of like as long as Hunter is around, everything is OK. When Hunter dies, then we're *all* old.

— "GINNY DANIALS," childhood friend of HST

I was fifteen or sixteen when I first read *Fear and Loathing in Las Vegas.* A lot of us were looking for somebody to ally with. And here's Hunter S. Thompson coming from Louisville, kind of a big brother. He didn't give a shit, drank his bourbon, smoked his cigarettes and ate his drugs in the face of everyone.

The whole thing about Hunter S. was that you didn't want to idolize him too much, because then you felt like if you ever met him, to idolize him would be almost to cheapen him.

So you almost took an opinion about Hunter S., "Oh, he's just one of us." Because somehow if you're like Hunter S. Thompson you know a little bit more about what's going on than just about everybody else you run into. He gave us an outline for the way our lives could be. He gave us a bit of a sarcastic edge. Hunter S. taught us to "DO WHAT YOU CAN GET AWAY WITH. AND ALWAYS BE SHARP ABOUT IT."

But let's not get too confused about this hero thing. Because Hunter S. Thompson is a mythical being. He's not a hero. He's a mythical being. Am I ready to hand Hunter S. on to my kids when I have them? Oh, absolutely! Absolutely!

— YOUNG LOUISVILLE ARCHITECT

So we shall let the reader answer the question for himself. Who is the happier man, he who has braved the storm of life and lived, or he who has stayed securely on shore and merely existed?

— HUNTER THOMPSON (written at age 16)

C H A P T E R
TWENTY-TWO

Good-bye—Good-bye.
—EDITH WHARTON

Famed Gonzo Journalist Grows New Liver

"He'll Live Forever," Say Doctors

Aspen, Colo., Feb. 29 (AP)—Hunter S. Thompson, the whiskey-drinking, womanizing, drug-taking outlaw writer, who for a quarter of a century has astounded medical experts by not dropping dead, solved the mystery yesterday at a press conference held at the Woody Creek Tavern in Woody Creek.

"Thompson has grown a completely new liver," said Dr. Bradley Hollingsworth, dean of the Indiana University Medical School and one of the world's foremost liver experts. Dr. Hollingsworth examined Thompson with a team of 31 American and European specialists. "There is evidence which leads us to suspect

that this is not the *first* liver Thompson has sprouted,"
Dr. Hollingsworth said. "It could be his third or fourth."

Thompson, who recently married his biographer,
Laetitia Snap, was too drunk to comment.

"He'll outlive us all," said Dr. Hollingsworth with a
nervous smile. Snap and Thompson are expecting their
first child in September.

SELECTED ANNOTATED BIBLIOGRAPHY OF WORKS BY AND ABOUT HUNTER S. THOMPSON

BY

CANDE CARROLL

CONTENTS

Books by Hunter S. Thompson

Hell's Angels: The Strange and Terrible Saga of the Outlaw Motorcycle Gang, New York, Random House; 1966

Fear and Loathing in Las Vegas; A Savage Journey to the Heart of the American Dream, New York, Random House; 1971

Fear and Loathing: on the Campaign Trail '72, San Francisco, Straight Arrow Books; 1973

Gonzo Papers, Vol. 1; The Great Shark Hunt; Strange Tales from a Strange Time, New York, Summit Books; 1979

The Curse of Lono, New York, Bantam; 1983 (with Ralph Steadman)

Generation of Swine; Gonzo Papers, Vol. 2: Tales of Shame and Degradation in the '80's, New York, Summit Books; 1988

Songs of the Doomed; More Notes on the Death of the American Dream. Gonzo Papers: Vol. 3, New York, Summit Books; 1990

Major Magazine Pieces, Newspaper Editorials, and Newspaper/Magazine Columns by Hunter S. Thompson *(in loose chronological order)*

Southern Star

Walter Kaegi, editor. Various columns and articles; 1947–1949

The Spectator

Athenaeum Literary Association; 1954 & 1955 *Open Letter to the Youth of Our Nation*; p. 23

Security; p. 49

Eglin Air Force Base Command Courier

The Spectator Weekly sports column and sports articles; 8/3/56 - 8/15/57

The Royal Gazette Weekly (Bermuda)

They Hoped to Reach Spain But Are Stranded in Bermuda; Trip of Americans Left Virgin Islands Three Weeks Ago; 7/10/60, p. 10 (interviews strongly suggest the article was written by HST. But the article "appears" to have been written by a Royal Gazette staff writer)

Chicago Tribune

California's Big Sur Lures Tourists to Solitude; 3/26/61, p. VI-6

Renfro Valley (Sunday Tribune); 2/18/62

Reporter

Southern City with Northern Problems; 12/19/63, pp. 26–29

National Observer

'Leery Optimism' at Home for Kennedy Visitor; 6/24/62, p. 11 (on President Valencia of Colombia)

Nobody Is Neutral Under Aruba's Hot Sun; 7/16/62, p. 14

A Footloose American in a Smugglers' Den; 8/6/62, p. 13 (smuggling from Aruba to Colombia, w/photos by HST)

Democracy Dies in Peru, But Few Seem to Mourn Its Passing; 8/27/62, p. 16 (Aftermath of Peruvian election w/photos by HST)

How Democracy is Nudged Ahead in Ecuador; 9/17/62, p. 13

Ballots in Brazil Will Measure the Allure of Leftist Nationalism; 10/1/62

Operation Triangular: Bolivia's Fate Rides With It; 10/15/62; p. 13

Uruguay Goes to Polls, With Economy Sagging; 11/19/62, p. 14

Chatty Letters During a Journey from Aruba to Rio; 12/31/62, p. 14 (correspondence, with HST sometimes begging for money, between HST and his editor)

Troubled Brazil Holds Key Vote; 1/7/63, pp. 1, 10

It's a Dictatorship, but Few Seem to Care Enough to Stay and Fight; 1/28/63, p. 17 (Paraguay's upcoming election)

Brazilian Soldiers Stage a Raid in Revenge; 2/11/63, p. 13

Leftist Trend and Empty Treasury Plague the Latin American Giant; 3/11/63, p. 11 (Economy post-election in Brazil)

A Never-Never Land High Above the Sea (Bolivia); 4/15/63, p. 11

Election Watched as Barometer of Continent's Anti-Democratic Trend; 5/20/63, p. 12

A Time for Sittin', Laughin', and Reverie; 6/3/63, p. 16 (folk festival in Covington, Kentucky)

What Lured Hemingway to Ketchum?; 5/25/64, pp. 1, 13

Whither the Old Copper Capital of the West? To Boom or Bust; 6/1/64, p. 3 (thoughts on the future of Butte, Montana)

The Atmosphere Has Never Been Quite the Same; 6/15/64, p. 1, 16 (awakening campus movement in the U.S.; Missoula, Montana)

Why Montana's 'Shanty Irishman' Corrals Votes Year After Year; 6/22/64, p. 12

Living in the Time of Alger, Greeley, Debs; 7/13/64, pp. 1, 16 (dateline: Pierre, South Dakota; men HST's met on the road)

Bagpipes Wail, Cabers Fly as the Clans Gather; 9/14/64, p. 12

You'd Be Fried Like a Piece of Lean Bacon; 9/28/64, pp. 1, 19 (forest fires in California in late summer, 1964)

People Want Bad Taste . . . In Everything; 11/2/64, p. 1, 15 (influx of topless joints in North Beach, San Francisco)

A Surgeon's Fingers Fashion a Literary Career; 12/21/64, p. 17

The Nation
Motorcycle Gangs; 5/17/65, pp. 522–6

Nonstudent Left; 9/27/65, pp. 154–8

Spider Magazine
Collect Telegram from a Mad Dog; 10/13/65 (poem)

The Distant Drummer
Obituary of Lionel Olay, The Ultimate Free Lancer; 1967

Pageant
Why Boys Will Be Girls; 8/67, pp. 94–101

Presenting: The Richard Nixon Doll; 7/68, pp. 6–16

Those Daring Young Men in Their Flying Machines; 9/69, pp. 68–78

The New York Times

Hashbury is Capital of Hippies; 5/14/67, p. 28

Fear and Loathing in the Bunker; 1/1/74, p. 19

Scanlan's Monthly

Letter to Warren about Jean Claude Killy Playboy Piece

The Temptations of Jean Claude Killy; 3/70 (vol 1, no 1), pp. 89–100

The Kentucky Derby is Decadent and Depraved; 6/70, pp. 1–12

Police Chief-The Indispensable Magazine of Law Enforcement; 9/70

Rolling Stone

#67 *The Battle of Aspen* (HST's run for sheriff); 10/1/70

#81 *Strange Rumblings in Aztlan* (Ruben Salazar); 4/29/71

#90 *Memo From the Sports Desk: The So-Called 'Jesus Freak Scare'* by Raoul Duke; 9/2/71

#95 *Fear and Loathing in Las Vegas: A Savage Journey to the Heart of the American Dream* by Raoul Duke; 11/11/71

#96 (continuation of) *Fear and Loathing in Las Vegas;* 11/25/71

#99 *Fear & Loathing in Washington: Is this Trip Necessary?;* 1/6/72

#101 *Fear and Loathing in Washington: The Million Pound Shithammer;* 2/3/72

#104 *Fear and Loathing: The View from Key Biscayne* (on Nixon); 3/16/72

#106 *Fear and Loathing: The Banshee Screams in Florida;* 4/13/72

#107 *Fear and Loathing in Wisconsin;* 4/27/72

#108 *Fear and Loathing: Late News from Bleak House;* 5/11/72

#110 *Fear and Loathing: Crank-Time on the Low Road* (Nebraska primary); 6/8/73

#112 *Fear and Loathing in California: Traditional Politics with a Vengeance;* 7/6/72

#113 *Fear and Loathing: In the Eye of the Hurricane;* 7/20/72

#115 *Fear and Loathing in Miami: Old Bulls Meet the Butcher* (Democratic convention); 8/17/72

HST was media critic beginning in 1985. When his *San Francisco Examiner* columns were reprinted in *Generation of Swine* and *Songs of the Doomed*, changes were made in headline wording and punctuation and sometimes body copy. The following citations are taken as the articles appeared originally in the *Examiner*

Revenge of the fish heads (Neil Frank, director of Hurricane Center and friends of Robert Vesco); 12/3/85

Saturday night in the City; 12/9/85

A generation of swine; 12/16/85

Apre moi, la deluge (the shock of Ted Kennedy's impending withdrawal); 12/23/85

The dim and dirty road (Ted Kennedy's bad driving and HST's too); 12/30/85

Off with their heads (Ted Kennedy withdraws, Hart in?); 1/6/86

How do you spell Hitler? (Khadafy, Castro and Selassie); 1/13/86

Crank time in Tripoli (Ricky Nelson's Death and Khadafy); 1/20/86

Nothing's moving on Lincoln Avenue (Reporting on the Super Bowl from Chicago); 1/26/86

Meat sickness (more on the Super Bowl); 1/27/86

Last train from Chicago; 2/3/86

Kill them before they eat (various news items including Haiti); 2/10/86

Four million thugs (Baby Doc flees Haiti); 2/17/86

Memo from the war room (bad business in the Philippines); 2/24/86

The Gonzo Salvage Co. (hiring a 36-ft. Cigarette boat on Sugarloaf Key); 3/3/86

Salvage is not looting (HST's in the Marine Salvage Business); 3/10/86

Dawn at the Boca Chica; 3/17/86

Let the cheap dogs eat (the pitbull dogfighting business); 3/24/86

Ox butchered in Tripoli ('Reagan' painted on ox's side); 3/31/86

Never get off the boat (cattle farming and snowed in at Denver's airport); 4/7/86

They called him Deep Throat (Khadafy, Pat Robertson and Watergate); 4/14/86

The pro-flogging view (letter to Steadman on raising children); 4/21/86

Just another terrorist (Marcos); 4/28/86

The woman from Kiev ("*some*" woman reported 2,000 dead at Chernobyl); 5/5/86

Two more years (V.P. Bush's upcoming run for President); 5/12/86

They all drowned (various subjects including draining Colombian Lagoon); 5/19/86

Four more games (NBA, Meese's war on Pornography, *Post*'s CIA article); 5/26/86

Last dance in dumb town (selling motorcycle at Woody Creek Tavern); 6/2/86

Rise of the TV preachers (Pat Robertson moving into national politics); 6/9/86

Dealing with pigs (The Meese Report on pornography); 6/16/86

Deported to Malaysia (wealthy elderly Chinese suicidal gentleman); 6/23/86

A clean, ill-lighted place (10th annual Erotic Film Awards); 6/30/86

Slow day at the airport (4th of July flight, San Francisco to Denver); 7/7/86

Lester Maddox lives (Meese pornography report and Maddox); 7/14/86

Sex, drugs and rock and roll (The Meese Report); 7/21/86

Dr. Thompson's odds for '88 race; Campaign '88: The early line; 8/4/86

Welcome to the tunnel (the President uses only *legal* drugs); 8/11/86

Strictly business (Rehnquist confirmation and need for new prisons); 8/18/86

Midnight in the desert (Conversation at Phoenix airport bar); 8/25/86

Showdown in the pig palace (laying odds on upcoming Senate races); 9/1/86

Down to a sunless sea (drugs/booze in Alaska, powermongers, dope fiends); 9/8/86

The Turk comes to TV news (interview with CNN's Ed Turner); 9/15/86

Bull market on The Strip (HST in Las Vegas picks up a few items at the Soldier of Fortune trade show and exhibition); 9/22/86

The South African problem (bill imposing sanctions against South Africa); 9/29/86

Loose cannon on the deck (South African sanctions and Iceland summit); 10/6/86

Let the good times roll (from Bernard Kalb to Oswald to Arafat); 10/13/86

A death in the family (all about the red fox); 10/20/86

The garden of agony (a busy week for politics); 11/3/86

Back to the Ormsby House (HST's Senate calls were startlingly accurate); 11/5/86

The white helicopter (HST's mail on the Red Fox question, and how the wife of French bank robber Michel Vaujour masterminded his escape from LaSante prison); 11/10/86

White trash with money (death of Don Boles, *Arizona Republic* reporter); 11/17/86

A night at the track (Greyhound racing in Phoenix); 11/24/86

The Lord and a good lawyer (Democrats' political strategy); 11/30/86

Ronald Reagan is doomed (fallout from the 'Iranian Transaction'); 12/8/86

God bless Colonel North (on Khashoggi and international arms trade); 12/15/86

Orgy of the dead (what it took to blow up the Jeep); 12/22/86

The year of the pig (no White House arrests over Christmas); 12/29/86

Mixup at the hospital (Sam Donaldson or Reagan, What will '87 be like?); 1/5/87

The gizzard of darkness (the Iran/Nicaragua scandal and the psychic); 1/12/87

Crazy Patrick and Big Al (odds on the '88 Republican ticket); 1/19/87

Trapped in Harding Park (Betting on the Broncos with barroom 'friend'); 1/26/87

The great white hope (on the next two years of madness on the political front. The new line and the field); 2/2/87

Expelled from the system (hazards that plague this generation); 2/9/87

Gone With the Wind (parallels between Watergate and Iran/contra toxin; 2/16/87

New blood on the tracks (Fitzwater and White House Press Secretaries); 2/23/87

The Lake of Fire (Bush replaced by Baker as GOP frontrunner); 3/2/87

Doomed love in the Rockies (HST misses Reagan press conference to help a sick neighbor); 3/23/87

The scum of the earth (TV preachers: Jim and Tammy Bakker and PTL Club); 3/30/87

The Losers' Club (Reagan, Mary Beth Whitehead, Dwight Gooden; US Embassy in Moscow security guards); 4/6/87

Hagler lacked buoyancy (Hagler loses fight in Las Vegas and Al Campanis leaves baseball); 4/13/87

The Loved Ones (John Hinckley and various other subjects); 4/20/87

The Death Ship (the international garbage crisis, National Waste); 4/27/87

The American Dream (Gary Hart labeled a sex fiend); 5/4/87

Caligula & the 7 Dwarfs (update on Democratic presidential hopefuls); 5/11/87

Memo to my editor (John Ehrlichman/Herbert Kalmbach transcript); 5/18/87

The time of the geek (how Gary Hart was *really* caught with seven women); 5/25/87

A wild and crazy guy (orgy at Bush's residence; arcade voter data from Pat Caddell); 6/1/87

Ollie's choice (second stage of Iran/contra hearings about to start); 6/15/87

The trickle-down theory (the Tower Report, the legacy of Ronald Reagan); 6/23/87

Four more years (electoral votes, who can count on what); 6/29/87

Dance of the Seven Dwarfs (PBS Democratic debate, William Buckley monitor); 7/6/87

It was you, Charlie (lunch at Woody Creek Tavern watching the hearings); 7/13/87

Fat men on horseback (Iran/contra players); 7/20/87

Cowboys at sea (Congress gets a new hero, George Shultz); 7/27/87

The honor of Dead Bill (interviews with Ed Meese); 8/3/87

The Last Taxi to Scotland (HST and Maria's horrific taxi ride to Denver for trip to Scotland for British motorcyclists speech at the Edinburgh Book Fair); 8/17/87

Gary Hart talks politics; 9/7/87

Swine of the week; 9/14/87

Here come de judge (on Bork's nomination to Supreme Court and Biden giving up his bid for president); 9/21/87

Wooing the degenerate vote (Nixon-Haig parlay for '88 looks strong); 9/28/87

The weak and the weird (V.P. Bush's European tour and Democratic field); 10/5/87

The time has come (Bush popularity, Bork defeat, Joe Biden revenge); 10/12/87

The worm turns (cancellation of Gorbachev's visit to Washington); 10/26/87

Never apologize, never explain (Reagan nominates Douglas Ginsburg for Supreme Court); 11/2/87

The end of an era (Reagan only has one year left as president); 11/16/87

The Continental Op (on Continental Airways and its operational reputation); 11/23/87

The waiver wire (the new wave of the future in the National Football League); 11/30/87

Pigs in the wilderness (an evening in Milwaukee); 12/14/87

They laughed at Thomas Edison, too (Gary Hart's return); 12/16/87

Back in the saddle again (Hart is back in but . . .); 12/22/87

Remembering Oscar; 12/28/87

Just say yes (comparing Ed Meese to Hermann Goering); 1/11/88

Acid Flashback No. 327 (Jimmy the Greek fired from CBS and HST offered the job); 1/18/88

The hangman cometh (Evan Meecham arraigned in Phoenix); 1/25/88

The wimp croaks in Iowa (on the dim fate of Jesse Jackson); 2/8/88

The fat is in the fire (HST compares his interest levels in Basketball and low-rent politics); 2/15/88

The seas of politics often lead to silliness (Bush picks Dan Quayle as running mate); 8/21/88, p. A–14

President Quayle?; 8/22/88

Weird today, gone tomorrow (obituary for Edward Bennett Williams, lawyer; and HST rumored to have been asked to be Dukakis' senior media consultant); 9/12/88

Post-hypnotic transgressions (comments on HST's criminal nature; then on to political comments); 9/19/88

Bush's big deal: Just a slip of the tongue? (Bush-Dukakis debate roundup); 9/27/88

There's no pulse (the campaign continues; The Great Debate turned out to be a false alarm); 10/3/88

When Quayle wrapped himself in JFK's mantle (the Quayle-Bentsen debate); 10/6/88

The meaning of life in 250 words; 10/10/88 (two versions, 10/10 & 10/11)

No hits, no errors in debate (PBS Bush/Dukakis debate and pre-debate Goldwater/McGovern election comments; also includes "Letter to the President"); 10/14/88

Last train from Camelot (with) I slit my own eyeballs (how HST wasn't heard from during the final days of the campaign); 11/7/88

The New Dumb ("the Democrats appear to be doomed"); 11/22/88

They also serve, who only stand and feed ("It was a pretty dull year to be a loser"); 12/6/88

Love in the age of greed (is Cromwell suicidal or insane?); 12/13/88

Year of the alligator (driving in the South; and Reagan's fun time in the White House); 12/21/88

Let's you and him fight (Bush just before inauguration; Gadhafi, Colonel North); 1/9/89

Fear & Loathing in Sacramento (gang-rape or birthday party at Ricci's); 1/30/89 (projected chapter in *Polo Is My Life*)

Strange ride to Reno (on the road with Jilly after escaping Sacramento); 2/6/89 (projected chapter in *Polo Is My Life*)

Omnia vincit amor (on the road with Jilly listening to George Bush on the radio); 2/13/89 (projected chapter in *Polo Is My Life*)

The death of Russell Chatham ("greatly exaggerated"); 2/27/89

Whiskey business (apologies for spreading the unfounded story about Chatham; and Bush rep calls offering HST John Tower's Secretary of Defense job); 3/6/89

I knew her when she used to rock & roll (the new wave of "rigid, Boy in the Bubble zeal that is sweeping the nation today"); 3/13/89

Another vicious attack (HST on medical leave in New Orleans from rabid animal bites, probably a huge red fox); 4/3/89

No more Semper Fi (on Spiro Agnew's legal difficulties); 4/10/89

Don't tread on me (on Alfred Nobel, bombs and bombing the Jeep); 5/22/89

Let the hundred flowers bloom (on Fred Astaire and Charles Atlas; and Raoul Duke being expelled from China); 5/29/89

(Chinese headline) (on Alfred E. Neuman's friendships with people in high places in Washington); 6/26/89

The bull market (HST and his polo-friend Avery order a p-51 Mustang); 7/31/89 (Avery might reappear in *Polo Is My Life*)

Welcome to the Abyssal Zone (on U.S. military power and studying up on the p-51 Mustang); 8/7/89

Nightmare on Thunder Road (Cromwell's problems after killing a gigantic attacking Quill Pig, and about Hatfield, the developer); 8/30/89

The rich are still hungry; 9/25/89

The German decade (Cromwell and the Nazis); 11/20/89

Medical bulletin #666—we think (HST recovering from being run over by a tractor pulling a Bush-Hog); 2/5/90

Boston Globe

Memoirs of a Wretched Weekend in Washington; 2/23/69, pp. 6–11

No Paranoia/Mecham; 1/27/88, p. 19

Robertson May Put Fat on Fire; 2/17/88, p. 17

A Blaze of Gibberish on Bush; 3/24/88, p. 15

Wearing the McGovern Tatoo; 3/30/88, p. 19

Sorting out the Weird Ones; 5/25/88, p. 19

Esquire

Lifestyles: The Cyclist; 1/67, pp. 57–63

Year of the Wolf; 2/91, p. 132

Where Were You When the Fun Stopped?; 3/91, p. 171

Death of a Sportsman (obituary, Peter Axthelm); 4/91, p. 152

London Observer

Fear and loathing at the Palace; 10/4/92, magazine section (on the state of the United Kingdom's Royal Family)

Selected Manuscripts, Monographs, Tapes, Films, Dramatic Presentations, and Art Exhibits by and about Hunter S. Thompson

Prince Jellyfish (novel excerpted in *Songs of the Doomed*); 1958/1959

The Rum Diary (novel excerpted in *Songs of the Doomed*); 1960/1961

Travelin' Lady Sorrels, Rosalie; on Sire (Polydor) Liner notes by Hunter S. Thompson; 8/71

The Aspen Wallposters Thomas Benton, artist/HST editor. Eight Wallposters were eventually published; 1970/71

America Steadman, Ralph; Straight Arrow Books, San Francisco. Introduction by Hunter S. Thompson; 1974

Fear and Laughter Stout, William (a comic book about HST's adventures); Krupp Comic Works, Kitchen Sink Enterprises, Princeton, Wisconsin; 1977

To Aspen and Back Clifford, Peggy; St. Martin's Press, New York. Introduction by Hunter S. Thompson; 1980

Where the Buffalo Roam, Universal Studios. Art Linson, Director; written by John Kaye; with Bill Murray and Peter Boyle (a movie based on the twisted legend of Dr. Hunter S. Thompson); opened 4/25/80

Fear and Loathing: On the Road to Hollywood Made for BBC. Shown in a series, as insight into "The American Dream Through the Hollywood Lens and the Journalist's Pen" on New York's Channel 13; 11/23/80

Hunter S. Thompson Reads his Songs of the Doomed; Simon & Schuster Audio, New York; 1990

Aspen Art Gallery; Mary Grasso, owner; 12-piece exhibit of HST art; 11/91.

Fear and Loathing in Las Vegas stage production, New Crime Productions, At the Gallery, Chicago. Co-director with Steve Pink and Producer John Cusack. With Jeremy Pivan as Dr. Gonzo. Adapted by Lou Stein. (adaptation first presented in London, 1982); 11/4/91–1/4/92

Soundbites From the Counter Culture (Atlantic)
Selections on the issue of free speech from HST, Burroughs, Henry Rollins, Jim Carroll, Biafra and others; 1990

Murder in High Places NBC 2-hour pilot movie (to be called "Out of Season") by John Byrum and Stan Rogow; Ted Levine as HST-like character; 6/9/91

MTV, "Twenty-five Years of *Rolling Stone*"; 11/18/92 (documentary celebrating magazine's anniversary)

ABC News, "PrimeTime Live: Down and Out in Aspen"; 2/27/92

An American Odyssey; Art Across America inspired in part by Jack Kerouac's Novel "On the Road," a Hofstra University History Course, 6-week road trip reading Whitman, HST and others; Sprint/92

Entertainment Tonight; 7:25 EST, 8/31/92 (HST, Greider, O'Rourke and Wenner interview Clinton for *Rolling Stone* magazine)

Biographies about Hunter S. Thompson

McKeen, William *Hunter S. Thompson* G.K. Hall, Boston; 1991

Perry, Paul *Fear and Loathing* Thunder's Mouth Press, New York; 1993

Snap, Laetitia, PhD *The Life of Hunter Stockton Thompson* Dutton, New York; 1993
   "By far the greatest American biography of the Twentieth Century."

Whitmer, Peter *When the Weird Turn Pro* Hyperion, New York; 1993

Selected Important Biographical and Literary Treatments of Hunter S. Thompson

Acosta, Oscar Zeta *The Autobiography of a Brown Buffalo* Straight Arrow Books, San Francisco; 1972

Anson, Robert Sam *Gone Crazy and Back Again* Doubleday, New York; 1981
"His curse was to be an old-fashioned moralist trapped in a world that, by its very immorality, continually threatened to destroy him."

Baldwin, Daniel R. *Thompson Hunting: A Search for Hunter Thompson, a Quest for the American Dream* MA Thesis, University of Iowa; 1983

Bradbury, Malcolm *The Modern American Novel*, Oxford University Press, Oxford/New York; 1983

Beave, H. *Great American Masquerade* Vision, London; 1985

Brownmiller, Susan *Against Our Will* Simon and Schuster, New York; 1975
"Years later, when he had quit mythologizing the Angels and had embarked on a more satisfying career of mythologizing himself through semifictional political-campaign reportage, the Prince of Gonzo told a fellow reporter, 'You know I was a real juvenile delinquent . . . got picked up on a phony rape charge, all that.' Out of this sort of stuff the image of the heroic male is formed."

Buhle, Paul *Popular Culture in America* Univ. Minn. Press; 1987

Conover, Ted *Whiteout, Lost in Aspen* Random House, New York; 1991
"Though the weather was warm and [Hunter] did not seem to have a cold, his nose ran constantly, in the thin, water way children of the eighties will recognize; Maria would reach over to wipe it dry for him."

Crouse, Timothy *Boys on the Bus* Random House, New York; 1972
"Standing outside the press room in the late afternoon, Hunter Thompson told Bob Semple how appalling it was to observe the White House Press, even for a few hours. 'They're like slugs on a snail farm,' he said, taking a nervous puff on his cigarette holder. 'Jesus, Ziegler treats them like garbagemen and they just take it."

Dickstein, Morris *Gates of Eden, American Culture in the Sixties* Basic Books, New York; 1977

Draper, Robert *Rolling Stone Magazine: The Uncensored History* Doubleday, New York; 1990
"Gonzo," Hunter Thomspon mutters, and shakes his great bald head. "Sometimes I wish I'd never heard of the goddamned word."—Draper

Gitlin, Todd *The Sixties; Years of Hope, Days of Rage* Bantam, New York; 1987

Hellmann, John *Corporate Fiction, Private Fable* (n.d.)

———— *Fables of Fact* Univ. Illinois Press, Urbana; 1981
"Thompson's self-caricature is a paradox of compulsive violence and outraged innocence, an emblem of the author's schizophrenic view of America." (on *Fear and Loathing in Las Vegas*)

Hollowell, John *Fact & Fiction, The New Journalism and the Nonfiction Novel* Univ. North Carolina Press, Chapel Hill; 1977

Johnson, Michael L. *The New Journalism* Kansas Univ. Press; 1971
"Thompson's book [Hell's Angels] is an especially significant document of the New Journalism, because it came about in large part because of his desire to correct the reportage of the established media, to get close to a way of life and write about it as it really was."—Johnson

Klinkowitz, Jerome *The Life of Fiction* Univ. Illinois Press, Urbana; 1977
"The quick cut, the strategic use of digression, the ability to propel himself through a narrative like a stunt driver, steering with the skids so that the most improbable intentions result in the smoothest maneuvers, the attitude of having one's personal craziness pale before the ludicrousness which passes for the normal in contemporary American life—on all these counts Thompson and Vonnegut share a basic affinity."

———— *The New American Novel of Manners: The Fiction of Richard Yates, Dan Wakefield, Thomas McGuane:* Univ. Georgia Press, Athens; 1986

Mailer, Norman *The Fight* Little, Brown, Boston; 1975

McRoach, J. J. *A Dozen Dopey Yarns. Tales from the Pot Prohibition Mandraxed Wombats and the Monster in Room 450* Australian Marijuana Party, Globe Press; 1979 (HST's visit to Australia)

Meyers, Paul Thomas *The New Journalist as Culture Critic* MA Thesis, Washington State University; 1983

Perry, James M. *Us and Them: How the Press Covered the 1972 Election* Potter, New York; 1973

Plimpton, George *Shadow Box* Putnam's, New York; 1977
"With him he carried a large leather flight bag with a *Rolling Stone* decal and a badge which read PRESS; he referred to it sometimes as his 'purse' and often as his 'kit'—full of pills and phials and bottles, judging from the way it clinked when he moved it."

Reeves, Richard *Convention* Harcourt Brace Jovanovich, New York; 1977

Scanlon, Paul *Reporting; The Rolling Stone Style* Anchor Press, New York; 1977
"Much of what Hunter reports, those events which seem most telling, just would not have happened had Hunter not been there. 'I like to get right in the middle of whatever I'm writing about,' he says, 'as personally involved as possible.' "

Smith, Adam (pseud of George J. Goodman) *Power of Mind,* Random House, New York; 1975

Steadman, Ralph *Scar Strangled Banger* Salem House, Topsfield, Mass.; 1987

Thompson, Toby *The 60's Report* Rawson, Wade Publishers, Inc., New York; 1979
"Hunter . . . had become culture hero to the sort of fraternity goons he regularly crucified in *Rolling Stone.*"

Trudeau, G. B. *The Doonesbury Chronicles,* Holt, Rinehart and Winston, New York; 1975

———— *Wouldn't a Gremlin Have Been More Sensible?* Holt, Rinehart and Winston, New York; 1974, 1975

———— *An Especially Tricky People* Holt, Rinehart and Winston, New York; 1975, 76, 77

———— *Stalking the Perfect Tan* Holt, Rinehart and Winston, New York; 1977, 1978

———— *"Any Grooming Hints for Your Fans, Rollie?"* Holt, Rinehart and Winston, New York; 1977, 1978

———— *"But the Pension Fund Was Just Sitting There"* Holt, Rinehart and Winston, New York; 1978, 1979

———— *We're Not Out of the Woods Yet* Holt, Rinehart and Winston, New York; 1978, 1979

———— *The People's Doonesbury, Notes from Underfoot, 1978–1989* Holt, Rinehart and Winston, New York; 1978, 79, 80

—— *"Speaking of inalienable rights, Amy ..."* Holt, Rinehart and Winston, New York; 1976

—— *And That's My Final Offer!* Holt, Rinehart and Winston, New York; 1979, 1980

—— *Ask for May, Settle for June* Holt, Rinehart and Winston, New York; 1981, 1982

—— *That's Doctor Sinatra, You Little Bimbo* Holt, Rinehart and Winston, New York; 1986

—— *Action Figure; The Adventures of Doonesbury's Uncle Duke* Andrews and McMell Publishers, Kansas City, MO.; 1992

Wallechinksy, David *The Book of Lists* Morrow, New York; 1977, pp. 245, 404

"12 Writers Who Ran (Unsuccessfully) for Public Office

John Greenleaf Whittier, 1842	*Victor Hugo, 1848*
Henry George, 1886	*Jack London, 1905*
H. G. Wells, 1921 and 1922	*Upton Sinclair, 1934*
Gore Vidal, 1960	*James Michener, 1962*
William F. Buckley, 1965	*Norman Mailer, 1969*
Jimmy Breslin, 1969	*Hunter S. Thompson, 1970"*

Wenner, Jann *20 Years of Rolling Stone; What A Long, Strange Trip It's Been* Straight Arrow Publishers, New York; 1987
"The first time I met Hunter S. Thompson, he arrived in my office, two hours late, wearing a curly, bubble-style wig and carrying a six-pack of beer in one hand and his leather satchel stuffed with notebooks, newspapers, tape recorders, booze, et cetera, in the other. He was wearing the wig during his bid to become sheriff of Pitkin County, Colorado."

Whitmer, Peter O. *Aquarius Revisited* Macmillan, New York; 1987

Witcover, Jules *Marathon: The Pursuit of the Presidency* Viking, New York; 1977

Wolfe, Tom *The New Journalism* Harper & Row, New York; 1973
"But the all-time free-lance writer's Brass Stud Award went that year [1966] to an obscure California journalist named Hunter Thompson, who 'ran' with the Hell's Angels for eighteen months—as a reporter and not a member, which might have been safer—in order to write *Hell's Angels: The Strange and Terrible Saga of the Outlaw Motorcycle Gangs.*' "

———— *The Electric Kool-Aid Acid Test* Farrar, Straus and Giroux, New York; 1968

Selected Major Magazine Interviews with and Stories about Hunter S. Thompson

College Papers

Felton, David *Hunter Thompson Has Cashed His Check*; Spring/80

Esquire

Salisbury, Harrison E. *Travels through America*; 2/76
    "You know when the last bomb goes off and the last cypress tree falls in the last mud bog there'll still be some, you know, weak, ugly, human voice saying, wait a minute, I'm here. I don't know—it's still in my interest to believe that right now. And that we're totally doomed, which I do on one level. But I think there's a perversity in people that I kind of like and have great faith in."—HST

Lemann, Nicholas *The New Hunter Thompson Stands Up*; 9/79

High Times

Rosenbaum, Ron *Hunter Thompson; The good doctor tells all . . . about Carter, cocaine, adrenaline and the birth of Gonzo journalism*; 9/77
    "When I arrived on board the huge yacht, I found Thompson ensconced on the command deck, munching on a handful of psilocybin pills and regarding the consternation of the snooty Newport sailing establishment with amusement."

Stratton, Richard *Hunter Thompson The Last Outlaw* cover; 8/91
    "Some theorize that the Thompson persona is theater. No one, they argue, could be this crazy and live to write about it. But what Dr. Thompson is really up to is Life as Art."

The Nation

Hinckle, Warren *Going for Gonzo*; 6/4/90
    "It was an extremely shaky constitutional ground for a search warrant, but in the Bush war-on-drugs climate it's hard to imagine a court having the fortitude to deny a drug search against Hunter Thompson."

Playboy

Commando Journalist; 11/73

Vetter, Craig *Interview;* 11/74
    "In Washington, the truth is never told in daylight hours or across a desk. If you catch people when they're very tired or drunk or weak, you can get some answers. You have to wear the bastards down."—HST

Checking in with Dr. Gonzo; 1/76

Vetter, Craig *Destination Hollyweird* (about the making of "Where the Buffalo Roam"); 6/80
    "When things get slow on the set, we *all* tell Hunter stories."—Bill Murray

Passavant, Tom *Aspen When It's Hot;* 8/88

Vetter, Craig *Aspen When It Was Cool;* 8/88
    "Thompson, who keeps roughly the hours of a vampire bat, arrived sometime after midnight, and from that moment on, the room was hot to a carnival of loons—bartenders and waitresses, cowboys and carpenters, politicians and artists, smugglers and athletes—all of whom described themselves as refugees from whatever is serious about the world."

Vetter, Craig *The Unmaking of the President 1992;* 10/92
    "His unusual technique notwithstanding, the Doctor has the art market pegged: 'It ain't art,' says the gonzo Gauguin, 'unless it's sold.' "

Psychiatry Digest Mandell, Arnold J., M.D. *Dr. Hunter S. Thompson and a New Psychiatry;* 3/76
    "... [Fear and Loathing in Las Vegas] is a message about the future of psychiatry."

Rolling Stone

#318 Steadman, Ralph *Gonzo Goes to Hollywood;* 5/29/80

#318 Felton, David *When the Weird Turn Pro;* 5/29/80
    "Perhaps no other living legend has been twisted, torn up and trampled on in so many ways during the making of a film."

#512 O'Rourke, PJ (interview with HST); 11/5/87
    "I would not be anything else, if for no other reason than I'd rather drink with journalists. Another reason I got into journalism: you don't have to get up in the morning."—HST

#581 Sager, Mike *Trial of Hunter S. Thompson;* 6/28/90

#582 Sager, Mike *Charges Dropped Against Hunter Thompson;* 7/12/90
" 'They fled like rats into the darkness,' Thompson said of the prosecution, prior to a lengthy 'celebration orgy' at Woody Creek Tavern. 'Everybody's house is a lot safer today. If we'd lost this case, they'd have been at your house next.' "

#277 Plimpton, George *Notes from the Battle of New Orleans;* 11/2/78
"In New Orleans I had seen Hunter briefly the night before the fight. He had said that he was on the track of 'Evil,' speaking of it as a palpable entity. 'You cover the fight; I'll handle the Evil.' "

#249 Powers, Charles T. *Literary Lasagna* (Elaine's); 10/6/77   ·

#194 von Hoffman, Nicholas, and Trudeau, Garry *Manifest Destiny in Pago Pago;* 8/28/75

#254 Felton, David *Lifer, My Years at Rolling Stone;* 12/15/77
"Hunter looked at me and Annie Leibovitz and raised a question I've heard him raise many times since. 'Now it seems to me we have two choices,' he said. 'We can either go to bed and call it a night. Or we can take the rest of this mescaline, get completely twisted and act like animals.' As always, it was a rhetorical question."—Felton

#632 Green, Robin *Naked Lunch Box;* 6/11/92

#632 Eszterhas, Joe *King of the Goons;* 6/11/92

#632 *The Contributors;* 6/11/92

Saturday Review

Whitmer, Peter O. *Hunter Thompson: Still Crazy After All These Years;* 1-2/84

Smart

Jenkins, Loren *Dr. Hunter S. Thompson and the Last Battle of Aspen;* Jan-Feb/90

Time

Allis, Sam, *An Evening With (gasp!)* . . . ; 1/22/90
"I gave up on the interview and started worrying about my life when Hunter Thompson squirted two cans of fire starter on the Christmas tree he was going to burn in his living-room fireplace, a few feet away from an unopened wooden crate of 9-mm bullets."

Griffith, Thomas, *Fear and Loathing and Ripping Off;* 7/19/76
"Despite Dr. Thompson's political wise-guyism and all the macho whisky-and-drug talk, this is not opium for the masses but Dr. Pepper for the credulous."

Stanley, Alessandra *When War Winds Down* Grenada w/Naipaul; 12/5/83
"The gonzo journalist is quirky, boisterous, happiest when surrounded by cronies in the hotel bar; the gentleman writer is quiet, refined, more comfortable at afternoon tea. But careering around the island, chasing slender threads of news, they seem a matched pair."

Kelly, James *In His Grandfather's Footsteps;* 2/3/86

Tresniowski, Alexander, and Cole, Wendy *Fear and Loathing in Aspen;* 12/9/91, p. 69

The Village Voice

Bradshaw, Jon *Hunter Thompson on a Bat;* 5/19/75, pp. 10–11

Cockburn, Alexander *Boredom and Nausea;* 5/24/76, pp. 28–29

Crouse, Timothy *Hunter Thompson Meets Judge Leff;* 5/24/67

Cockburn, Alexander *Expert Witness;* 7/31/78

Stokes, Geoffrey, and Simonson, Kevin *Gonzo's Last Stand;* 5/15/90

A Small Selection of Important Newspaper, Magazine and Journal Reviews of Hunter S. Thompson's Works

Reviews of *Hell's Angels*
Louisville Courier-Journal and Times

Maurer, David W. *'Hell's Angels': Rejects of Society Who Live for Violence and Kicks;* 2/3/67
"It is good sociology, written in a style that few sociologists ever master. An experienced, sophisticated writer for one so young, Thompson demonstrates a profound understanding of the drives, social and psychological, which motivate these mixed-up misfits who have it in for the square world—and everyone in it."

New Republic

Elman, Richard M.; 2/25/67
"... it asserts a kind of Rimbaud delirium of spirit for nearly everybody to which, of course, only the rarest genuises can come close ... I suspect that Hunter S. Thompson is a writer whose future career is worth watching."

The New York Times

Litwak, Leo *Hell's Angels;* 1/29/67
"His language is brilliant, his eye is remarkable, and his point of view is reminiscent of Huck Finn's."

Nichols, Lewis *In and out of Books;* 3/5/67
"Reviewers have spoken of its authenticity, and in town the other day, author Thompson offered up a possible reason. 'I've a lot in common with the Angels, the main difference being I've a gimmick.' The gimmick is, he writes."

Reviews of *Fear and Loathing in Las Vegas*

London magazine

Raban, Jonathan *The New Mongrel;* June, July/73
"No hood or cop could be as unbuttoned, as obscene and sensitive and open, as Hunter, motherfucking his way over the typewriter keys like an attentive secretary to his own subconscious."

National Observer

Putney, Michael *A Freaky Huck Finn Assaults Fleshpots;* 8/5/72, p. 23
"If you do suspend your disbelief and climb out on that precarious psychic limb with Thompson and, once there, slosh down great quantities of Wild Turkey and Chivas Regal, vicariously smoke grass, snort coke, shoot smack, break open amyls, and go without sleeping for, say, 70 hours at a stretch, *then* and only then *Fear and Loathing* comes off as a mad, manic masterpiece."

The New York Times

Lehmann-Haupt, Christopher *Heinous Chemicals at Work;* 6/22/72
"The whole book boils down to a kind of mad, corrosive prose poetry that picks up where Norman Mailer's 'An American Dream' left off and explores what Tom Wolfe left out. Besides, its—gulp—funny."

Woods, Crawford *Best Book of the Dope Decade*; 7/23/72

"A desperate and important book, a wired nightmare, the funniest piece of American prose since *Naked Lunch* ... These are the tracks of a man who might be dismissed as just another savage-sixties kook, were it not for the fact that he has already written himself into the history of American literature, in what I suspect will be a permanent way."

Reviews of *Fear and Loathing: on the Campaign Trail '72*

Columbia Journalism Review

Booth, Wayne C. *Loathing and Ignorance on the Campaign Trail*; 11, 12/73

"The style derives what liveliness it has mainly from a slashing contempt for every institution and almost every person—except of course those few who have kept themselves pure."

Harper's

Vonnegut, Kurt Jr. *Political Disease*; 7/73

"From this moment on, let all those who feel that Americans can be as easily led to beauty as to ugliness, to truth as to public relations, to joy as to bitterness, be said to be suffering from Hunter Thompson's disease."

Los Angeles Times

Greenberg, Peter *Haunting of Hunter Thompson*; 6/10/73

"Eventually, Thompson's drug anecdotes become almost as predictable as his use of the words 'fear and loathing.' In the end, however, Thompson reveals himself again as a rebel with a cause—this time to take us fishing with him in a raging stream of consciousness. With any luck at all, you'll catch some big ones."

The Nation

D'Arazien, Steven *Wild Man's View of the Campaign*; 8/13/73

"Thompson discards any pretention of godlike objectivity. Rather than disguising his natural, human bias, he put it 'up front.' "

The New York Times

Seligson, Tom *Tripping of the Presidency '72*; 7/15/73

"[Fear & Loathing: on the Campaign Trail] is the best account yet published of what it feels like to be out there in the middle of the American political process."

Saturday Review

Kanon, Jonathan *Madness & Filigree*; 4/21/73
"Fear & Loathing: on the Campaign Trail '72 is open to attack from just about any traditional standard of political journalism . . . Hunter Thompson is an original; there is no one quite like him . . . It is the best political reporting in some time."

Washington Post

Greider, William *Amok-Raking Journalist*; 5/13/73, Book World
"My own opinion of this book is impossibly warped by exposure to Dr. Thompson in person."

Reviews of *The Great Shark Hunt*

Chicago Tribune

Algren, Nelson *Savage Image of America*; 7/15/79
"No other reporter reveals how much we have to fear and loathe, within and without, yet does it so hilariously. He covers events with the passion of Louis Ferdinand Celine dressed like a ski bum."

Indianapolis News

Brown, L. T. *Thompson Leads Hairy Breed of Journalism*; 9/8/79
"Every newspaper and magazine needs a Hunter Thompson, just as probably as every publisher *does not want* a Hunter Thompson: 'What's this on the expense voucher? Two kilos of WHAT?' "

Los Angeles Times

Wolff, Geoffrey *Walking Bomb Writes*; 8/12/79
"Thompson has fastened on fear and loathing as the yin and yang of our culture."

Mother Jones

Klein, Joe *The New! Old! New!! Journalism!!!*; 12/79
"Even if Thompson never ingests another drug for literary effect, he is one of the few writers extant who can rest assured that people will be reading his work 200 years from now."

New Republic

Plummer, William *Great Shark Hunt*; 8/25/79
"During the reign of Richard Nixon, Thompson set out to be to journalism what François Villon once was to poetry."

The New York Times

Buckley, William F., Jr.; 8/5/79
> "Hunter Thompson is indisputably a hugely important sociological phenomenon ... [he] elicits the same kind of admiration one would feel for a streaker at Queen Victoria's funeral."

The Village Voice

Gornick, Vivian *The Gonzo and the Geeks;* 11/19/79
> "Thompson's talent—and it really is his only talent—lies in his ability to describe his own manic plunge into drink, drugs, and madness through a use of controlled exaggeration that is truly marvelous ... But ... these moments are surrounded by pages and pages, and still more pages, of compulsive writing without purpose or destination."

Wall Street Journal

Perry, James M. *A Madhouse Writer in a Peach Daiquiri Era;* 9/5/79
> "He is the bane of every traditional political reporter at work in America today."

Washington Post

Wills, Garry *Hunter Thompson: Rollercoasting through the 60's/70's;* 8/19/79
> "Thompson never preaches. But that means he never instructs. He amuses; he frightens; he becomes a dandy at flirting with doom. But he is a good way of visiting Nick Adams country; and even if he never does anything else, his achievement is substantial."

Reviews of *The Curse of Lono*

Denver Post

Carlton, Michael *Fear & Loathing in Hawaii;* 11/6/83
> "Unless you are totally devoid of a sense of humor (or are the president of the Hawaii Visitors Bureau), *The Curse of Lono* will delight and entertain you fully—especially on a rainy December night in Kona."

Louisville Courier-Journal and Times

Scott, Archie *Curse of Lono;* 12/4/83
> "Thompson, with characteristic paranoia, finds paradise rife with racial tensions and violence that reduces the melting pot to a myth."

Publishers Weekly

Crichton, Jennifer; 7/1/83
> "Thompson's book was more than a year past deadline when Ian Ballantine, acting as free-lance editor ... flew out to Aspen four times to work with Thompson on finishing up *The Curse*. In Aspen, he daily donned his New York business suit and tried to appear 'as if I were a man who knows about making money.' "

Wall Street Journal

Gannan, Franklin-Reid *Gonzo Style Journalism Goes Hawaiian*; 1/9/84
> "If your vision of Hawaii is Thomas Magnum working out on a surf ski borrowed from the King Kamehameha Club, give *The Curse of Lono* a wide berth. But if you can subscribe to the Thompson motto—'When the going gets weird, the weird turn pro'—here's the perfect tropical toddy to warm up a winter's night."

Reviews of *Generation of Swine*

Chicago Tribune

Dretzka, Gary *Swine Is Lean on Dr. Gonzo*; 7/19/88
> "The short, tightly structured newspaper format seems to work against Thompson's rambling but full-bodied style. He's a distance horse, not a sprinter, the outrageousness is still there in abundance, but he can't stretch out and pace his act."

National Review

Vigilante, Richard *Lost Generation*; 9/16/88
> "The book is obsessively political. Thompson has always had strong prejudices, but these days that's all he has."

New Leader

Lekechman, Robert *Swine*; 11/28/88
> "Thompson is fun to read, less as a prophet than an irreverent commentator on our deplorable politics. No non-gonzo treats American politicians with the scorn and of course loathing that too many of them merit."

New York

Koenig, Rhoda *Generation of Swine*; 7/3–10/89
> "One does not, though, read Thompson for his prophetic skills but for his sober, unflinching anarchy ..."

The New York Times

Mitgang, Herbert *Art of Insult;* 8/11/88
> "He's a little more strident this time out, but if you happen to share his public enemies, Mr. Thompson's your man."

USA Today

Kellman, Steve *Swine;* 11/88
> "Thompson's rant is informed by a powerful moral indignation, rage at the perversion of the American Dream."

Reviews of *Songs of the Doomed*

Baltimore Sun

Stepp, Carl Sessions *Hunter Thompson: rantings by a voice from the 1960s;* 1/6/91
> "Is it amusing or pathetic? Stimulating or maddeningly manipulative? With Mr. Thompson, you never know. That is his hold on us, and perhaps his tragic flaw."

Boston Globe

Reidy, Chris *Thompson's Brazen Bonfire of Inanities;* 11/23/90
> "Like his evil genius, Richard M. Nixon, Thompson shows signs of making a comeback . . . It's all here in *Songs of the Doomed*—the senseless violence, the four-letter words and the four-day benders."

The New York Times

Rosenbaum, Ron *Still Gonzo After All These Years;* 11/25/90
> "Reading *Songs of the Doomed* reminds us how good he was at his best, and how good he still can be when he's given the freedom—and expenses—to hit the road, rather than stewing in his own bitterness in Woody Creek."

Rocky Mountain News

Middleton, Harry *Thompson's Lost the Edge;* 10/28/90
> "There is something slightly sad about reading Hunter Thompson these days. It's like looking through an old scrapbook, remembering things past, the way we were before the world forced us to grow up. However, Thompson, as a writer at least, seems inexorably fixed in time."

Washington Post

Nicosia, Gerald *What a Long Strange Trip;* 11/18/90
   "What saved Thompson from becoming one more failed alcoholic
   and drugged-out writer, and instead turned him into a pioneer of
   the only genuinely new and original literary form of our time, the
   so-called New Journalism, was an absolute commitment to telling
   the truth, not only about the world he lived in, but also about himself."

A Small Sampling of Secondary Newspaper, Magazine and Journal Reviews of Hunter S. Thompson's Works
(particularly concentrating on "The Great Shark Hunt")

Arizona Daily Star

Levin, Rob *'Shark Hunt'—a Thompson sampler;* 11/18/79
   "... one look at his collection of material in 'The Great Shark
   Hunt' should persuade doubters of his reporting and writing ability. The book is a sampling of Thompson's best work, ranging from
   the early '60s to the Rolling Stone days of the late '70s."

Atlanta Journal & Constitution

Monroe, Doug *Thompson Laments America the Doomed;* 1/6/91,
   p. N-10
   "Nobody says it meaner."

Baltimore Sun

Hall, Wiley A., 3rd *Hunter Thompson and world as he sees it (Swine
   rev);* 9/4/88
   "... buried in each column is the caustic commentary, always on
   target, that makes Hunter Thompson Hunter Thompson."

Birmingham News

Carlton, Bob *It's more of a jaunt than savage journey, but promise is
   there;* 7/31/88 *(Swine rev)*
   "The good news is that while Thompson is not the unchained animal that Dave Barry is, he's certainly not the Beaver Cleaver that
   Bob Greene has turned out to be. On his good days, he's an armed-
   and-dangerous P.J. O'Rourke. On his bad days, he's like Jerry
   Falwell on codeine."

Boston Globe

Devine, Laurie *Uppers and downers* (*Shark* rev); 9/16/79, p. A-7
> ". . . even though Thompson the writer and the man is wildly un-disciplined, immature, self-indulgent, self-destructive and distract-edly discursive, he also is one of the best writers around."

Feeney, Mark *The Good Doctor* (*Swine* rev); 6/19/88, p. A-17
> "Walter Lippmann may be the patron saint of punditry, but Hunter S. Thompson is its dark, delirious underbelly."

Buffalo News

Montgomery, David *Hunter Thompson Flails Away At the Foibles of Life in the '80s* (*Doomed* rev); 7/24/88
> "Thompson has no illusions about the weekly crank of news copy."

Charlottesville Progress

Prior, Richard *'The Great Shark Hunt': Rebellious Invective*; 10/7/79
> "Well, there sure are a lot of folks out there who would no more breathe the names Celine and Hunter Thompson in the same sentence than they would Herman Melville and Mother Goose, particularly the crew which Thompson labeled with relish as the 'waterheads' and 'senile hags' who run the 'Columbia Journalism Review.' "

Chicago Tribune

Petersen, Clarence *Swine*; 8/13/89
> "There is something here to offend just about everyone, which is fair enough when you consider that just about everyone offends Hunter Thompson."

Johnson, Steve *Gonzo at 50* (concert hall lecture); 12/7/89, p. Sec5-1
> "With his avowed fondness for pharmaceuticals and a liver that must look like the sort of thing you'd find in a jar on the shelves of a junior high school biology class, Thompson has performed more than one man's share of abuse on his 50-year-old body, and lived to celebrate it."

Dretzka, Gary *60's thru Thompson's Lens* (*Doomed* rev); 2/5/91, p. Sec5-3
> ". . . if you buy into the Thompson living-legend mystique—and, judging by attendance at his speaking appearances, many still want to—this book will provide some enjoyable moments."

Cincinnati Enquirer

Besten, Mark *Thompson reflects upon arrest by 'scum'* (*Doomed* rev);
11/4/90
"Should Thompson soon find a new pack of dogs at the door, as
seems possible if not likely, let's hope that clearer heads once again
prevail so that he won't have to write the Great Jailhouse Novel.
His is a major American talent, and this is his most comprehen-
sively autobiographical book to date. Nice work, Hunter, and
hey—be careful out there."

Cleveland Plain Dealer

Frakes, James R. *Loathings of Hunter Thompson in new anthology*;
10/5/79
"If Hunter S. Thompson, 'America's Quintessential Outlaw Journalist,' had never existed, I don't think anyone would have felt
compelled to invent him."

Cleveland Press

Stella, Charles *Great shark Hunter digests politicians* (*Shark* rev); 9/6/79
"Thompson views politics as the hucksterism that it is and that sensible vantage point gives his reflections honest merit lacking in
other reposts by writers who seem to believe that political candidates are descended from Mt. Olympus, when in truth most of
them climb out of some kind of Tammany Hall."

Columbia (SC) The State

Sebak, Richard *'The Great Shark Hunt' Is A Bit Disappointing*; 8/26/79
"Centuries from now, if people haven't forgotten how to read, it
won't surprise me if they use this book to find out what was *really*
going on in America in the flipped-out 1960s and the baffling 70s."

Rick Sebak, Bookaholic television segment; (air date) 9/27/79
"He *knows* how to make his observations and his opinions as important as the events he's covering."

Courier-Post

Kent, Bill *A Journalist for these crazed times* (*Shark* rev); 9/23/79
"Like the Kerouac crowd of the an[sic] earlier generation, the
Thompson we see is a man our mothers would rather not have us
meet."

Figaro

Middleton, Harry *Gonzo Shark Hunting and Other Tales;* 12/17/79
"Any chronicle of the Sixties will have to include some of Thompson's frenzied, atomized history of those years, even though now, a decade later, his hopped-up, rampaging prose is already losing its pizzazz, races along as directionless as a tailless kite."

(Grand Junction) Westworld

Shaw, Mildred Hart *Book-shelf* (*Shark* rev); 9/2/79
"To coin a phrase, you don't have to be insane to enjoy Hunter, but it would probably be a great help. He is wordy, disconnected most of the time, obscure, profane, irreverent, frequently irrelevant, and, apparently, usually writing on the knife edge of hysteria."

Guardian

Vidal, John *No-show time for Gonzo;* (weekend arts) 1988; (date unconfirmed), p. 10
"Everytime I've been with Hunter I've been a wreck at the end of it. I always had that feeling that when I went on a job with him I might never come back."—Ralph Steadman

Journal of Popular Culture

Green, James *Gonzo;* Summer/75, p. 204
"If there is an experimental, radical or lunatic branch to respond to the experimental, radical and lunatic fringes of society, certainly Hunter Thompson's GONZO journalism must move to the head of the class ... some would have it move to the corner with the trash."

English, John W *What Professionals Say;* p. 232
"Hunter Thompson, though, had been doing New Journalism with his Hell's Angels book long before a movement was recognized, and only retroactively got credit for it."—Roger Rapoport

Los Angeles Herald Examiner

Carlson, Timothy *Ravings of a '70's evil-watcher* (*Shark* rev); 8/9/79
"The language is funny, if you take it as hysterical overkill. It makes sense as a kind of therapy against the injustice and perfidy taking place in the White House under Nixon, which sent Thompson back to the Third Reich and Joseph Conrad's 'Heart of Darkness' for appropriate parallels."

Los Angeles Times

Greenberg, Peter S. *The haunting of Hunter Thompson*; 8/12/79, p. 9

Toure, Yemi *Newsmakers* (rev of art exhibit); 11/26/91, p. E-1

Louisville Courier-Journal and Times

Kaukas, Dick *Generation of Swine*; 9/4/88
> "He is arguably the most notorious and celebrated journalist Louisville has ever produced, and he has been a kind of weird celebrity on the national media stage ever since he wrote about the Hell's Angels in the late 1960's and harassed presidential candidates in the campaign of 1972."

Minneapolis Tribune

Nolen, Wm A., MD *Thompson Gleefully guilty of every crime but dullness* (*Shark* rev); 9/16/79, p. 14-G
> "... I'd give a substantial pile of money to see what these articles looked like before the lawyers for Rolling Stone, Random House, the New York Times Magazine and the other original publishers censored them."

More: A Journalism Review

Gonzo Goes to War; 7/75, p. 22

Drosnin, Michael; 7–8/76, p. 18

Nashville Tennessean

Badger, David *Thompson's Latest Gonzo Volume Depicts the Hunter After the Shark*; 8/26/79
> "... while Thompson frequently dismisses his own prose as 'gibberish' or 'fish-wrap journalism,' his style and expression remain unique."

New Brunswick Home News

Genovese, Peter *Savage caricature in 'Shark Hunt'*; 9/30/79
> "For those who've never heard of Gonzo Journalism, let it suffice to say it is a kind of writing that has few practitioners, fewer socially redeeming qualities and no rules whatsoever."

New Haven Advocate

Mix, David *Thugs, Waterheads and Montebanks: A History of Gonzo Journalism;* 10/10/79

New Haven Register

Wyman, Carolyn *Thompson remains true to 'Gonzo' style;* 4/15/89

Newport News Daily Press

Allen, David *(Shark* rev); 9/9/79
> "Thompson throws objective reporting out the window, usually along with the television, armchair and any other piece of sleazy motel furniture that offends his drug- and drink-crazed eyes."

Newsweek

DeFrank, T.M. *Catcher in the Wry;* 5/1/72, p. 65
> "Guys write down what a candidate says and report it when they know damn well he's lying."—HST

Kroll, Jack *Writing High* (Where the Buffalo Roam); 5/12/80

New West

Movie Review; 5/19/80, p. 38

Fearless Toasting in Movieland; 5/8/78, p. 6

Fullington, Greg *Shark Hunter;* 9/24/79, p. 88

New York

Denby, David *Faint "Heart";* 5/12/80, p. 62
> "Kerouac (who died in 1969) and Thompson have contributed more than their share of bull slinging to the creation of a personal myth."

McGill, Deborah *The New Journalism Revisited;* 12/80, p. 91
> "Thompson is a windbag on the subject of Nixon and Republicanism, and half of his collected works is not writing but ranting. One wouldn't mind if the other half weren't so keen."

The New Yorker

Angell, Roger *Where the Buffalo Roam* (rev); 5/12/80, p. 112

New York Review of Books

Plimpton, George *Last Laugh*; 8/4/77, p. 29

The New York Times

Lask, Thomass *Book Awards, Hunter S Thompson withdraws*; 3/17/75, p. 24

Buckley, Tom *Behind the Best Sellers; Hunter S. Thompson*; 10/14/79
"There has been both profit and method in Hunter Thompson's madness ever since Rolling Stone discovered, in 1970, that there was an enthusiastic audience for his brand of journalism—fiction about real people, fantasy, invective and self-celebration, all supposedly written under the influence of drugs and alcohol."

Haas, Charlie *Curse of Lono* (rev); 1/15/84, p. VII-19
"The Gonzo manner seems down to a formula at times, and, most disappointingly, the fantasies that provide vicarious vindication in *Fear and loathing* seem bilious and undirected here."

What a Long Strange Trip it Was; 12/9/90, p. VII-3

Ottawa Citizen

Gordon, Charles *Gonzo news from outlaw, doped writer* (*Shark* rev); 10/6/79
"Thompson discovered early that you could learn just as much about a place by interviewing its freaks and junkies as you could by interviewing its mayor or chamber of commerce president. Thompson was later to learn that the piece could be more interesting if *he* was the freak and junkie he interviewed, and he refined the technique, taking his strange head to events, then looking inside it."

Palo Alto, Peninsula Times Tribune

Ford, Jan (*Shark* rev); 10/27/79
"No one could have consumed the quantities of drugs he claims to have and still put pen to paper, or finger to typewriter."

Patriot Ledger

Williams, Paul *Two writers look at similar subjects in different ways* (*Shark* rev); 8/31/79
"When the weird get going the going turns to prose."—Williams

People

Fink, Mitchell *Fear & Loathing & Drinking on the Lecture Trail*; 4/22/91, p. 37

Sunday Peninsula Herald

Thomas, Kevin *'Gonzo' Journalist at Work* (*Shark* rev); 9/2/79, p. 8-C
"If life is indeed nothing more than a continuing series of sins and redemptions, then Hunter Thompson really has been living."

Philadelphia Magazine

Mascaro, John *Generation of Swine*; 10/88, p. 79

Playboy

Books; (*Shark* rev); 9/79
". . . the collection underscores the point that Thompson is working from a dementia no one in his right mind would want to share."

Lupica, Mike *Books: Shooting from the Lip*; 6/88, p. 22

Richmond News Leader

Baker, Ira *Thompson's 'Gonzo Papers' Have Little to Offer*; 10/10/79
"Unless you are a confirmed Thompson fan and know what you are getting into, The Great Shark Hunt will be a waste of time and money. There are limits to the sound and fury one can take."

Richmond Times-Dispatch

Slack, Charles *Vintage columns make 'Swine' worth reading*; 7/7/88

Roanoke Times & World-News

King, Nina *Hunter Thompson on the trail*; 9/17/79
"An occasional reading of Hunter S. Thompson can clear the mind and sharpen the wits. But 602 pages is about 600 pages over the line, guaranteed to bring on a state of raving incoherency in which the reader is likely to confuse his or her navel (or the random knot-hole) with the secret of eternal life."

Rochester Democrat & Chronicle

Leonard, John *Super Geek. More strange snippets from Thompson's works*; 8/26/79
"It is nice to think of him naked on his porch in Colorado, drink-

ing Wild Turkey and shooting at rocks. Somewhere, beyond John Denver, he smells injustice. Scales grow on his torso, wings sprout on his feet. Up, up and away . . . it's Captain Paranoid! The Duke of Gonzo 'Super Geek.' "

Sacramento, Suttertown News

Holt, Tim (*Shark* rev); 9/21/79, p. 11

San Francisco Chronicle

Stone, Judy (film rev) *Selling of Gonzo Journalist*; 5/2/80

Holt, Patricia *Full of Danger and Weirdness* (Lono rev); 11/6/83
"Some readers will find these [Mark Twain or Captain Cook's biography] excerpts boring, however, compared to the wicked insanity perpetrated by Thompson himself, and possibly suspect that a lot of the quoted material has been added as filler to a basically thin narrative."

Robertson, Michael *Thompson and Steadman viewed*; 12/27/83

Ross, Michael E. *American Dream's Underbelly*; 12/23/90

San Jose Mercury News

Clark, Tom *Bashing the swine*; 7/3/88

Savannah News-Press

Sunday Magazine *Gonzo Journalist's Weird Adventures*; 9/9/79, p. 5f

Toledo Blade

Thomas, Kevin *Autopsy On Our Culture*; 9/23/79
"In each story—rather adventure—he leads us on a scattered but very personal journey of experience. The bottom line is that he's really a Charles Kuralt for crazy people."

Toronto Star

Kucherawy, Dennis *Welcome to the No Decade* (Doomed rev); 2/2/91

Tulsa World

Maurer, Mitch *Thompson's Ramblings Land Well off the Mark*; 7/3/88

USA Today

Election '92 ... His Generation: (Greider, Wenner, O'Rourke and HST interview Clinton for Rolling Stone); 8/28/92

> "Said Thompson, known in the past for mixing mind-altering substances and firearms, reported "Clinton was not comfortable being in the same room with me."

Allen, Bruce *Misadventures of Kesey and Thompson*; 11/29/90, p. 5-D

Washington Monthly

Nocera, Joseph *How Hunter Thompson Killed New Journalism*; 4/81, pp. 44–50
> "College students are especially susceptible to writers who project an unusual and compelling vision of the world."

Washington Post

Allen, Henry *For Hunter S. Thompson, Outrage is the Only Way Out* (*Las Vegas* rev); 7/23/72
> "Thompson's real subject is outrage."

Edens, Michael *Thompson, More Gone Than Gonzo* (*Swine* rev); 8/2/88

Brace, Eric *Personalities: Gonzo Art*; 11/26/91, p. B-3

Washington Times

Gonzo artist aims at J. Edgar Hoover; 11/25/91, p. A-2

Wilmington Sunday News Journal

Leonard, John *Notes of a 'gonzo' journalist* (*Shark* rev); 8/28/79

Winnipeg Free Press

MacKay, Douglas *What now for dope set's Don Quixote?* (*Shark* rev); 10/13/79
> "Will the new Hunter Thompson continue to write? Or will he just be a caricature of his former self, a Doonesbury cartoon character,

a loony reporter portrayed in the movies by comedian Bill Murray?"

Winnipeg Tribune

Allentuck, Andrew *Through the seventies on a suitcase of drugs;* 10/20/79
"Hunter S. Thompson is one of the most interesting and perhaps one of the most important contemporary stylists of the essay."

Winston-Salem Sentinel

Mashburn, Rick *The Doktor Mutters; Do We Understand?* (*Shark* rev); 8/17/79
"If his writing of the Watergate hearings sounds a little bloodthirsty, it is still a fair and honorable account of a hot and giddy summer when a whole nation was glued to the tube to watch the greatest soap opera of all time."

Worcester Telegram

Hafey, Richard J. (*Shark* rev); 9/23/79
"When Hunter Thompson is observing, he can be superb. But when he makes himself an integral part of his story, he is a bore."

A Very Small Selection of Newspaper and Magazine Stories about Hunter S. Thompson

Aces & Eights

(interview) Hunter S. Thompson; vol. 1, no. 2, spring/92

Advertising Age

McDonnell, Terry *Industry Still Has Room for Dreamers . . . ;* 10/23/89
"Thus I was able to launch Smart in early August 1988—for less cash than Vanity Fair spent on its anniversary party that year. All of this money came from friends and contributors. Writers George Plimpton, Hunter Thompson, P.J. O'Rourke and Peter Maas all purchased shares, and several recognizable media executives including William Randolph Hearst III are also investors."

American Spectator

Marin, Rick *Bad Time/Gonzo*; 12/90

Aspen Anthology

Vetter, Craig *Member of the Lynching*; Winter/76
> "The reporters from the big dailies are like the President in that they don't ever get to talk dirty in public or print the really juicy stuff."

Aspen Daily News

Note: Eve O'Brien's articles on HST have appeared in newspapers in many other cities including Denver and San Francisco. We have chosen not to list all of them here.

O'Brien, Eve *Woman Says Alleged Assailant Thompson Was 'Hero'*; 3/1/90

——— *Thompson Version of Events Questioned*; 3/2/90

——— *Confiscations Back Up Thompson's Rep*; 3/2/90

Forbes, Frank *Drugs, Sex, Lies and Videotape* (letter); 3/5/90

Wyatt, Candy M. *No One Is Above The Law* (letter); 3/12/90, p. 3

O'Brien, Eve *Hunter Thompson May Face Felony Drug Charges*; 3/14/90

925-News Tipline *Hunter Thompson Applauded By Tipline Callers In Face Of 'Lifestyle Police'*; 3/13/90
> "Just because Hunter is some sort of celebrity, what gives him any special rights? He should be prosecuted for any crimes he commits."—Caller

Bruno Kirchenwitz *Give Hunter His Brain Candy Back*; 3/21/90

(AP) *Hunter Thompson Says World Turning Into Repressive, Fearful Place*; 3/24/90
> "What can you say about a generation that's grown up thinking that rain is poison, sex means certain death and anything that's fun will give you cancer?"—HST

O'Brien, Eve *Hunter Thompson Saga Moves 60's Song-writer To Lift His Pen Again*; 3/30/90

Brian, Evil *Gonzo Writer Evicted From Rehab Center*; 3/31/90

O'Brien, Eve *Hunter Thompson Doesn't Like People Singing his Song*; 4/2/90

(staff report) *Thompson Celebrates In Style*; 5/31/90

O'Brien, Eve *Probe Ordered Into DA Investigator's Alleged Misdeeds*; 6/1/90

———— *DA Reacts To Criticism*; 6/1/90

Bourne, Michael *Thompson's Friends And Neighbors Warned Him To 'Lay Low' Before His Arrest*; 6/1/90
     "It was pretty obvious to people who live in the (Woody Creek) valley and who go to the tavern that there was a federal presence."—Zino Beattie, neighbor

(staff and wire reports) *Judge Dismayed As He Dismisses Charges*; 6/1/90

They Said It, We Printed It; 6/2/90
     "We were not out to get Hunter Thompson because of his lifestyle. We had a witness who said she saw Hunter doing cocaine in his house."—Chip McCrory, prosecutor

Thompson Has That Letdown Feeling After Charges Dropped; 6/6/90
     "I was getting in the mood to get on their level. We would have crushed them like eggs, rotten eggs."—HST

Bourne, Michael *D.A. Under Budget Scrutiny After Thompson Case*; 6/12/90

O'Brien, Eve *Thompson Wants Records Sealed*; 6/12/90

Smith, Brent Gardiner *Biographer of Hunter Thompson Looking For A Little Input*; 5/28/92

Aspen Magazine

Cowen, Jay *Hunter S. Thompson, Gonzo Sportsman*; Midsummer/89, p. 45

Aspen Times

Primary Vote Tuesday; 9/3/70

Sheriff Candidate Hunter Thompson Discusses Law and Order; 9/17/70
     "Sod the streets at once."

'Stone' article describes 'freak-power' in Aspen; 10/1/70

National press gawks at local race; 10/8/70

Sheriff candidates invited to meeting; 10/8/70

"All it takes is a quack complaint to launch them into an 11-hour search and felony court. This is like Berlin in 1933."—HST

Support for Hunter Thompson comes from unlikely sources; 3/22/90

Roaring fork digest—Hunter S. Thompson Tape adds to drama; 4/5/90

Huffman, Mark *Lawyers: victim's reluctance immaterial;* 4/12/90

Roaring fork digest—Hunter S. Thompson 2 trials requested; 4/26/90

Roaring fork digest—Hunter S. Thompson Case file sealed; 8/16/90

Associated Press

Domestic News: People in the News (A drunken driving charge against HST was dropped, but he pleaded guilty to running a stop sign and admitted "raving" at a state trooper); 8/7/81

Slater, Wayne *Celebrating 25 Years of Kerouac's 'On the Road';* 7/21/82

Barclay, Delores *Doonesbury is Dropping Out;* 9/11/82

Domestic News: People in the News (HST has hit the campaign trail for Rolling Stone again); 4/8/84

Domestic News: People in the News, Bozeman, Mont. (Author HST, who has turned his biting, new journalism style on high and low alike, was bitten on the finger after a talk before about 1,000 people at a tavern); 4/20/85

Domestic News: People in the News, San Francisco (HST sentenced to three years' probation and $800 who found him guilty of drunken driving in an incident that injured three people); 7/13/85

Doonesbury Marks Passing of Character Based on Hunter Thompson; 1/23/86

Writer Charged With Gun Violation (HST charged with illegally firing a shotgun at a city golf course); 8/20/87

Money Jar Filling for Defense of Hunter Thompson on Firearms Charge; 9/18/87

Domestic News: Names in the News (Counterculture journalist HST canceled tonight's scheduled speaking engagement at the University of Arizona because of alleged death threats, his agent says); 4/14/88

Aspen Dispute Heats Up With Fish Poisoning (Floyd Watkins' plan to open his ranch to commercial trout fishing has angered his rural neighbors and led to complaints about gunshots, vandalism and the poisoning of two ponds filled with dozens of large fish); 8/10/87

Johnson, Allan *That goofy Dr. Gonzo to appear at the Funny Bone*; 9/21/90

Smith, Sid *Fear and Loathing ignores reality on drug trip's fringes*; 11/18/91

Cincinnati Enquirer

Besten, Mark *Thompson reflects upon arrest by 'scum'*; 11/4/90

Daily Telegraph

The Bonds of Friendship (Steadman and HST); 4/18/90

Denver Post

Sinisi, J. Sebastian *America's repressive 'age of fear'*; 3/23/90

—————— *Unruly crowd gets gonzo entertainment*; 3/24/90
"As a writer, I'm biased as hell. But being biased and accurate at the same time is being gonzo."—HST

Trial of Aspen writer caught global notice; 6/30/90

Tinker, Greg *Aspen goes Hollywood; NBC filming in jet-set village; Freedom of speech? Hunter S. Thompson will drink to that*; 4/3/91

Detroit Free Press

Niemiec, Dennis and Bruni, Frank *Palmer-Slater Talks About Porno Past*; 4/9/90

Detroit News

Sweeney, Ann *Gail Force*; 5/5/90 (about Palmer-Slater)

—————— *It's Hard to Leave Porn World Behind*; 5/21/90

Allen, Bruce *Thompson, Kesey still around*; 12/10/90

Houston Post

Denson, Bryan *Hunter S. Thompson tells all, sort of, in Tower Theater event*; 6/14/90

Hotline

Hunter Thompson and top NC Dems in Inner Circle; 3/22/90

Independent

Thompson denies sex and drugs; 4/11/90

Profile: Over the tip with Fear and Loathing; Hunter S. Thompson, de doctor of letters; 4/14/90

Wheen, Francis *Interesting if true; 4/15/90*

Midgley, Simon *Around the World; Fear and Loathing; 6/1/90*

Ithaca Journal

Hunter bags the biggies; 11/25/91

Legal Times

Fear and Loathing (on NACDL's help, Keith Stroup); 8/13/90

Los Angeles Times

Cohen, Jerry *Freak Power Candidate May Be Winner in Sheriff's Race; 10/7/70*

> "I think we can win because of the nature of the opposition (his two rivals are the incumbent sheriff, a Democrat, and the under-sheriff, a Republican). They're both cookie-cutter types, gas station attendants who were given a gun. They'll split the vote. The realities of life are far beyond them. I want to set a style of law enforcement for the 1970s, not the 1880s."—HST

(exclusive to the Times from a Staff Writer) *Sod the Streets; Freak Party Platform; 10/7/70*

> "Change the name 'Aspen' by public referendum to 'Fat City.' This would prevent greedheads, land-rapers and other human jackals from capitalizing on the name 'Aspen.' " —HST

Lochte, Dick *Gonzo journalist in bookland; 6/29/80*

DuFresne, Chris *As Hunter Might Say, There's Haight-Ashbury and Hate 49ers; 10/24/85*

Goldstein, Patrick *Pop Eye; Paging Hunter Thompson* (Drug testing at Rolling Stone); 7/6/86

Zonana, Victor F. *Bay Area Battle: Reviving the Examiner; Will Hearst III Makes Feisty Comeback Bid with a Bit of a Flash; 12/22/85*

Hunter Thompson fined $800 for drunk driving; 7/15/85

Gendel, Morgan *Night of the Living Gonzo;* 10/5/86

Pryor, Larry *Aspen Chipping In to Get Gonzo Golfer Off the Hook;* 9/20/87

Finke, Nikki *Election '88 Forecast: Gonzo style;* 10/18/87

—— *The New Hunter S. Thompson;* 10/18/87

Pryor, Larry *Scandals Somehow Led to Vice* (Gordon Liddy vs HST at Brown Univ.); 11/22/87

Dr. Thompson's Savage Journey into Politics; 4/6/89

Lewis, Randy *Gonzo review; Hunter Thompson Holds Forth* (at Bogart's in Long Beach); 4/6/89

Nibbles & Bits: Journalist Hunter S. Thompson's scheduled performance Tuesday at the Coach House has been postponed until Thursday because Thompson reportedly injured himself when he fell off tractor; 5/31/89

Lewis, Randy *Thompson to Invade Nixon's Old Territory;* 6/1/89

(Times staff and wires) *Woman Alleges 'Gonzo' Assault;* 3/1/90

Morain, Dan *Gonzo Time (scandals discussed);* 4/23/90

Richards, Florence *Selective Enforcement of Drug Laws at Issue;* 5/6/90

(Times staff and wire services) *Eggs on His Foes;* 6/9/90

Stein, Mark A. *The Wrath of Ralph; Ralph Steadman's Political Cartoons are Gone. His Gut-Level Sensibilities Have Been Transferred to Opera;* 8/17/90

Morain, Dan *Pornographer Arrested in Partner-Brother's Slaying;* 3/1/91

Toure, Yemi *Newsmakers* (Durango appearance); 3/21/91

Washburn, Jim *Third No-Show is Strikeout for Hunter Thompson;* 4/22/92

Louisville Courier-Journal and Times

Freeman, Don, *Scoop to Mutts;* 1/11/48
> "The reporters, who are paid on a piece-rate basis, average 10 cents an issue, with the two 'stars' getting about 15 cents. This is somewhat below the national salary level of reporters, Kaegi admits; but after all, the paper is young."

Boy on First Job at Bank Finds 1st Pay Goes Too Far-Away; 7/2/53
"I didn't have it long enough to realize it was really mine."—HST

Lost $50 Greets Owner Returning to Restaurant; 7/3/53
"Alonzo Robinson, an employee at the restaurant, found the money on the floor and waited for its owner to appear. He learned the owner's name from a Courier-Journal story reporting the loss. Thompson gave Robinson a reward."

3 High School Seniors Held in Robbery; 5/11/55

3 High-School Students Held For $8 Robbery in Park; 5/11/55
"Police said Monin gave them this account of the robbery: He, a girl, and another couple were parked near Hogan's Fountain in Cherokee Park. An automobile pulled up behind Monin's car. Two boys got out, and one asked Monin for a cigarette. When Monin held out a package of cigarettes, one of the boys grabbed it out of his hand and reached inside the car and took the keys from the ignition. Another boy approached and held his hand in his pocket as if he had a gun. The boys then forced Monin to give them his billfold. They took $8 from it and threw it down. The three drove off as another automobile approached."

Youth Fined in Scrape Halting his Graduation; 6/12/55
"Male Principal W.S. Milburn said he placed Stallings and Thompson under 'indefinite suspension pending their re-entry through the superintendent's office.' "

Youth Ordered Jailed for 60 Days Pending Action in Robbery Case; 6/16/55

Tearful Youth Is Jailed Amid Barrage of Pleas; 6/16/55
"When Jull ordered Thompson taken to jail, he explained to those in the courtroom that a juvenile could not make bond. And if anyone attempts to bail Thompson out when he becomes 18 on July 18, Jull said, Juvenile Court will order him brought before the court immediately for final disposition of his case."

'Doing Better' Youth Given His Freedom; 8/18/55
" 'You are not on probation,' Judge Jull told Hunter S. Thompson, 2437 Ransdell, 'but you will be watched.' "

It's Tough For A Dog To Have A Globetrotter For A Master; 1/3/62
"Since he bought Agar, Thompson has acquired a sort of 'family' responsibility, but they are both born rovers. . . . "

Double Play: A New Kentucky Author is making his debut with a double bang.: 1/5/67

Ex-Louisvillian Loses Colorado Sheriff Race; 11/4/70 and 11/5/70

Cox, Bill *Rolling Stone's fearless, far out political reporter;* 12/17/72
"Thompson himself might be accurately compared to one of those $700 electric typewriters that sit quietly until you accidentally rest the side of your hand on the 'return' and 'backspace' keys at the same time, setting off a frenzy of clacking and whirring to wake the dead."

Filiatreau, John *Who is Raoul Duke?;* 10/23/75
"Most journalists only talk about objectivity, but Dr. Duke grabs it straight by the ———— throat."

Christensen, John *On The Trail Of The Outlaw Journalist;* 1/22/77
"The domestic tranquility depends on Thompson's small, blonde wife, Sandy. 'She's magnificent,' said the admiring mother-in-law. 'She makes his appointments, cancels them, takes messages, pays the bills, cooks the meals, keeps house, lies for him, does whatever is necessary. She's a fantastic person. God knows, anybody who could live with Hunter for 14 years has to be superhuman.' "

Filiatreau, John *Gonzo journalism: Fun of a sort;* 8/26/79
"He can get away with his outrageousness because his personal savageries are always in full view, and he doesn't ask to be taken seriously."

Reid, Ford *Journalist brings his audacity to UK stage;* 9/20/80
" 'I'm doing this (a speaking tour) for the money,' he said. 'It honestly puzzles me and embarrasses me. When you grow up in Kentucky wanting to be a writer, this is not exactly the end you had in mind.' "

Elson, Martha *Alums Recall Castlewood Athletic Club Days;* 5/29/91
"Among those attending—including many prominent Louisville businessmen and professionals—was journalist Hunter S. Thompson, who, perhaps in tribute to the old days of the club, wore a plaid short-sleeved shirt and sports coat."

Simmons, Ira *Waxing Nostalgic; Hunter Thompson Reflects on His Boyhood;* 5/25/91
" 'It's a very emotional thing with me,' Thompson said at the reunion. 'When we were growing up, we didn't know what bonding was—but that's what it was. We were a gang, a damn good gang—and we still are.' "

Kaukas, Dick *Gray but Gonzo; Hunter S. Thompson is 53. Now he'll start growing up. Right?;* 9/8/92

Keepnews, Peter *Monster of Woody Creek (interview)*; 11/25/90

Cohen, Roger *That Rare Avis at Owl Farm* (profile); 12/12/90

Specter, Michael *'Gonzo' Godfather Swings at Clinton*; 4/7/92
"It's just a disgrace to an entire generation."—Hunter, when asked about Mr. Clinton's decision not to inhale.

Ottawa Citizen

Hale, James *Basic Black examines gonzo journalist Hunter S. Thompson*; 8/11/91

Lewis, Charles *20 Years Later, Hunter Thompson Becomes Tiresome*; 1/19/92

People

Small, Michael *Spaced out Journalist Hunter Thompson and singer Jimmy Buffett . . .* ; 10/1/84

Port Huron Times Herald

Omer, Sevil *Palmer says trial 'rather a hassle'*; 5/19/90

Verdin, Tom *Ex-porn queen angry. Palmer-Slater says authorities botched investigation of author*; 6/1/90

PR Newswire

(dateline Cleveland) *Thompson Named Health Editor to Bathroom Journal*; 7/23/87

Today the Doctor . . . Tomorrow, You; 5/16/90

Rocky Mountain News

Caine, Winston *Hunter Thompson Charged*; 4/10/90

San Francisco Chronicle and Sunday Examiner

Women's Wear Daily *Covering Politics and Getting High*; 7/10/72

Hunter S. Thompson arrives at Fla. divorce trial; 11/17/82

Appearance in Bay area, a gonzo sellout; 2/9/84

Weider, Robert S. *Fear & Loathing Goes to Cal*; 3/11/84

Liberatore, Paul *Writers' views on Democratic National Conv*; 7/18/84

Selvin, Joel *Journalist Wins Election Bet/Loses Card*; 11/8/84

$800 drunk driving fine; 7/13/85

Hunter S. Thompson joins Examiner staff; 9/22/85

Hinckle, Warren *F&L at the Examiner;* 5/29/88

Hamlin, Jesse *Mitchell Bros throw party on 'Spot';* 3/28/85

Hunter Thompson Denies Assault; Gonzo journalist says he rejected woman's sexual advances; 3/2/90

HST denies assault; 3/2/90

Shoales, Ian *Brushfire of the Arrogance;* 2/3/91

Zane, Maitland and Leary, Kevin *How the Mitchells Revolutionized the Porn Business;* 3/1/91

Caen, Herb *Eat More 3-Dot Journalism;* 7/17/91

Lundgren, Mark *The Duke Gets His Way;* 10/10/91

Spin

Conrad, Harold *Fear and Loathing in Hunter Thompson;* 5/86
"And don't ask me where the money is."—HST

Sunday Times

Kiley, Sam *Delirious Doc looks for an explosive encore;* 6/3/90, Overseas News

Toronto Star

Blackadar, Bruce *Doctor of Gonzo is Back on the Outrageous Trail;* 1/18/92

United Press International

'Uncle Duke' Lives as the 53rd Hostage!; 1/24/81

Hunter Thompson, journalist ordered to appear in court; 6/22/81

Hunter S. Thompson, a 'new journalism' pioneer who wrote Fear and Loathing on the Campaign Trail . . . will appear in court next month on drunk driving charges; 6/30/81

Author Hunter Thompson's only appearance in the Bay Area has been sold out almost three weeks in advance; 2/9/84

Loathing: Montana State University has moved next week's lecture by intoxicant-loving Hunter S. Thompson 12 miles off campus in keeping with an alcohol awareness program; 4/12/85

Schwed, Mark *Gonzo on the Night Shift;* 6/15/85

Trott, William C. *Gonzo's Geek from Gables;* 10/4/85

Outlaw Journalist Hunter S. Thompson is Getting Primed for More Fear and Loathing on the Campaign Trail (University of Massachusetts); 4/9/87

Franckling, Ken G. *Gordon Liddy Debates Hunter S. Thompson;* 11/21/87

Thompson (Univ. Arizona reconsiders his invitation); 12/17/87

Vancouver Sun

Potter, Greg *A gonzo pilgrimage to the strip of fools;* 7/6/91

———— *Junkies flying on U.S. Publicity Wave: Even Hunter S. lends gonzo ear to beautiful music;* 5/20/92

Washington Post

Johnson, Haynes *Good Dr. Thompson Called New Hampshire 12 years ago;* 3/4/84

Aarons, Leroy F. *Hippies May Elect Sheriff;* 10/18/70

Greider, William *Amok-Raking Journalist;* 5/13/73

Rovner, Sandy *Fear & Loathing at Rolling Stone;* 5/30/75

Wadler, Joyce *The Rages of Ralph Steadman;* 12/31/83, p. C-1

Flush with success; One woman's search for a creative outlet (Post's 'rogue' hydrant painting of HST); 9/2/90, p. B-8

Streitfeld, David *Hunter Thompson Balancing on the Edge;* 1/7/91

Washington Star

Coburn, Randy Sue *An adrenalin junkie seeks to change his act;* 10/4/79
  "So what sort of story are you going to do? Is it essentially madman tracked down in his lair—one of those things?"—HST to Coburn

Washington Times

Elvin, John *On the Town; . . . Still Crazy;* 6/18/90, p. A-6

Washington City Paper

McCormack, Lisa *Gonzo Brain Death;* spring/92

"You want Bad? How about your dick falling off in your hand the next time you walk up to a public urinal & zip down your pants. . . . So what? You could have yr. nuts ripped OFF by a 5000 horse power industrial belt-sander while you're trying to masturbate during your lunch hour."—HST when asked for a comment on '92 campaign and election

Special thanks to Joe Porletto and Hal McCabe of Ithaca College.

Thanks to Meryl White and Anthony Cosgrave of Cornell University Libraries; Pat Chapman of *The Louisville Courier-Journal,* Paul Johnson of Aspen, and C. Moss of the *San Francisco Examiner* for their enthusiastic research assistance.

Thank you to Kihm Winship and Steve Fowler for the loan of research materials.

And a most special thanks to Ms. Laetitia Snap, who was able to work under unreasonable pressures and shared her strength to the utmost.

Author's Note

Ms. Maura Wogan, the publisher's lawyer and partner in the august firm of Frankfurt, Garbus, Klein and Selz, has threatened to flog me with a bull's pizzle if I do not state that Laetitia Snap is a fictitious character and that some of the incidents Snap said happened, did not.

E. Jean Carroll